THE DISINTEGRATION
OF NATURAL LAW THEORY

BRILL'S STUDIES
IN
INTELLECTUAL HISTORY

THE DISINTEGRATION
OF NATURAL LAW THEORY

Aquinas to Finnis

BY

PAULINE C. WESTERMAN

BRILL
LEIDEN · NEW YORK · KÖLN
1998

This book is printed on acid-free paper.

Library of Congress Cataloging-in-Publication Data

Westerman, Pauline.
    The disintegration of natural law theory : Aquinas to Finnis / by
Pauline Westerman.
      p.   cm. — (Brill's studies in intellectual history ; v. 84)
    Includes bibliographical references and index.
    ISBN 9004109994 (cloth : alk. paper)
    1. Natural law—History. I. Title. II. Series.
K415.W47   1997
340'.112—dc21   97–38234
                                          CIP

Die Deutsche Bibliothek - CIP-Einheitsaufnahme

Westerman, Pauline:
The disintegration of natural law theory : Aquinas to Finnis / by
Pauline Westerman. – Leiden ; New York ; Köln : Brill, 1997
    (Brill's studies in intellectual history ; Vol. 84)
    ISBN 90–04–10999–4

ISSN 0920-8607
ISBN 90 04 10999 4

PRINTED IN THE NETHERLANDS

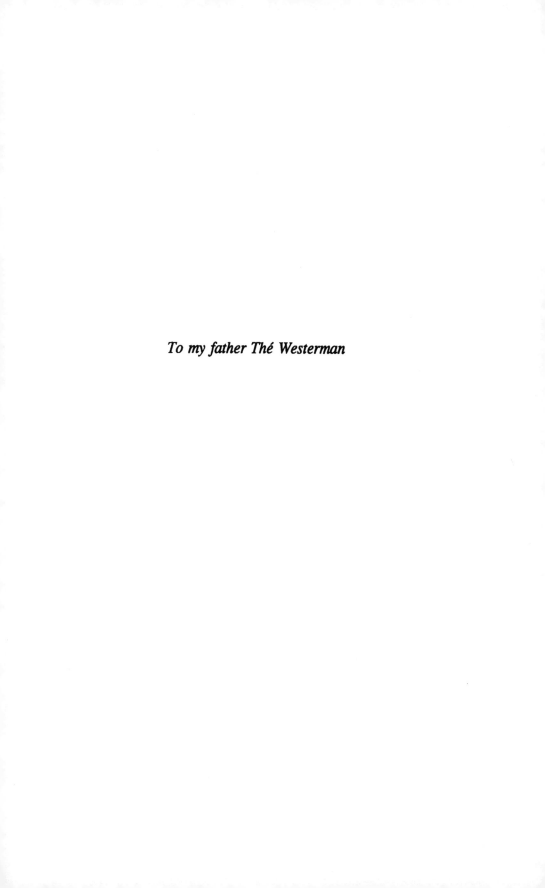

To my father Thé Westerman

CONTENTS

ACKNOWLEDGEMENTS

In writing this book I have been supported by a number of people, who were willing to offer their comments on its various aspects.

Some of these commentators were prepared to read both the penultimate version and the ultimate version. Professor Ernst Kossmann's advice has been very inspiring to me. I want to thank him as well as his wife for the many stimulating conversations we had at his home and for their unfailing support. I am also indebted to Professor Arjo Vanderjagt who read both versions in a very precise manner and was always willing to assist me whenever asked. My dear colleagues (and friends!) Dr Anne-Ruth Mackor and Dr Thomas Mertens were also prepared to read both versions. Despite their different philosophical orientations, they often agreed in their criticism, which was always a infallible sign to me that I had to change my account on those points. My partner Dr Paul de Laat could not escape the plight of being included in this category of readers as well. Despite the fact that my subject is very alien to his own specialism, he read all my versions carefully, and with acute insight. Moreover, he prepared the camera-ready copy of the manuscript as a whole. I want to thank him for that, as well as for all those other ways in which he supported me.

I am no less indebted to the readers who read one version only. I especially want to thank Professor Damiaan Meuwissen. He read the ultimate version and devoted much attention especially to the chapters on Aquinas and Finnis. I am very grateful to him for his willingness to support me, both intellectually and morally, during the last stage of this book. The final version was also read by Professor Willem Witteveen and Professor Arend Soeteman. I thank them for the promptness with which they offered me their help and encouragement. Professor John Griffiths, who read the penultimate version, helped me to avoid, as best I could, the pitfalls of scholasticism. Both my dear friends Dr Sjaak Koenis and Dr Rein de Wilde read the entire penultimate draft. They made me aware of the fact that I am not a historian of ideas, and should never try to become one. Their criticism as well as the ensuing debates resulted in the views expressed in the introduction.

Three readers originally intended to read the entire book, but circumstances prevented them from doing so. Professor Desiré

Scheltens offered me assistance by reading the chapters on Aquinas and Suárez. His emphasis on the theological assumptions underlying Suárez's analysis is reflected in this book and I am grateful for his constant encouragement. Also Janke van der Sluis read the chapters on Aquinas and Suárez. I profited from her knowledge of medieval philosophy and her precise reading. These chapters were also read by Professor Sandy Stewart. I want to thank him for his advice in the first stage of writing this book, when I was mainly exploring Hume's attack on natural law theory.

There are several readers to whom I turned for their specialized advice on one particular author. Dr Leonard Besselink, specialized in Grotius's theory of natural law, was willing to comment upon my chapters on Grotius and thanks to his nuanced criticism I was able to attenuate the statements in these chapters. Of very great help indeed was the expert advice on Pufendorf which I received from Dr Fiammetta Palladini. She read my penultimate version of those chapters with great care and her fundamental comments were extremely valuable and inspiring.

Finally, I would like to thank Tony Foster for his careful reading and corrections of my English and Theo Joppe of Brill Publishers for his efficient assistance when the manuscript was prepared for publication.

Groningen, augustus 1997.

ABBREVIATIONS

De Ver.   *De Veritate* (Aquinas, 1256-9)

DL   *Tractatus de Legibus ac Deo Legislatore* (Suárez, 1612)

DOH   *De Officio Hominis et Civis Juxta Legem Naturalem Libri Duo* (Pufendorf, 1673)

FE   *Fundamentals of Ethics* (Finnis, 1983)

JBP   *De Jure Belli ac Pacis Libri Tres* (Grotius, 1625)

JNG   *De Jure Naturae et Gentium Libri Octo* (Pufendorf, 1688)

JP   *De Jure Praedae Commentarius* (Grotius, 1604)

Lev.   *Leviathan: on the Matter, Forme and Power of a Commonwealth Ecclesiasticall and Civil* (Hobbes, 1651)

NLNR   *Natural Law and Natural Rights* (Finnis, 1980)

SHN   *De Statu Hominum Naturali* (Pufendorf, 1678)

ST   *Summa Theologiae* (Aquinas, 1266-73)

INTRODUCTION

I

It would be an overstatement to describe the appearance of John Finnis's book, *Natural Law and Natural Rights* in 1980 as an event that shook the world, but it certainly brought about a wave of commotion in the world of legal theory. Proponents and opponents alike found Finnis's enterprise impressive, although few went as far as Neil MacCormick who refers to his reading of Finnis as a kind of religious conversion:

> I have seldom read a work of philosophy with a greater sense of excitement and discovery than that which I experienced on a first breathless run through the pre-first edition of *Natural Law* [...]. It remains for me an intellectual landmark; one of those few books which bring about a permanent change in one's understanding; a shift in one's personal paradigm.[1]

MacCormick, Regius Professor of Public Law and the Law of Nature and Nations at Edinburgh, relates how Finnis's book lifted his initial doubts on the appropriateness of the name of the venerated chair he occupied. It induced him to a 'better appreciation' of natural law theory and to attenuate the—legal positivist—doctrine of the separation between law and morals.

Although MacCormick is probably the most famous example, he is not the only one whose ideas have been affected by Finnis's attempt to rehabilitate natural law theory. Since the first edition of *Natural Law and Natural Rights*, numerous volumes and articles have appeared, defending or criticising this new natural law theory. It seems that nowadays any legal theorist who wants to be taken seriously has to come to terms with natural law theory.

The influence of Finnis's book is not surprising. Here at last, there is an attempt to give a definite *meaning* to the empty phrase[2] with

---

[1] MacCormick, 1992, pp. 105-6.
[2] I am not taking into account Fuller's attempt to provide for a 'procedural' natural law. Cf. Fuller, 1964.

which, since Second World War, legal theorists had tried to allow for a connection between law and morals. Here at last, 'natural law' is not an inarticulate battle-cry against legal positivism, but a theory dealing with the problem of obligation, the creation of rules and the formation of customs, the validity of law, and the claims of law in a modern state. Moreover, it seemed to incorporate many of the views expounded by legal positivists such as H.L.A. Hart, Finnis's teacher, and Joseph Raz's writings on practical reasoning. And not only did it promise to overcome the standstill in legal theory between 'natural law' and 'legal positivism'; it equally announced resolution of the deadlock in modern moral theory, and reconciliation of the competing claims of 'consequentialism' and 'deontology'.

However, Finnis's book does not merely stimulate systematic discussions on legal and moral issues and their connection. It also implies a reconsideration of the *history* of natural law theory. Finnis claims that in order to rehabilitate natural law theory as a promising way of understanding law, we should cut away the weeds that have overgrown the original conceptual framework of Aquinas. This view, developed in collaboration with moral philosopher Germain Grisez, who set out to rehabilitate Aquinas in order to develop a new ethical theory for the Roman Catholic Church, is at the root of Finnis's natural law theory.

According to Grisez and Finnis, a pure and fertile concept of natural law can be regained by a drastic reinterpretation of Aquinas. A reinterpretation that can be carried out only if we remove the distorting filter of Neo-Thomism through which Aquinas is commonly interpreted. But not only should we dismiss the Neo-Thomist additions to Aquinas, such as the theories of the 16th-century Spaniards Vázquez and Suárez; we should also discard the Protestant formulations of natural law theory, found in the works of Grotius, Pufendorf, Culverwell and Clarke. Finnis and Grisez claim that all these later modifications of natural law theory distorted and thereby weakened Aquinas's theory to such an extent, that it was easy for David Hume to pronounce a final death-sentence.[3]

In itself, this somewhat dramatic proposal to discard tradition in order to go back to a purer state of affairs is not unique. The idea that at some moment in the history of philosophy things went badly wrong and that a cure can only be found by going back to the roots,

---

[3] NLNR pp. 46-8.

is a recurrent theme in the history of philosophy. Around the time that Finnis's book appeared, Alasdair MacIntyre engaged in a similar project and likewise attacked the fragmentation in contemporary moral discourse.[4] Both men, different as they may appear, assume that we should return to the happier times of Aristotle and Aquinas in order to bring moral theory to a more inspiring level than it is now-adays. Both men criticise modernity for its stress on the individual as a rights-holder, and its emphasis on procedures rather than virtues. Both thinkers stress the importance of the community, in which cit-izens can participate and in which moral discourse is guided by a practical orientation on the good life. Both criticise the distinction between private and public and the modern tendency to relegate morals to the private domain only.

What is unique, however, in Finnis's attempt, is that he explicitly refuses, in contrast to MacIntyre, to underpin his bold proposal with a profound criticism of the tradition he wants to discard. One might expect the proposal for purification to be accompanied by an exten-sive historical analysis of the distortions. One might want to know, where and how natural lawyers like Suárez and Grotius went astray. Yet, such an approach is rejected:

> No effort is made to give an ordered account of the long history of theorising about natural law and natural rights. For experience suggests that such accounts lull rather than stimulate an interest in their subject-matter.[5]

But not only is Finnis afraid of writing dull books. His book is meant as a discourse on natural law itself, not on the 'doctrines of natural law'.[6] Unlike doctrines, these 'principles of natural law [...] have no history'.[7] They are eternally valid and transcend historical discourse. That is why he does not engage in writing a history of the doctrine and relegates his remarks on previous doctrines to—extensive—foot-notes. This procedure has been welcomed by most legal theorists. Greenawalt is relieved that despite Finnis's attention to 'esoteric disputes among competing schools of natural law', 'most of what he

---

[4] MacIntyre, 1981.
[5] NLNR p. v.
[6] NLNR p. 25.
[7] NLNR p. 24.

says is of contemporary relevance',[8] and MacCormick praises Finnis for having done more than 'merely playing the historian of ideas'.[9]

We might agree with them that it is better to invent something new than to cover old ground again, but the problem is: if we lack an adequate grasp of the old theories, how do we *know* that a certain theory is 'new' and not just a set of old ideas parading as new ones? How can we be sure that Finnis fares so much better than the old thinkers, who erected grand-scale theories about natural law? What is it that immunises Finnis and Grisez against the diseases that allegedly had infected natural law tradition since Aquinas's death in 1274?

Perusing the extensive footnotes, it is possible to form an image of Finnis's criticism. Suárez, for instance, is blamed for having under-rated the importance of practical reason. He is said to have turned the model of theoretical reason into the dominant one. In Suárez's theory the principles of natural law achieved the status of—indisputable—theoretical certainties. A distortion, Finnis thinks, of the practical principles Aquinas had in mind. As a corollary of that criticism, both Catholic and Protestant natural lawyers are blamed for having attached much more importance to nature than Aquinas. Especially the Protestant writers are blamed here, for they are said to have limited the scope of nature to that of 'human' nature alone. The new natural lawyers think that this emphasis on human nature, due to Stoic influences, has rendered natural law theory unnecessarily vulnerable to the charge of naturalistic fallacy; the charge of making illicit inferences from nature to morals, or from 'is' to 'ought'-statements.

These are useful insights, and they give rise to much thought. If Finnis and Grisez are correct in their analysis of the traditional natural lawyers, and I shall argue that in some important respects they are, what does that tell us? Does it imply that there were a lot of confused theorists who, by mere thoughtlessness, squandered Aquinas's heritage? This must be the implication, since Finnis and Grisez think that they can set it right, and that they can avoid the pitfalls of their forerunners. But is this a plausible view? Is it not probable that the natural lawyers had *good reasons* for their alterations and modifications?

In order to account for the deviations from Aquinas's original programme, two possible explanations present themselves: a historical

---

[8] Greenawalt, 1982, p. 136.
[9] MacCormick, 1991, p. 232.

and a theoretical one. In a historical explanation it is assumed that since any theory of natural law is closely connected with political and social practices, theoretical modifications should be regarded as reflections of political and institutional changes. And indeed, there are many studies to be found which situate the theories of the 'great' natural lawyers, such as Suárez, Grotius or Pufendorf in their intellectual and social contexts.

This kind of literature, though extremely valuable for a better insight in the history of the theory of natural law, is almost completely overlooked by Finnis. The reason for this is clear: Finnis does not think these interpretations have any bearing on his own theory. It is his view that a good theory of natural law should be independent from historical contingencies. It is the eternal truth he is after, principles that are universally and eternally valid. To point out that, until now, these eternal truths have always been framed in a vocabulary that reflects the social contexts in which they are formulated would merely strengthen his belief that indeed the old natural lawyers were wrong. They should not have led themselves astray by contingencies; they should have remained faithful to Aquinas's programme.

Such a line of defense is not possible if we try to provide for a theoretical explanation for the modifications in natural law theory. In a theoretical explanation, the modifications of traditional natural lawyers can be accounted for by pointing out that they were not coincidental, but that they can be regarded as solutions to some conceptual difficulties in Aquinas's programme. If it can be argued that the reformulations of the natural lawyers can be regarded as 'forced moves',[10] in the sense that they are the only acceptable solutions to certain problems which arose on the basis of Aquinas's legacy, this would be a serious challenge to Finnis's theory, which is entirely based on that legacy. It would be a challenge that would force the modern natural lawyers to point out why they think they can escape these age-old and persistent dilemmas. In short: a theoretical explanation would urge the modern natural law theorists to make absolutely clear *why* their new theory of natural law is so much better than that of their forerunners. They can no longer content themselves by asserting that they are simply cleverer than their theoretical ancestors.

---

[10] The term 'forced moves' is borrowed from the completely different context of the writings of Dennett, 1995, p. 128.

In comparison with the abundant historical and idea-historical literature on past formulations of natural law theory, reconstructions in purely theoretical terms are relatively scarce. The few instances I could find of such an approach were mostly German, but these frequently suffer from the German tendency to span centuries of theorising with a few sweeping statements.[11] These analyses are inspiring, but often too broad to do justice to the particular kind of 'distortions' for which the natural lawyers are blamed by their 20th-century successors.

There seems to be only one option left, which is to try to do what Finnis and Grisez have failed to do: to take seriously the modifications of the traditional natural lawyers, and to try to interpret their theories as rational attempts to solve certain problems that are inherent in the theoretical framework which was handed over to them.

As I became immersed in that part of intellectual history, I gradually became aware that the attempt to reconstruct the additions, alternations and reformulations of subsequent natural lawyers made one thing uncomfortably clear: that there is very little room for escape from a number of persistent difficulties in the concept of natural law itself. That indeed, despite Finnis's attempt to brush aside history and to do it all over again, he cannot avoid being entangled in exactly the same kind of problems as his forerunners. I came to believe that, had Finnis taken the trouble to write a history of the concept of natural law, he could indeed have 'lulled the interest in the subject-matter', thereby saving himself and others a lot of time and trouble.

II

The outcome of this attempt to reconstruct the various reformulations of subsequent natural lawyers as rational solutions to problems within Aquinas's legacy is a story of decline. It sketches the gradual increase of insoluble problems. It shows how one concept is diversified into several concepts, which are mutually exclusive or at best hard to reconcile. It tries to discover why former options are no longer accessible to subsequent natural lawyers. In short, this story tells how the solid foundations of Aquinas's edifice were gradually undermined.

---

[11] One of the best books in this genre is Welzel, 1951.

In this sense, this book is different from most idea-historical studies, which tend to focus on concepts and theories that have been successful to the present day and play a vital part in contemporary discourse. In view of this modern success or widespread propagation, these studies inquire into the origins of these notions. What are the origins of our rights-theories.[12] What is the historical basis for modern political thought in general?[13] What are the origins of international law?[14] What are the origins of our view of America?[15] In these studies, the past is studied in so far as it contributes to modern political thought.

The difference between a story of decline and a story of success accounts for the different approach to the historical authors discussed in this book. If one is intent upon unravelling the modest beginnings of modern concepts, one should try to gain insight in the precise meanings and intentions of the classical authors in relation to the social contexts in which their theories originated.

It is in view of the latter approach that the so-called 'contextualist' method was proposed and advocated by historians such as J.G.A. Pocock and Quentin Skinner.[16] This method has many virtues. It makes us aware of the dangers of ascribing anachronistic views to past authors and of studying texts isolated from contexts. Skinner's views are valuable reminders of the impossibility\of a proper historical understanding of classical philosophical texts, if one has not the slightest idea of the world the authors lived in, or of the specific problems they addressed.

We should keep in mind, however, that these useful reminders, warnings and prescriptions are intended as guidelines for a kind of history of ideas which is different from the aims I have in view. Skinner's methodology is useful for someone who, in Skinner's words,[17] sets out to unravel the 'historical identity of texts'. The historian of ideas has to have a keen eye for historical contingencies,

---

[12] E.g. Tuck, 1979.

[13] E.g. Skinner, 1978.

[14] E.g. Scott, 1934; Soder, 1973.

[15] E.g. Chiappelli, 1976.

[16] For a short overview, see Skinner, 1969. A more extensive discussion of his views is to be found in: Tully, 1988b, and Pocock, 1985. Further discussion in: Rorty et al., 1984.

[17] See Tully, 1988b, p. 273.

shifting problems, intellectual circles, networks, pamphlets and minor philosophers.

This implies that Skinner's advice is of limited significance to someone who wants to examine the theoretical claim that Aquinas's legacy should be restored.[18] As I noted above, the new natural law theory can hardly be affected by historical insights in the social and cultural contingencies that shaped the theories of the Catholic and Protestant natural lawyers. If we want to question Finnis's view that one can erect a theory of natural law which avoids the mistakes of past natural lawyers, we need to focus on the kind of theoretical dilemmas and difficulties inherent in natural law theory. For instance: are there *theoretical* reasons for Suárez to supplement his natural law theory with an 'additional divine will', which had been absent in Aquinas's writings? Or, to take another example, was Grotius's solution to take human nature as a starting-point indeed 'merely' the reflection of Stoic influence or can it be understood as a forced move, as the only way out of the dilemma between voluntarism and intellectualism?

In order to find an answer to this type of question, it is necessary *not* to content oneself with explanations that refer to social and cultural contexts. In order to understand the available theoretical options, the difficulties with the various foundations and the emerging inconsistencies, we should abstract from those data which are vital for a truly historical understanding of the origins of a certain theory.

That is why I have decided to sin against most of the recommendations of the contextualists. In the *first* place, I deliberately deal with the various natural lawyers as abstractions. In this book one will seek in vain for biographical details, sketches of cultural and social contexts, or for other information concerning the period, or the intellectual circles surrounding the natural lawyers. Suárez and Pufendorf, even Grotius, are presented merely as people who wrote books. These people have no legs, no desires or needs, let alone parents, enemies, or bank-accounts. They are neither physical nor social beings. As far as I am concerned, Grotius was never imprisoned in the Loevesteyn-castle. That does not imply that I have not picked the fruits of other

---

[18] Some historians of ideas also find Skinner's recommendations too restrictive. Cf. e.g. Haakonssen's introduction to Haakonssen, 1996, where he remarks that the historian should *also* understand ideas as 'intellectual phenomena with their own logic' (p. 11).

peoples' work, less abstract-minded than I am. I should even confess here that I went to see Suárez's birth-place in Granada. But the images thus conveyed were only used as instruments. They only helped me to avoid—at least I hope they did—the worst kinds of anachronisms. And when they are occasionally allowed to creep into my analysis, it is just in order to make understandable that some—theoretically possible—options were not available to the authors discussed.

In the *second* place, I deliberately disregard the various social and political *functions* natural law theory was meant to fulfil. This is obviously highly unrealistic. Natural law theory was not developed for its own sake. It was not formulated and reformulated with no other aim than to perplex subsequent generations of philosophers. On the contrary, modifications in the doctrine of natural law testify to the fact that indeed it was used as a tool for different purposes. Aquinas—partly—used it to assert the authority of the Catholic Church, Suárez developed the concept in order to provide the Spanish Crown with the necessary legitimation, Hugo Grotius used it as the foundation of an international legal order and Pufendorf mainly used it in order to demarcate moral philosophy from theology.

But I decided to abstract from these different functions, because I feared they would impair a clear view on the theoretical dynamism of the concept. Apart from the fact that there is an abundance of litera-ture to be found on the formation of moral and political theories as an answer to pressing social problems, and that there is no need to burden the reader with repetitions, I feared that focusing on the social and political functions of natural law theory would render my task too easy. For instance, it is tempting to regard Suárez's repeated empha-sis on the certainty and inflexibility of natural law, as a theoretical reflection of the absolutist claims of the Papacy following the Council of Trent.[19] However, useful as this information may be for a histor-ian of ideas, such an answer does not suffice for someone who wants to unravel the theoretical factors that contributed to Suárez's solution. The Council of Trent in no way enhances my understanding of the conceptual difficulties with which Suárez had to deal. Therefore I decided to look *first* for some theoretical explanation. Social explana-tions come in only when theoretical explanations cannot be found.

---

[19] Skinner, 1978, II, p. 145.

In the *third* place, and here at last I think Skinner would agree with me,[20] have tried to avoid explanations that refer to 'influences'. Again, the assumption that the natural lawyers were not influenced by other writers on the subject is not realistic. It is not meant to be. I do not for a moment doubt that the various elements to be found in natural law theories are borrowed from earlier writers. Suárez's divine will is reminiscent of Occam's voluntarism, Grotius's hypothesis that the validity of natural law is independent from God's existence, might indeed be traced back to Gregory of Rimini. Pufendorf's scepticism concerning human nature can justly be ascribed to the influence of Hobbes. These are all useful insights, that deserve to be examined.

Here again, an explanation in terms of influences makes matters too easy. Do we really understand Grotius's statement once we have explained it as a trace of Gregory of Rimini? We do not. The question remains why this old view is put forward with such force, and why Grotius did not select another book from his vast library.

There is another difficulty with the search for influences that would have hindered my enterprise. Most interpretations in terms of influences focus on only one element of the theory in question. It is *only* Grotius's statement on the validity of natural law that is traced back to Rimini, not his entire theory. And by the selection of one such element, the structure of the theory as such, as a combination of various elements, is overlooked. I think therefore that the pedigree of the distinct elements of a given theory does not help in clarifying the plausibility of the conceptual alterations in the history of the doctrine of natural law. In order to understand these theoretical innovations, we should focus on the relationship between the various elements. It is the combination that counts, not the separate elements. Do these elements fit together, or are there any tensions to be found? Is it possible to reconcile a certain element with the combination of other elements? Those are the questions I shall deal with.

This does not imply that this book never refers to any influence at all. That would be nearly impossible. But these influences are never taken as sufficient explanations in themselves. They merely serve to indicate what, in my view, has happened on the chess-board of natural law theory, the pieces that have been taken, and the opening that has been chosen. Influential forerunners are merely taken into

---

[20] Cf. Skinner's criticism of 'Einfluss'-studies, 1969, pp. 25-6.

account in order to understand the kind of forced moves required by
the author in question.

III

One might wonder whether it is *possible* to arrive at a theoretical
understanding on the basis of such a deliberate refusal to be guided
by some sound methodological requirements for the history of ideas.
Is it possible to abstract from social reality? Is it possible to focus on
theoretical innovations and continuities without taking into account
that these theories had some function to perform? Is it not true that
the almost exclusive focus on theoretical possibilities and impossibil-
ities at the expense of practical considerations suffers from the mis-
conception that a theory can be separated from social practices? And,
more importantly, is it not true that the very *definition* of what should
be counted as 'natural law theory' depends on the definition given by
the classical authors themselves; definitions that were to a large extent
dictated by concrete circumstances, habits and vocabularies?

These objections are justified. I am the last to deny that the definition of theoretical concepts and the roles they play are inseparable
from the demands of time and place. I also agree with Skinner's view
that there are no perennial philosophical problems. Although the
various authors all claim to build a theory of natural law, and
although they view themselves as being engaged in the same project, I
shall show in this book that there are considerable differences
between their theories.

The question then arises whether this book does not rest on the
mistaken assumption of continuity. Is it not true that the arrangement
of five authors in a row suggests that they are considered to contribute to one tradition, whereas they simply do not? Is it not equally true
that the differences are more striking and also more interesting than
their continuity?

I agree with that objection. But I maintain that in order to discern
and assess these differences, it can be helpful to act *as if* these various
theories all contribute to the same tradition. That tradition does not
'exist', it cannot readily be 'found'; it is a construct of our own
making. But the hypothesis of a continuous tradition may clarify the
shifts and ruptures more adequately than when we already start from
the assumption of discontinuity. In this sense, the assumption that
there *are* perennial philosophical problems, though unrealistic, has a

certain heuristic advantage. Unrealistic assumptions may be pernicious for an empirical historical investigation (and they easily lead to
anachronisms in the search for 'origins' of contemporary political
thought), but I believe they are of great value for a theoretical reconstruction. For the sake of argument it can be useful to abstract from
reality and to start from *idealised notions* of what is to count as
'natural law theory'.[21]

Of course, one should keep in mind that the history one tells is not
the history of something 'real', as Finnis seems to assert when he
talks about the 'existence of natural law'.[22] It is the history of a
construct of one's own making. It is the continuity that one is able to
discern only on the basis of a *decision* about what should be counted
as relevant and what not. Since this entire book is based on such a
decision, it is worthwhile to spend a few words on the kind of working-definition of 'natural law theory' I use. Such a definition should
not be too vague. It should not include almost every theory that in
some way or another has something to tell about nature and/or
morals. As I shall point out in the introduction to chapter IX, a vague
definition leads to such an inflatory use of the term 'natural law', that
it can be identified with moral philosophy as such without further
difficulty, and lose any specific meaning.

In order to have an instrument that is not too blunt I have decided
to base my working-definition on four assumptions, which, according
to my initial understanding of natural law theory, are crucial to any
natural law theory. These are the following assumptions:

> a) there are universal and eternally valid criteria and principles
> on the basis of which positive law can be justified and/or
> criticised;
> b) these criteria and principles are grounded in nature, either
> physical nature, or more specifically, human nature;
> c) human beings can discover those principles by the use of
> reason;
> d) for positive law to be morally obligatory, it should be jus-
> tified in terms of these principles and criteria.

---

[21] For a formal analysis of idealisation as a methodology in *empirical* investiga-
tions, see the Polish philosopher Nowak, 1980.
[22] NLNR p. 25.

This working-definition should not be seen as a strait-jacket. Rather, the four assumptions serve as a few fixed points which might enable us to compare the various theories and to assess some important shifts. That is why the discussion of each author is concluded by a short analysis in terms of these assumptions. But as we shall see, the assumptions are gradually enriched by the interpretations of the various authors.

This gradual enrichment of my initial working-definition, however, does not imply that my book can be read as a history of natural law theory. In the first place, it is not a *history*, but an abstract and theoretical reconstruction. In the second place it is not a history of *natural law theory* but of an idealised notion on what should be counted as such a theory of natural law.

As such it can be read in—at least—two ways. Either as a—theoretical—contribution to the interpretative studies that already exist. As such, the chapters can be read separately by readers, interested in the work of a particular author. Or as one long story of decline and as an argument against contemporary attempts to rehabilitate natural law.

IV

Since the working-definition serves only as a—modest—tool for evaluation, it cannot justify the selection of the writers presented in this book. It is true that there are certain writers, generally regarded as 'natural lawyers', who are excluded by my initial decision to define natural law theory in terms of the above-mentioned four assumptions. As I shall argue in the introduction to chapter IX, Hume is excluded by assumptions a) and d) and Kant is excluded by assumption b). But I could also have included many more writers. Locke and Hobbes present themselves, Culverwell and Clarke, but also someone like Christian Wolff.

The decision to confine myself to Aquinas, Suárez, Grotius, and Pufendorf is to a large extent inspired by Finnis's book and the systematic argument I want to raise against Finnis's confidence concerning the possibility of a rehabilitation of natural law theory.

The first part of this book deals exclusively with Aquinas's theory. I chose Aquinas as a starting-point, and not—historically more accurate—Aristotle, since he is the main source of inspiration for contem-

porary natural lawyers.[23] The first chapters should therefore be read
not only as an interpretation of Aquinas, but also as a preliminary
sketch of natural law theory, on the basis of which the contributions
and modifications of later theories can be assessed.

The second part deals with these later modifications, particularly
those of 16th and 17th-century writers, which are scorned for having
'distorted' Aquinas's legacy. It is in this part that the conceptual
fissures underlying natural law theory are revealed. Three authors are
selected. Suárez was chosen, because he is Finnis's main scape-goat.
He is blamed for rigidity, the undermining of practical reason, and
the gap between voluntarist and intellectualist accounts of natural law.
I shall point out that although this interpretation is to a large extent
justified, there were certain theoretical constraints which prompted
Suárez to these modifications.

Grotius was chosen for two reasons. In the first place because
Finnis regarded his 'intellectualism' as one of the main factors that
contributed to Hume's attack on natural law. In the second place,
because I have gradually come to believe that Grotius's theory provides a solution for the problem of obligation that had haunted
Suárez's account. I have come to the conclusion that rather than
having provoked the death of natural law, Grotius's theory shows that
natural law theory can only be rescued in the form of a theory of
natural rights. This solution is rejected by Finnis, and I hope that the
chapter on Grotius will reveal why Finnis has to pay a price for this
rejection.

Pufendorf, finally, is hardly mentioned by Finnis at all. The reason
I chose to include him in this book is that I think Finnis could have
profited from a more thorough reading of Pufendorf. I initially started
reading Pufendorf, since he regarded himself as a successor of
Grotius. But that is not the reason I have included him. If I had used
that criterion, Locke and many others would have been suitable
candidates as well. I decided to include Pufendorf's contribution to
the debate, because I believe it shows clearly what happens if one
rejects Grotius's solution to the obligation-problem. The analysis of
Pufendorf provides us with the keys to an understanding of the failure
of Finnis to develop natural law theory. Like Finnis, Pufendorf was
unsatisfied with Grotius's dissolution of natural law into natural
rights. Like Finnis, he wanted to restore natural law theory as a

---

[23] Boyle, 1992, p. 7.

unified and comprehensive conceptual framework. Pufendorf's struggle to formulate such a theory foreshadows the enormous theoretical difficulties Finnis encounters. These difficulties are examined in part III, which deals exclusively with the contemporary theory of natural law as developed by Grisez and Finnis.

This selection of authors disregards the conventional distinction between so-called 'scholastic' natural lawyers and 'modern' or 'rationalist' natural lawyers. It seems to me that the distinction between these schools may be useful for *other* debates; for instance if one wants to contrast right-based theories with vocabularies that revolve around virtues. It may be that the distinction is an adequate reflection of present-day concerns such as the debate between communitarianism and liberalism. I am not in a position to judge the utility of the distinction in the light of these concerns.

But for my purpose there was no need to assume any 'watershed' between Scholasticism and rationalist accounts of natural law. Finnis emphasises a dividing-line between Aquinas and all his followers: both Suárez and the Protestant writers are blamed for being unfaithful to Aquinas's programme. Since I wanted to understand the successive formulations of natural law as solutions to problems inherent in—my reconstruction of—natural law theory, an artificial boundary between the authors discussed would have unnecessarily obscured all those ruptures and continuities which do not coincide with the great divide between scholasticism and rationalism, such as for instance the differences between Pufendorf and Grotius, which, according to my interpretation, are more dramatic than the differences between Pufendorf and Suárez.

V

As I noted, studying the works of these authors enriched the naive working-definition with which I set out to analyze the theories of the natural lawyers presented here. I came to understand the variety of ways in which these assumptions could be filled in, and the relationship between these assumptions and other topics, such as the role of practical reason, the role of conscience, the question concerning the origins of political society, private property, and the like. Not all of these notions and topics recur in every chapter—that depends on the author in question. It is of no use to talk about the notion of *synderesis* for example in the discussion of philosophers who do not use it.

But my initial understanding has also become impoverished. It appeared that most of the natural lawyers took these assumptions much less seriously than I had believed, or than they themselves professed to believe. I did not notice this clearly until I started writing. It then transpired that the discussion of each author could best be arranged in two chapters. There seemed to be a kind of 'natural division' in the work of the natural lawyers: that between 'fundamentals' and 'applications'.

Each first chapter on a particular author deals with the internal conceptual framework of the natural law theory in question. It relates how the various fundamental components and elements are interrelated and combined in that particular theory. Each second chapter deals with the question how this theory of natural law works out in 'practice', i.e. how this concept of natural law was *used* in the actual assessment of law, private property, the state, civil (dis)obedience as well as private moral issues.

I was surprised to find that these second chapters seem to have little relation with the first ones. More often than not, the professed ideals were relinquished when they were applied to practice. Despite pages, volumes even, of minute theorising on the status and certainty of natural law, its obligatory force, how it can generate moral rules and how it should be applied to practice, the natural lawyers consistently fail to live up to their own programme. Interestingly, the applications reveal that there is a *different* programme being carried out, hidden from our view by the dominance of the traditional vocabulary of natural law theory.

In the case of Suárez, this different programme centres around custom-formation; in the case of Grotius, it is the concept of the state as rights-holder and in the case of Pufendorf it is the possibility of rational reconstruction that is explored in this second programme. Finnis is no exception to this rule. We will see not only that he fails to implement natural law theory, but that the programme he is actually carrying out, is a Neo-Kantian programme. If there is continuity to be found in natural law theory, it is apparently in the constant failure to *do* something with natural law theory.

I do not think that the discrepancies between the first and the second chapters can be attributed to disingenuousness on the part of the natural lawyers. We should not regard their theories as a cover for 'true intentions'. On the contrary, the ideals and programmes professed are, I believe, to a large extent serious attempts to provide for a foundation of their political and moral views. But these foundations seem to fail just *because* they are foundations. As such, they cannot shed light on the practices with which the philosophers have to deal. We should therefore not blame the natural lawyers for being unable to do something with natural law. It is inherent in the kind of—foundational—aspirations of the theory.

Leibniz once criticised the kind of natural law theory prevailing in his time, by writing that 'it is more celebrated by words than applied to affairs'.[24] It seems to me that the validity of his criticism is of a more universal nature than Leibniz thought. Each natural law theory, examined in this book, suffers from the same defect. Writing this book was therefore in a sense a disappointing experience. Nobody has expressed this disappointment better than Lloyd Weinreb, in the opening sentences of a recent article:

> The philosophy of Thomas Aquinas has been called the *philosophia perennis*—the perennial philosophy. If that is applied specifically to natural law, the philosophy most closely identified with Aquinas, one may be driven to conclude that it is like the perennials that are pictured heavy with blossoms in seed catalogues but, planted in one's garden, come back year after year with never a bloom at all.[25]

I hope that this book will make clear that the lack of blossoms is not due to coincidental climatological circumstances or poor gardening practices, but that the plant *is* simply a perennial that never flourishes.

---

[24] Leibniz, 1706, p. 66.
[25] Weinreb, 1996, p. 195.

PART I

CHAPTER I

AQUINAS'S VARIATIONS ON A DIVINE THEME

That Aquinas's philosophy is taken as an inspiring starting-point for a modern theory of natural law may come as a surprise to anyone who has been brought up with the interpretation of Aquinas's theory, standard in legal positivist circles, as a prime example of the 'naturalistic fallacy': the mistaken belief that norms can be inferred from facts.

Legal positivists differ in their diagnosis of the underlying assumptions that are responsible for this mistake. Hans Kelsen thinks that it is brought about by the assumption that there is a 'will' immanent in nature. According to Kelsen, natural law theory is a specimen of 'animistic superstition' or of a belief in God's will as immanent in nature.[1] H.L.A. Hart, who rejects this view, claims that it is not the belief in God that is accountable for naturalistic fallacies, but the teleological conception of nature:

> [...] on the teleological view, the events regularly befalling things are not thought of *merely* as occurring regularly, and the questions whether they *do* occur regularly and whether they *should* occur or whether it is *good* that they occur are not regarded as separate questions.[2]

These differences notwithstanding, both authors agree that in Aquinas's theory the principles of natural law are simply inferred from the observance of certain regularities in nature. These inferences are thought to be of a rather unimaginative type: 'human beings *do* naturally seek company, therefore they *should* live sociably'.

On the basis of such an interpretation, Aquinas's theory is certainly not a promising starting-point for any contemporary legal theorist. Not only because of logical fallacies; not only because it is difficult nowadays to assume widespread consensus on the existence of God, but also because our concept of nature seems no longer adequate to play the role required. Nowadays, many people would recognise their

---

[1] Kelsen, 1963, p. 129.
[2] Hart, 1961, p. 185.

own views in the opinion of J.S. Mill that nature is reckless, utterly indifferent to suffering, and incapable of setting a moral example:

> In sober truth, nearly all the things which men are hanged and imprisoned for doing to one another, are nature's everyday perform-ances.[3]

If Aquinas is once again to be taken as a starting-point for a new theory of law and morals, his theory should *not* be interpreted as a mere attempt to infer norms from nature.

That is why Finnis's new theory of natural law is based on the re-interpretation of Aquinas by Germain Grisez. Grisez, trained as a logician who is well aware of the difference between is and ought-statements, attempts to show that Aquinas is not guilty of a naturalis-tic fallacy. It is his view that Aquinas never translated natural regular-ities into value-judgements. Instead, Grisez claims that Aquinas's theory contains a valuable and hitherto underestimated method for 'practical reasoning': the kind of deliberation required in order to arrive at sound conclusions about good and evil and the courses of action to be taken. It is on the basis of this interpretation of Aquinas, adopted and developed by Finnis, that Aquinas is allowed to play such an important role in Finnis's own proposal of a modern natural law theory.

The contemporary theory of natural law proposed by Finnis and Grisez will be discussed in the two final chapters of this book, but as far as their interpretation sheds some light on Aquinas, it is clear that their views will be discussed here as well. In fact, whatever the defects may be of contemporary natural law theory, their interpreta-tion of Aquinas is certainly inspiring. It focuses on a number of issues that are commonly neglected in 'naturalistic' interpretations of Aqui-nas. On the other hand, I shall argue that the contemporary natural law theorists tend to overdo things. In their ambition to detect a theory of practical reasoning, they tend to underrate the natural foundations of Aquinas's theory. So whereas legal positivists see only nature and hardly any reason, Grisez and Finnis perceive only reason and no nature.

---

[3] Mill, 1874, p. 28. Mill's view of nature was not influenced by Darwin, since he had not read Darwin when writing this essay.

In this chapter I shall first try to assess the structure of Aquinas's philosophy of natural law by examining the relationship between practical reason and nature. In the next chapter, I shall pay attention to the question how Aquinas's theory of natural law can be translated into requirements for individual as well as collective decision-making.

1. *Conflicting interpretations*

The debate about the question whether Aquinas is guilty of a naturalistic fallacy or not focuses nearly entirely on the status of Aquinas's so-called 'first principle of natural law'.[4] Aquinas defines this principle as: 'Good is to be done and pursued, and evil avoided',[5] and adds that it should be regarded as a self-evident principle, from which all the other precepts of natural law are derived.[6]

At first sight, the status of this principle seems to be rather unambiguous. If someone tells us to avoid evil and to do good, we generally take that as a moral principle. In itself, this principle is of course too general to inform us on what is to be *counted* as good and evil. If we want to use the principle as a starting-point for the derivation of more specific precepts, we should have some more information. Since Aquinas's concept of reasoning is inspired by Aristotle's model of the syllogism, we might expect him to use the first principle as a *major*, to be accompanied by informative *minors*.

Major: Good should be done and pursued, and evil avoided.[7]
Minor: x is good, y is evil.
Conclusion: x should be done, y should be avoided.

And, indeed, if we look at the passage in which Aquinas introduces his first principle, it seems as if Aquinas proceeds to formulate these informative *minors*. Immediately after his formulation of the first principle, Aquinas points to man's natural inclinations: man naturally inclines to self-preservation, to procreation, to sociability

---

[4] Grisez, 1965.
[5] 'Bonum est faciendum et prosequendum, et malum vitandum.'
[6] ST I, II, 94, 2.
[7] Taken as a *moral* injunction, 'should be' is more appropriate than 'is to be'.

and to truth about God. This combination of the first principle together with the enumeration of natural inclinations, gives rise to the interpretation that, according to Aquinas, we can only comply with the first principle of natural law by consulting our natural inclinations. Since we *do* have a natural tendency to live sociably, we *should* live sociably.

This kind of interpretation seems to match with Hart's formulation of teleological ethics: the observation of natural inclinations gives rise to a formulation of moral propositions. It can be argued, however, that precisely the first principle prevents Aquinas from falling into naturalistic traps. Norms are not derived from nature, but from the normative injunction, expressed in the *major*. Nature is not the foundation of morals, but only plays a role where it informs us about our natural inclinations. Aquinas seems to argue consistently from 'ought' to 'ought', whereas 'is'-statements play only an intermediary role.[8]

Finnis and Grisez, however, are not satisfied with this line of defense. They think that even this more modest role for nature is too large. Whether the whole theory is erected on a general 'ought' or not, in both cases nature would be decisive in informing our practical judgements on desirable courses of action. According to Finnis, that was not at all what Aquinas had in mind when he formulated the general first principle. Finnis points out that for Aquinas—as for Aristotle—, practical reasoning was meant to be 'practical all the way through', i.e. independent from a—theoretical—investigation of nature.[9]

How then should we interpret Aquinas's first principle of natural law? According to the modern natural law theorists, we should not understand it as a moral principle at all.[10] We should take it as a *formal* principle, which governs practical reasoning. It should not be read as a normative injunction, but as a methodological guideline for reasoning on moral affairs.

The textual context, in which the first principle is introduced, supplies some evidence for this claim. Here, Aquinas repeatedly refers to the parallel between the way we reason about theoretical

---

[8] The theory proposed by Adler is inspired by such an interpretation of Aquinas. Cf. Adler, 1981.

[9] Finnis, 1983 (abbrev. FE), p. 14.

[10] Grisez, 1965, p. 368; NLNR p. 34; Boyle, 1992, p. 25.

matters and the way we reason about practical affairs. To Aquinas, both theoretical and practical reason find their starting-point in first principles, which are self-evident.[11] The first principle of theoretical reason is—a reformulation of—the principle of non-contradiction: 'There is no affirming and denying the same simultaneously'.[12] It is a basic guideline for proper reasoning concerning nature. The first self-evident principle of practical reason is the principle that good should be done and evil avoided. It is a self-evident guideline for proper reasoning on moral matters.

Since Thomas repeatedly draws this parallel between the two kinds of reasoning, it is indeed plausible to argue, as Grisez does, that the two self-evident principles have the same methodological status, which implies that:

> Just as the principle of contradiction is operative even in false judgments, so the first principle of practical reason is operative in wrong evaluations and decisions.[13]

On the basis of the analogy with theoretical reason, Grisez and Finnis argue that the first principles of theoretical and practical reason alike have the function to direct the process of reasoning. Without these principles, reasoning would be chaotic.

This, however, does not imply that those who follow these guidelines, necessarily arrive at truths, or—in the practical domain—at morally good actions. The first principle,, understood as a formal principle, is a *sine qua non* for all reasoning about moral matters, but does not guarantee that this reasoning is sound, or that it gives rise to desirable and morally defensible lines of action. The principle merely expresses the fact that practical reason, unlike theoretical reason, is 'active'; it seeks to realise a certain end. As such it is a necessary condition for sound practical reasoning, but not a sufficient one.

The dispute whether the first principle of natural law is formal or moral appears to be less innocent than it seems at first sight. If we take the first principle as a general, moral injunction, which is further specified in the natural inclinations, Aquinas can be interpreted as a

---

[11] Cf. Kühn, 1982.
[12] ST I, II, 94, 2, concl.
[13] Grisez, 1965, p. 369.

philosopher who regards moral rules as the outcome of inferences from natural inclinations. But if we interpret the first principle as a methodological rule, Aquinas's theory can be regarded as a theory of practical reasoning, which rests on the presupposition that man is to some extent free to deliberate on his *particular conception* of the good.

2. Exemplar *of divine wisdom*

In order to gain a clearer view on these matters, I think we should abandon the somewhat technical discussion on the first principle, and widen the scope of our inquiry. What exactly is the status of natural law and its relationship to that other important concept in Aquinas's writings: the eternal law? I think that once we succeed in answering these questions, we might be able to shed some light on the discussion concerning the first principle.

Natural law is defined by Aquinas as the participation (*participatio*) of rational creatures in the eternal law.[14] Natural law is 'the light of natural reason by which we discern what is good and what evil', or 'the impression of divine light upon us'.[15] We should, therefore, understand natural law not as 'law' in the ordinary contemporary sense of the word, but as an epistemological *gateway*, by means of which rational beings have access to the eternal law.[16]

This raises the question what exactly the subject-matter is to which we have access by means of natural law. What does Aquinas understand by 'eternal law'? According to Aquinas:

> [...] the Eternal Law is nothing other than the exemplar of divine wisdom as directing the motions and acts of everything.[17]

What then is meant by 'exemplar'? Aquinas explains his view by means of a metaphor. He writes that we can compare the eternal law God has in mind with the *exemplar* an artist has in mind when he sets

---

[14] ST I, II, 91, 2, concl.

[15] Ibid.

[16] The other available gateway is divine law, the direct expression of the eternal law as revealed by God Himself in the Scriptures.

[17] ST I, II, 93, 1.

out to produce a work of art. In fact, the eternal law as the guiding idea for God's creation is elucidated by a whole series of terms:

> And so, as being the principle through which the universe is created, divine wisdom means art [*ars*], or exemplar [*exemplar*], or idea [*idea*], and likewise it also means law [*ratio*], as moving all things to their due ends.[18]

In order to define the eternal law, a whole set of concepts is clustered here. How are we to understand this cluster as elucidations of the *lex aeterna*? In view of the emphasis of God's role as Artificer, I think we should take the metaphor of art more seriously than most interpreters tend to do. If we want to gain a proper understanding of eternal law, it seems we should inquire into the precise meaning of *exemplar* and to form an idea of the role the concept played in the medieval conception of art.

If one considers the sculptures and paintings of the Pre-Giotto period, it is tempting to think that for a medieval artist an *exemplar* was no more than a conventional pattern to be copied. If the medieval artist was asked to portray a particular bishop, he did not try to represent this particular individual bishop, but drew a conventional figure, recognisable as a bishop by his attributes, crozier and mitre.[19]

But if we understand *exemplar* in this way we cannot understand why Thomas equates eternal law with the exemplars God has in mind. If God created the universe on the basis of isolated stereotypes, individual creatures would be mere copies of those stereotypes. On the basis of such a view it might be understandable that Aquinas equates *exemplar* with *ars* and *idea*, but we cannot understand why these terms are further equated with *lex* and *ratio*, directing things to their due ends. If people already resemble the stereotypes God has in mind, why would there be need for a law to direct them? Or, again in the words of Mill:

> If the natural course of things were perfectly right and satisfactory, to act at all would be a gratuitous meddling, which as it could not make things better, must make them worse.[20]

---

[18] ST I, II, 93, 1.
[19] Cf. Gombrich, 1950, p. 147.
[20] Mill, 1874, p. 19.

However, this was not the only way *exemplar* was used in medieval art. Although it is true that there were certain well-defined
conventions to be followed, medieval art cannot be seen as a mere
repetition of stereotypes. It could not be like that, because according
to medieval standards all art had to fulfil a definite function. A work
of art was only considered to be successful if it was judged to be
suitable for its intended purpose. In order to judge artistic works on
the basis of this criterion, one had to consider the work of art as a
whole. The question then is not whether all the isolated elements of a
painting (the Madonna, the bishop, or the angel Gabriel) faithfully
represent the conventional images. Rather, the question is whether the
painting as such is suitable for its purpose (for instance, as altar-
piece).

Apart from the criterion of suitability, a work of art had to meet
the requirement of proportion. According to Umberto Eco, proportion
is the most important criterion according to which works of arts were
judged.[21] The elements should be represented in a harmonious
whole. Like the criterion of suitability, this criterion can, of course,
only be applied to a work of art as a whole. It seems then that the
exemplar Aquinas has in mind, refers, not to an isolated pattern to be
copied, but to the idea of a work of art as a harmonious and propor-
tionate whole, which is suitable to the end it is meant to serve. The
term *exemplar* refers to order, not to a particular element. In Eco's
words:

> Order is not so much a model to be copied as a compulsion that must
> be satisfied.[22]

If the *exemplar* which human artists have in mind is considered as
such a 'compulsion' for order, this must be all the more the case
where Aquinas speaks about eternal law as the *exemplar* in the mind
of God. The *exemplar* in both man-made works and in God's creation
might be thought of as something which

> [...] presides over its construction and regulates it in a law-governed
> way.[23]

---

[21] Eco, 1988.
[22] Eco, 1988, p. 98.
[23] Eco, 1988, p. 101.

Both God and the human artist have an overall plan in mind for a harmonious whole directed to a specific purpose or end.

If we understand *exemplar* in this sense, it is clear why Aquinas clusters notions like *idea* and *exemplar* with those of *ratio* and *lex*. These are not different things. The *exemplar* God has in mind directs the way the world is *and* should be. In short, the world is created in such a way that it is best fitted to these ends. It is because of the directive power of the *exemplar* that it can properly be called 'law'. And, in accordance with the above-mentioned aesthetical criteria, Aquinas remarks that law (*lex*) is a rule (*regula*) and measure (*mensura*). It is a rule, since it directs the elements to their appropriate ends, a measure, in so far as it makes sure that the elements stand to one another in due proportion.[24]

'Law', like 'exemplar', refers to an overall plan for the construction and regulation of a work of art (or, in God's case: the created universe). In the words of the famous writer on medieval psychology and moral theory Odon Lottin:

> [...] la loi, avant d'être un principe d'obligation, est un principe d'ordre, règle de vie, norme de moralité.[25]

The eternal law is an ordering principle regulating God's creation, rather than a set of coercive precepts.

In aesthetics there is a term for such an ordering principle: 'style'. I think that the term 'style' is more appropriate to clarify Aquinas's concept of 'eternal law' than the term 'law'.[26] It does justice to Aquinas's conception of God as Artificer, and it excludes all kinds of misunderstandings, provoked by the term 'law'.

As we shall see in the chapters on Suárez, one such misunderstanding is to think that God Himself is *obliged to obey* the eternal law. Suárez thought that the concept of eternal law implied a serious blasphemy. The mere assumption that God would have been governed by a 'law', would entail the view that He was not free, omnipotent and sovereign, but that He was and is bound to obey some precepts, that are not of His own making.

---

[24] ST I, II, 90, 1.
[25] Lottin, 1931, p. 97.
[26] We should be cautious, however, not to identify 'style' with 'personal style'.

The term 'style' prevents such a misunderstanding. It is true that God is 'bound' to it, just as an artist who decides to paint in an impressionist style can be said to be 'bound' to a certain degree of consistency and cannot suddenly revert to classicism in one and the same picture. But it does not imply that God would not have been free in His choice of style. The adoption of a style does not curb His sovereignty. On the contrary, style as an ordering principle is the *sine qua non* for creativity. It gives a general direction to the artistic process, and provides for a certain amount of unity and coherence within the artistic product. It is on the basis of these qualities that William James remarks that:

> Aesthetic union [...] is very analogous to teleological union. Things tell a story. Their parts hang together so as to work out a climax.[27]

If we understand eternal law as divine style, it is clear why Aquinas could view the world as a unified, ordered whole. He conceived it as the expression of God's—self-imposed—style.

3. *The divine style applied*

But there are other advantages of the term 'style' as well. The most important one is that it clarifies the various ways in which created beings 'participate' in the eternal law. At first sight, it seems to be Aquinas's view that only rational beings can participate in the eternal law. According to Aquinas 'law is something that belongs to reason'.[28] Usually this view is taken in the ordinary sense that a subject has to know and understand the law in order to comply with the law.

But this interpretation raises some difficulties. According to Aquinas, irrational beings are also bound by the eternal law: '[...] Even non-rational creatures share in the Eternal Reason in their own way'.[29] They share in the eternal law by 'inward moving principles'. Apparently law is *not* strictly connected to rationality.

As we shall see, subsequent natural law theorists were troubled by this inconsistency. If law can only direct rational beings, how can we

---

[27] James, 1906, p. 77.
[28] ST I, II, 90, 1, concl.
[29] ST I, II, 91, 2, ad 3.

say that animals are bound by the eternal law as well? We can do that only by making the most of Aquinas's assertion that animals are subject to eternal law *per similitudinem*, as a figure of speech.

However, if we interpret eternal law as style, it is easier to understand what Aquinas had in mind. He regarded God's creation as an artistic product. As such, all creatures share in the eternal law in the sense that they are the—visual—*expressions* of the divine style, in just the same way as we might say that Monet's waterlilies are an expression of 'impressionism'. In this sense, both rational and irrational beings are an expression of the divine style.

But rational creatures participate in the divine style in an additional sense as well. Being endowed with reason, they can *recognise* the divine style in themselves and in other creatures and they can—and therefore they must—adopt that style in the regulation of their own affairs. That is why Aquinas writes that rational beings 'join in and make their own the Eternal Reason through which they have their natural aptitudes for their due activity and purpose'.[30] 'Natural law' is indeed nothing other than a name for the rational participation in the eternal law. It expresses the possibility for rational beings to apply the divine style to their own dealings.

Whereas irrational beings are merely the expression of the divine style, rational beings are both expression of that style, as well as capable of adopting that style to their own affairs. This is why Aquinas writes:

> Taken as a rule and measure, law can be present in two manners, first, and this is proper to the reason, as in the ruling and measuring principle, and in this manner it is in the reason alone; second, as in the subject ruled and measured, and in this manner law is present wherever it communicates a tendency to something, which tendency can be called derivatively, though not essentially, a 'law'.[31]

The two meanings of the word 'law' referred to here are at the root of our later distinction between a normative law and a descriptive law (as in 'laws of physics'). It is only by means of the analogy with aesthetics, by understanding 'law' as 'style', that we are able to see why these meanings are not logically distinct in Aquinas's writings.

---

[30] ST I, II, 91, 2, concl.
[31] ST I, II, 90, 1, ad 1.

Law in the descriptive sense, refers to 'tendencies' and qualities which are inherent in God's stylistic expressions. Normative laws, on the other hand, are the result of our own rational application of the divine style to human affairs.

It is important to note that rationality is indeed required in order to adopt that style. We are not expected merely to copy God's artefacts. To adopt a style is more than the repetition of stereotypes. Conventional examples may constitute a certain style—and there is certainly no style without such examples—but style is more than the sum-total of stereotypes. Why? Because a style does not contain precise directions in order to perform specific actions. An artistic style is not to be seen as a recipe on 'how to paint a portrait'. The term 'style' rather denotes a general way of making or doing things. In fact, 'style' is better fitted to express the kind of rationality required to 'partake in the eternal law' than 'law', for it shows that rational beings are expected to look beyond the examples and conventions. Just as a good painter does not merely copy Monet's waterlilies, but can adopt that style in painting a modern industrial landscape, a rational being is required to do more than doggedly follow God's precepts.

If we understand 'natural law' as the adoption of the divine style, we can also understand why natural law does not only prohibit us to commit evil, but also enjoins us to pursue and to do good. Many interpreters have drawn attention to the fact that Aquinas did not merely think of natural law as a set of prohibitions, but also of counsels.[32] Nowadays, we might be inclined to regard that as a correct representation of what any legal system is about. But as I shall show in III.1, law's function as a source of actions was not always recognised. The term 'style' is illuminating because it reveals how both counsels and precepts hang together. For instance, the stylistic requirement of unity of time, place and action, which any successful classicist playwright had to meet, was not merely a constraint; it also opened a vast array of possibilities that would otherwise have remained unexplored. Style can be a source of creativity, in the same way that law can be a source of actions, associations and arrangements which would have been impossible without law.

So the term 'style' enables us to understand why Aquinas's concept of law comprises so many elements. It makes clear why he links law with rationality (the understanding and adoption of a style); why he

---

[32] Cf. Grisez, 1965, p. 367; Lottin, 1931, p. 75.

nevertheless allowed irrational beings to be part of eternal law (as expressions); and finally why he thought of law as comprising both precepts and counsels.

But the analogy with art not only clarifies why so many notions are *included*; it also reveals why a certain topic is *excluded* from Aquinas's discussion on law. The topic which is excluded is the question to what extent rational beings are obliged to follow the natural law. Aquinas does not explicitly address the problem of obligation, when speaking about natural law. As we shall see, this 'omission' would ultimately prove fatal for any subsequent theory of natural law. The problem that haunts Suárez's analysis of natural law is that natural law only seems to *indicate* good and evil, but does not *oblige* us to do good and to avoid evil.

The interpretation of eternal law as divine style clarifies why Aquinas did not differentiate between these two functions. Natural law is not a set of moral rules, precepts and prohibitions. It denotes the capacity of human beings to adopt a style. The question is therefore not to what extent we are obliged to follow precepts, but to what extent we are obliged to adopt God's style. As to this latter question, there seems to be no problem involved. Aquinas thought that since our rationality is an impression of the divine light, we have no other alternative than to adopt His style. There is no variety of styles between which we can choose.

That does not mean that we cannot go wrong in the adoption of that style. Just as there are a lot of bad impressionist painters, there are a lot of people who inadequately adopt the divine style to their own doings. But that does not imply that we need an additional source of obligation for the fact that we should adopt the style. We cannot do otherwise. The problem of obligation, therefore, only surfaces when natural law is regarded as a set of precepts. Then, of course, promulgation of those precepts does not entail an obligation to follow them. But if we take natural law as referring to the possibility to adopt the only available style, there is no need to argue that we are obliged to adopt that style.

4. *The role of nature*

Once we understand the eternal law as a divine style, and natural law as the capacity of rational beings to adopt that style, we are able to resolve the debate whether the first principle of natural law is moral

or formal. If we regard the first principle as a general stylistic requirement, Grisez seems to be right. The first principle is indeed not
a general recipe or precept. It does not exhort us to paint only por-
traits. Nor is it purely 'formal', as Grisez maintains. It does not
merely give us a guideline such as 'make always preparatory sketches'.

In fact, the analogy with style reveals that the discussion between
'moral and 'formal' rests on a misunderstanding on what methodology
is about. If we share the view of some philosophers of science that it
is possible to detect various styles of scientific reasoning,[33] we might
say that methodological rules and guidelines are constitutive of such a
style. These rules do not decide which theories are 'true', but they
serve as criteria according to which the question can be decided
which theories *can* be true and which are not. In this sense, Grisez's
assumption that the first principle is neutral and 'pre-moral' is exaggerated. Style and substance cannot be separated. The principle that
good should be pursued and done and evil avoided, does not specify
which particular act is morally praiseworthy, but it certainly asserts
that some actions (pursuing evil) can never count as morally good
acts. The first principle is indeed methodological, but as such it
serves as a general evaluative criterion as well.

We have seen that the debate concerning the first principle entails
a debate concerning the role of nature. If we take it as a moral
principle, nature provides the specifications of 'the good' referred to
in the first principle. If we interpret the principle as a formal one,
'the good' merely refers to the fact that practical reason is active, but
that we can do without nature in order to arrive at sound conclusions
about the courses of action to be taken. According to Grisez and
Finnis, nature plays no important part at all. The mere distinction
between theoretical and practical reason, each with its own fundamental and self-evident principle, testifies to Aquinas's awareness of the
fact that moral judgements are the outcome of practical reasoning, not
of any theoretical investigation of nature.

From end to end of his ethical discourses, the primary categories for
Aquinas are the 'good' and the 'reasonable'; the 'natural' is, from the

---

[33] Fleck, 1935, was the first to introduce the concept of style in the analysis of
science. For a more recent overview see: Hollis and Lukes, 1982. Of course, these
theories start from the assumption that there are several possible styles of reasoning,
whereas Aquinas did not allow for such a variety.

point of view of his ethics, a speculative appendage added by way of metaphysical reflection, *not* a counter with which to advance either to or from the practical *prima principia per se nota*.[34]

This interpretation deviates from the standard-view shared by both Neo-Thomists and legal positivists, that the 'good' as the end for mankind, is informed by Aquinas's catalogue of natural inclinations.

I think that also here, the analogy with art is capable of resolving the dispute. If we regard natural law as the expression of the possibility for rational beings to adopt the divine style, it is clear that the general first principle is not sufficient in itself. There is no style, neither artistic nor scientific, that contents itself with the formulation of methodological guidelines alone. Schönberg's style cannot be transmitted by only explaining the atonal system; one should hear his music in order to compose in his style. Someone who has never seen an impressionist painting is not able to paint in that style. The study of scientific methods does not turn someone into a good scientist. Apart from guidelines, one should have access to the works of art in which a certain style is expressed.

God must have been aware of this wisdom as well. And that is why Aquinas thinks that we human beings can 'grasp' his style by looking at the products of the Supreme Artificer. So we might say that it is in ourselves, as God's creatures, that we find the examples of God's style, the greater part of which he has equally expressed in animals and plants. An investigation of these inclinations and ends in nature is therefore a heuristic device in order to know and to adopt God's style.

This interpretation allows me to adopt a middle-course between the conflicting interpretations. It is true that natural inclinations should not be seen as examples to be copied. Aquinas did not conceive of reason as a mechanical translation of is-statements into ought-statements. An understanding of God's style is more than following successful examples. In this sense, the contemporary natural lawyers are right to reject the kind of automatic inferences legal positivists have in mind when they speak about natural law. But Finnis and Grisez exaggerate matters by claiming that we should not rely on information about nature *at all*, or that nature is entirely irrelevant for practical reasoning.

---

[34] NLNR p. 36.

5. *Fullness of being*

In order to assess the importance of the information nature provides, it should be noted that the first principle of natural law is embedded within two metaphysical assumptions. The first is a general statement concerning the nature of 'the good'; the second refers to the inclinations that are implanted in all creatures.

The general assumption is introduced just before Aquinas's formulation of the first principle:

> [...] the first principle for the practical reason is based on the meaning of good, namely that it is what all things seek after.[35]

And it is here that Aquinas draws a parallel with theoretical reasoning: just as the first principle of practical reasoning is based on the meaning of 'good', the principle of non-contradiction is based on the meaning of 'being' and 'non-being'. The principle is evidently supported by the metaphysical assumption that all things seek after the good. But this is not the only definition of the good. He also identifies the good with 'an end':

> [...] every agent acts on account of an end, and to be an end carries the meaning of to be good.[36]

In order to understand the equation of 'good' with 'end' we have to bear in mind the hierarchical and teleological framework of Aquinas's theory. 'Good' is not simply the opposite of 'evil', but is seen as a quality of being. The well-known Thomistic adagium 'bonum et ens convertuntur' can only be understood on the basis of Aquinas's view that good is fullness of being, and evil the lack of being:

> [...] the good and evil of an action [...] depends on its fullness of being or its lack of its fullness.[37]

---

[35] ST I, II, 94, 2.

[36] Ibid.

[37] ST I, II, 18, 2. This quotation is taken from the Pegis edition, 1944, since the Blackfriars edition translates *plenitudo essendi* as 'completeness of reality' which gives the expression an objectivist flavour that might be misleading.

And:

> Thus a blind man has a quality of goodness for being alive, yet it is an evil for him to lack sight.[38]

It is clear that Aquinas does not conceive of the relation between good and evil as a dichotomous relationship. It is Aquinas's view that there are degrees of 'goodness' which run parallel with degrees of 'being'. In order to do justice to that view, we should not visualize his views as a horizontal, linear relationship of which good and evil are the extremes. The relationship between good and evil should be represented as a pyramid, in which each step higher means more fullness of being (good), and each step lower implies less fullness of being (evil). The definition of the good on which the whole edifice of natural law is erected, is informed by Aristotelian metaphysics in which all things strive towards fullness, perfection and the actualiz-ation of their potentialities. Viewed in this light, we can now under-stand why Aquinas formulates the first principle. It requires people to conduct their practical reasoning on the basis of the assumption that it is fullness of being we strive after and that we should not hamper that natural inclination.

The pyramidal representation of good and evil as more or less fullness of being implies that good and evil are notions, relative to the position one occupies at the scales of the pyramid.

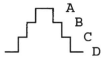

If you find yourself at a level of being which corresponds to stage B, any action which leads to a descent to C is to be considered as a morally bad action. Of course, for those who start at D, the ascent to the same stage C is quite an improvement; the actions leading to such an ascent should be regarded as morally good.

The first principle ('good is to be done and pursued, and evil avoi-ded') is, of course, of no avail in determining the position one occupies on the scales. It only tells us that the general direction *should* be upwards, because it *is* in the nature of all beings to move

---

[38] ST I, II, 18, 1.

upwards. And in this *general* sense, Hart is certainly right in his sketch of teleological thinking. It seems that Finnis and Grisez cannot cut loose the first principle of natural law from the teleological metaphysics in which it is embedded.

However, if nature's role would be confined to the general statement that it is in the nature of things to move upwards on the scales of being, we might not really find that a helpful clue in deliberating on desirable courses of action. Although such a general role of nature would be theoretically significant, it might indeed be discarded as something that is not very relevant to our actual practical deliberation.

Aquinas, however, does not rest at this general statement. Immediately after the introduction of the first principle Aquinas adds more detailed metaphysical assumptions. Here he indicates the position on the scales occupied by mankind. To quote him in full:

> The order in which commands of the law of nature are ranged corresponds to that of our natural tendencies. Here there are three stages. There is in man, first, a tendency towards the good of the nature he has in common with all substances; each has an appetite to preserve its own natural being. Natural law here plays a corresponding part, and is engaged at this stage to maintain and defend the elementary requirements of human life.
>
> Secondly, there is in man a bent towards things which accord with his nature considered more specifically, that is in terms of what he has in common with other animals; correspondingly those matters are said to be of natural law which nature teaches all animals, for instance the coupling of male and female, the bringing up of the young, and so forth.
>
> Thirdly, there is in man an appetite for the good of his nature as rational, and this is proper to him, for instance, that he should know truths about God and about living in society. Correspondingly whatever this involves is a matter of natural law, for instance that a man should shun ignorance, not offend others with whom he ought to live in civility, and other such related requirements.[39]

This passage indeed reveals that there is no fundamental gap between man and the rest of God's creation. As far as we have the inclinations to self-preservation and procreation we are, like the other creatures,

---

[39] ST I, II, 94, 2. It is not clear to me why in the Blackfriars edition *praeceptum* is translated as 'command' instead of 'precept'. It gives the passage an unnecessarily voluntarist ring.

expressions of the divine style. But we have also something extra which elevates us to a position of more perfection than the lower strata. That implies that although we have higher aims in life than the animals, we are not absolved from the duty to preserve ourselves and to procreate.

This raises the question what we should do if the various natural inclinations conflict with one another. What should someone do who is confronted with the choice between self-preservation and truth of God? What is the Christian supposed to do who is confronted with the choice either to die or to convert to Islam? Should the lower aim (self-preservation) come first or is it the other way round and is Aquinas advocating an attitude in which man should always seek his higher aims, and pursue the truth about God in the afterlife, at the cost of hindering the lower aims?

Finnis and Grisez simply *deny* that Aquinas's hierarchical ordering has any moral implications, if we are confronted with such a dilemma between competing inclinations. Finnis claims that

> [...] Aquinas's threefold ordering quite properly plays no part in his practical (ethical) elaboration of the significance and consequences of the primary precepts of natural law [...].[40]

This looks like an easy way out. In this view, Thomas gives us no clue whatsoever about the priority of goals in case they conflict. Goods such as self-preservation, knowledge, or social life are all simply conceived of as 'basic goods' and it is for practical reason to decide which of these goods should have priority in case of conflict. Therefore Finnis thinks that the principles based on these inclinations should be regarded as just some more guidelines, complementing the first principle of practical reasoning. He therefore speaks about the first principles of natural law not being derived from any statement of fact.[41]

This is, however, an unsatisfactory solution. Time and again Aquinas differentiates between ends that are desired for their own sake and ends that are desired for the sake of some further goal. This is clearly expressed in the *Commentary on the Ethics*:

---

[40] NLNR p. 94.

[41] As we shall in IX.4, the rejection of any hierarchical ordering here causes enormous problems for their own moral theory.

> Some ends we choose only for the sake of something else; e.g.
> riches—which we do not desire except in so far as they are useful for a
> human life [...]. It is clear that all these ends are incomplete. But the
> best and last end should be complete. Hence if there is only one thing
> that is complete, it should be the last end which we are seeking. But if
> there are many complete ends, then the most complete of them should
> be the best and last.[42]

According to Aquinas, ends such as self-preservation and procreation cannot be regarded as complete ends. The 'most complete end'
in Aquinas's vocabulary,[43] is knowledge of God. This is truly an
end which is desirable for its own sake. We might therefore expect
Aquinas to give priority to the more complete end if it conflicts with
a less complete end. This does not imply that Thomas shows con-
tempt for these lower aims. They are not 'merely' instrumental.[44]
On the contrary, less complete ends are 'sub-ends'. They have a value
in themselves, since they are the realisations of the tendencies that are
implanted by God. The only thing that is required from us is that we
should be aware of the incompleteness of these ends in our practical
reasoning. To think that self-preservation should be given priority
over knowledge of God is simply making a mistake in the assessment
of the degree of completeness of these aims. To give priority to those
lower ends is to forsake the divine spark in us which enables us to
adopt the divine style. To pursue less complete ends at the expense of
a more complete one is to treat oneself as merely an artistic product;
not as the artist one can—also—be.

6. Desired and desirable

We might wonder whether this interpretation of the role of nature, as
outlined above, is so much different from the standard Neo-Thomistic
interpretation, that the first general principle should be viewed as a
major, which, coupled with informative *minors*, gives rise to moral

---

[42] Bk. I, lect. 9, in Martin, 1988, p. 171.

[43] Nowadays, one might be inclined to think that completeness admits of no
degrees, but also here Aquinas's gradual and hierarchical ordering has to be taken into
account.

[44] As we shall see in chapters IX and X, this is how incomplete ends figure in
Finnis's account.

rules. The observation of the various natural inclinations towards ends informs us about the morally desirable ends to pursue. It seems then, that all my talk of eternal law as 'style' and natural law as our adoption of that style is no more than an unnecessary 'aesthetisation', a futile attempt to make Thomism somewhat more palatable to the taste of the post-modern reader and to conceal the undeniable fact that indeed, it was Aquinas's view that we can infer norms from nature without more ado.

At first sight, this appears to be the case. In the preceding section we have seen that Aquinas offered two definitions of 'the good'. The first is 'that which all things seek'; the second equates the good with an end. The two definitions recur in *De Veritate*:

> Since the essence of good consists in this, that something perfects another as an end, whatever is found to have the character of an end also has that of good. Now two things are essential to an end: It must be sought or desired by things which have not attained the end, and it must be loved by things which share the end, and be, as it were, enjoyable to them.[45]

There seems to be an ambiguity involved here. On the one hand, Aquinas conceives of the good as that which is 'perfective' of man's nature, in the sense that it helps man to realise his ultimate end. In this sense the good is thought to be objectively *desirable*. On the other hand, he stresses that the good must be loved and found 'enjoyable'; in other words, the good must be *desired*. The juxtaposition of these two definitions suggests that Aquinas simply conflated the factually 'desired' with the normatively 'desirable'.

In order to clarify the troublesome position of this twofold definition, it is useful to look into a passage in the *Summa*, where Aquinas comes to speak about the three ways in which reasoning can be called theoretical or practical.[46] Reasoning can be called theoretical or practical as regards its *object*, its *method* and its *end*. For instance, if a builder considers how a house can be built, but does not actually build that house, his object is practical, but his end is theoretical. His reasoning is partly theoretical, partly practical.[47]

---

[45] *De Veritate*, 21, 2.
[46] Cf. also McInerny, 1981, p. 39.
[47] ST I, 14, 16.

In order to understand the differences between practical and theoretical reason it is worthwhile to see what they look like, if they are completely theoretical or practical in all three aspects. Based on Aquinas's assertions on how the two kinds of reason run parallel, the following order can be reconstructed:

	theoretical reason	*practical reason*
object	being and non-being	the good
method	principle of non-contradiction	good is to be done etc.
end	the truth	the good

We immediately perceive a remarkable incongruity here. For we see that in the domain of theoretical reason 'object' and 'end' are different: being and truth do not coincide. But in the domain of practical reason the good is both object *and* end of practical reasoning. It is that which all men seek *and* the ideal to which we *should* strive. It seems as if this little exercise indeed reveals the profound confusion between 'is' and 'ought'; between 'desired' and 'desirable'.

Oddly enough, the definition of the good as both 'that which all men seek' and 'the end', does not raise any scepticism among Neo-Thomists. They even conclude that the twofold definition of the good proves that there is no inference here from the desired to the desirable. This is the position of Ronald Duska,[48] who concludes from the above-quoted passage that an end can be counted as 'good' if it fulfils both the criterion that it is actually desired *and* that it is desirable (because of its perfective qualities):

> Aside from being desired and enjoyed, any candidate for being called 'good' must also be perfective.[49]

Duska concludes, that by stressing both elements Aquinas avoids the pitfalls of the position in which the desirable is simply inferred from the desired and it equally avoids the (non-naturalist) position in which the desirable is completely independent of what is actually desired by people.

I believe that this interpretation is too easy. If the problematical relationship between the normatively desirable and the factually

---

[48] Cf. Duska, 1974.
[49] Duska, 1974, p. 153.

desired could have been solved by a mere juxtaposition of the two, it is hard to understand why such a long and fierce debate would have ensued. The problem is that Aquinas needs a criterion in order to decide which good is more 'complete' or more 'perfective' of our being than another good. The question is whether this criterion itself depends on the degree in which this end is actually desired by people or not. If so, there would be reason to think that according to Aquinas the most desirable good is the good which is most desired.

The above-quoted passage from the *De Veritate* does not help us decide whether this is indeed the case. More information is given by Aquinas in a passage in the *Summa,* where our purpose in life is discussed. There, Aquinas draws a highly important distinction, which I quote in full:

> We can speak of the ultimate end in two senses, namely to signify first what it means, and second that in which it is realised. As for the first, all are at one here, because all desire their complete fulfilment, which, as we have noted, is what final end means. As for the second, however, all are not unanimous, for some want riches, others a life of pleasure, others something else. We draw a comparison here with the palatable, which is pleasurable to every taste. Some find this in wine most of all, others in sweetstuffs or something of the sort. All the same, by and large, we esteem that most palatable which most appeals to cultivated tastes. And likewise we ought to account that good the most complete which is finally sought by those with well-tempered affections.[50]

In this passage, the desired and the desirable are not merely juxtaposed but serve as answers to two different questions. Asked for a *definition* of the ultimate end (the so-called first sense) he merely repeats his definition of the good, which is simply that which all men seek. Aquinas says that 'all are at one here'. Of course they are: if we define the good as the desired, it is a somewhat trivial truth that it is the good that we all desire. The real problem arises as soon as we start to look for an objective criterion in order to answer the question whether the desired is that which *should* be desired. About that answer there is lack of consensus, Aquinas says. No objective cri-

---

[50] ST I, II, 1, 7.

terion seems to be available. In that case we should follow those with a 'cultivated taste': we should follow the virtuous man.[51]

This solution is surprisingly similar to the criterion J.S. Mill invoked in order to decide which kind of happiness should be pursued:

> Of two pleasures, if there be one to which all or almost all who have experience of both give a decided preference [...] that is the most desirable pleasure.[52]

Mill tried to refute the criticism raised by his opponents that utilitarianism simply inferred desirability from the desires of 'swine', by arguing that a cultivated person who is acquainted with lower pleasures as well as higher pleasures would opt for the higher ones. Mill and Aquinas both share the view that the ends which are truly desirable are desired by persons with a cultivated taste.

This does not turn Aquinas into a utilitarian, although I believe that there are more similarities between the two doctrines than is commonly recognised. The main difference between the two philosophers is that Mill does not provide us with an answer to the question how we can recognise the truly cultivated man. His treatise vaguely evokes the picture of the educated gentleman, but it is unclear what exactly this gentleman's abilities should be. Apart from that, the claim that the gentleman should also be acquainted with the lower pleasures is confusing. In order to be persuaded that indeed 'it is better to be a Socrates dissatisfied than a fool satisfied',[53] we have to know for sure that Socrates had some experience with brothels, drugs or laziness and consciously opted for philosophy as a higher pleasure.

All these confusions are absent in Aquinas's account, for the cultivated person we should follow is not merely marked by 'taste'. His moral behaviour is not only marked by 'well-tempered affections' but, more importantly, by the fact that the ends he pursues are guided by practical reasoning:

> The natural inclination to the good of virtue is a kind of beginning of virtue, but is not perfect virtue. In fact, the stronger this inclination is, the more perilous can it prove to be, unless it be joined by right reason

---

[51] Cf. also O'Connor, 1967, p. 28.

[52] Mill, 1863, p. 8.

[53] Mill, 1863, p. 9.

[...] just as, if a running horse be blind, the faster it runs the more heavily will it fall, and the more grievously be hurt.[54]

On the basis of these quotations it is not difficult to assess the relationship between good as the object of practical reasoning and good as the end of practical reasoning. They do not simply coincide. The object of practical reasoning is the good towards which we have a natural inclination (that which all things seek). That good simply refers to that which is desired. But although this is 'the beginning' of true virtue, and as such can serve as an *indication* where the good should be sought, it is not enough. 'Good' as the *end* of practical reasoning is that which is truly desirable. In order to assess the desirability of our desires, we should rely on practical reasoning and on the moral behaviour of the well-informed man. In order to avoid confusion, I believe that Aquinas's views on the differences between practical and theoretical reason can be reconstructed as follows:

	theoretical reason	*practical reason*
object	being and non-being	the desired good
method	principle of non-contradiction	good is to be done etc.
end	the truth	the desirable good

Just as the truth is the result of sound reasoning about being, the desirable is the product of sound reasoning concerning the good we naturally seek.

It is important to note that taken in this sense the desirable is not simply inferred from the desires people have. These desires do not serve as the only basis from which ought-statements are derived. Aquinas is not a naturalist *pur sang*. The style-metaphor is more apt to describe the more complex kind of reasoning Aquinas had in mind than the standard interpretation in which rules are the product of simple inferences.

But at the same time Aquinas avoids the pitfalls of those who claim that the determination of the ends one should pursue is completely independent of what people desire. As we shall see in IX.6, this is the view Finnis reverts to. In the modern theory of natural law, the actual desires of people are discarded as irrelevant. Aquinas avoids both pitfalls, not because he equally values both the desirable and the

---

[54] ST I, II, 58, 4, ad 3.

desired (as Duska would have it) but because the process of reasoning forms the missing link between the two.

7. *Conclusion*

The debate whether Aquinas's theory should be regarded as a set of inferences of norms from nature, or as an attempt to develop a theory of practical reasoning, which is independent from nature, seems to be marked by a tendency—on both sides—to underestimate the unifying potential of the concept of eternal law.

In this chapter we have seen that once we take seriously Aquinas's view of God as Artificer, the eternal law is not strictly speaking a 'law', but can be more adequately understood as a style that regulates and directs God's creation. Such an interpretation clarifies the position occupied by the various creatures within the eternal law. The natural inclinations which animals, plants and human beings have in common, can be seen as artistic products: as expressions of the divine style. The natural inclination to rationality (in angels and human beings) enables these beings to participate in the divine style, i.e. to adopt that style in regulating and ordering their own affairs. Natural law is nothing more than a term denoting that capacity of rational beings.

The reading of eternal law as style makes clear that God Himself is not obliged to 'obey' that eternal law. He simply created the world according to a consistently applied self-imposed style. Nor is it necessary to suppose that natural law needs extra obligatory force for us to comply with that law. There is no need for us to look for an additional expression of God's will. Aquinas simply presupposes that we have no other alternative than to adopt the divine style, albeit imperfectly. The very promulgation of the style entails its obligatory force. There is no gap between *reason and will*.

Secondly, since rational beings are not able to adopt a style on the basis of some general stylistic requirements alone (such as the first principle of natural law), we should rely on the additional information concerning God's style that is furnished by His products: the inclinations in all created beings. In order to reason well, we should be informed by the expressions of God's style that can be found in both human nature and in the natural inclinations we share with the irrational beings. As the term 'style' suggests, we should not use this information as examples to be copied in a mechanical way, as Hart supposed. But neither is it advisable to discard nature, as Grisez and Finnis do, as an important source for information and to rely on our rationality alone. The concept of eternal law, if we regard it as style, does not allow for a gap between *nature and reason*.

The absence of any gaps between reason, will and nature implies that it is Aquinas's view that God's will is manifest in the particular style He adopted. In this sense, Kelsen is certainly right that natural law theory depends on the assumption that God's will is immanent in nature. But it is not only an expression of *will*: God's style is also *reasonable*, in the sense that it is accessible to human reason. Finally, His style is *natural* to the extent it is expressed in the creation. In this sense, what God wills is reasonable and natural at the same time.

Obviously, that does not imply that what *we* human beings will is reasonable and natural at the same time. Although there is no other option available than to adopt God's style, it is not certain whether we apply that style in a successful way. We can try to connect our natural inclinations to the rational perception of what is really 'perfective' of our nature, but whether we succeed in doing that and opt for the correct course of action in pursuing the good depends on the way we actually proceed within the parameters of the divine style. Are we successful as artists, working in the image of God? To that question we turn in the next chapter.

CHAPTER II

AQUINAS'S AWARENESS OF CONTINGENCY

In the preceding chapter, I argued that Aquinas's theory cannot merely be regarded as a theory of practical reasoning. To stress the importance of reason at the expense of the role of nature would entail a serious underestimation of Aquinas's views that man is *naturally* endowed with reason and that nature provides the examples of God's style we are supposed to adopt.

However, this emphasis on the vital role of nature in Aquinas's theory once more seems to render Aquinas's position vulnerable to the attack of the legal positivist. My analysis of the role of practical reason as proceeding from the factually desired to the normatively desirable would only confirm his suspicion that, indeed, the kind of reasoning proposed by Aquinas is fallacious. But is it? The answer to that question seems to depend on how we regard practical reason. If it is only a serving-hatch through which information about nature is transmitted and processed into ought-statements, the legal positivist is right: in that case practical reasoning is no more than a derivation of norms from nature.

As may be gathered from the preceding chapter, I think that Aquinas allowed the practical reasoner more room for manoeuvre than that. Aquinas's emphasis on rationality seems to exclude an interpretation of practical reason as merely the ability to translate is-statements into ought-statements. It suggests that more is required from the practical reasoner than only copying God's examples.

But exactly what is this 'more'? In what sense is practical reason 'more' than the ability to infer ought-statements from is-statements? In order to assess Aquinas's views on practical reasoning, it seems that we should examine more carefully the three component parts of practical reasoning Aquinas distinguished: *synderesis* (sections 1-3), *conscientia* (section 4) and *prudentia* (section 5).[1] The analysis of these parts of reasoning will reveal not only how Aquinas conceived of individual deliberation on moral matters, but also how he con-

---

[1] For thorough analyses see Lottin, 1948, II, I, pp. 103-350; d'Arcy, 1961; and Potts, 1980.

ceived of the legislative process and the role of natural law in legislation (sections 6-7).

1. Synderesis: *the angel's eye*

As we have seen in the preceding chapter, Aquinas regards natural law as an expression of the possibility for rational beings to 'participate' in the eternal law. I argued that we should interpret this 'participation' as the ability of rational beings to grasp the divine style and to adopt that style in the regulation of their own affairs. Aquinas has a term for the ability to grasp that style, *synderesis*, a term which has now become obsolete for the obvious reason that the notion has lost its function in contemporary discourse.

The term refers mainly to that part of the human soul which is not affected by original sin. It is the spark of divinity which is not even extinguished in the breast of Cain.[2] Aquinas tells us that *synderesis* is a passive and innate disposition by which we can understand the starting-point or 'seed-bed of all subsequent knowledge', the first principle of practical reasoning. Therefore Aquinas speaks of *synderesis* as the 'law of our intellect'.[3]

This perception of the divine style is described by Aquinas in optical metaphors. *Synderesis* is conceived of as pure 'vision': the immediate perception of the truth. In this respect, *synderesis* is comparable to visual perception by the senses, where there is also an immediate and direct contact with the outer world.[4] But whereas ordinary sight is shared with the lower creatures, the higher form of sight called *synderesis* is what we share with angelic creatures:

> It is proper to the nature of an angel to apprehend the truth without inquiry or running over the matter, but proper to human nature to reach an apprehension of truth by inquiring and by running from one point to another. As a result, the human mind, at its highest, comes near to something of what is proper to an angelic nature, i.e. by apprehending some things immediately and without inquiry [...]. Thus in human nature, in so far as it comes near to that of angels, there must be

---

[2] Potts, 1980, p. 10.
[3] Cf. ST I, II, 94, 1, ad 2, and *De Ver.* 16, 1.
[4] Cf. Kühn, 1982, p. 409.

apprehension of the truth without inquiry both in theoretical and practical matters.[5]

Synderesis is human apprehension at its highest peak. It is that part of human existence which touches that of the angels. *Synderesis* is the angels' eye. This angels' eye grasps things at a glance. The total picture is immediately seen and understood. There is no 'running from one point to another', there is no movement involved, as in reasoning. It is essentially immobile, indeed just like the contemplation of a picture. And it is this absence of movement which is thought to be the best guarantee for the absence of error. It is this ability that sets human beings apart from irrational creatures and links them with the higher creatures.

This pinnacle of human understanding involves freedom as well. Human beings share angelic freedom in as much as they share angelic perception. *Synderesis* renders our actions voluntary. In so far as we have the angels' eye, we can be properly said to 'move ourselves'. By the immediate grasp of the divine style, we can shape our world according to that style. And in this respect we are different from irrational creatures, who are moved by principles implanted in them by God. Their actions can be called involuntary, for they are moved by others.[6] Of course, *synderesis* is also implanted in us: our rationality is not our own product. But thanks to that implanted ability to reason, we are elevated beyond the rank of mere artistic products: we can start to work as artists ourselves. *Synderesis* is therefore a prerequisite for human freedom.

2. Unquestionable parameters

It is by virtue of *synderesis* that we can freely choose how we are to pursue and to do good. It enables us to shape our lives according to our free will. But this freedom does not imply that we are free to doubt the principle itself that is grasped by *synderesis*. We may deliberate about how to pursue good, we may deliberate about our personal conceptions of the good, but *that* we are bound to pursue good and to strive upwards on the scales of goodness and being is not

---

[5] *De Ver.* 16, trans. Potts, p. 124.
[6] ST I, II, 6, 1.

open to criticism. As I emphasised in the preceding chapter: there is only one option for man and that is to apply the divine style. Since there is no alternative, there is no discussion possible about the divine style perceived by *synderesis*. The divine style itself, expressed in the general first principle, as well as in the tendencies of all creatures, is excluded from debate. According to Aquinas, the first principle

> [...] cannot be called in question, but must be presupposed in every inquiry.[7]

The principles perceived by *synderesis* form the beginning and end of any form of practical reasoning. They are like fixed points, without which variation would be impossible. We might compare the ultimate principles with the position of immobility and rest from which one departs when one takes a step, and to which one returns as well. It would be impossible *to walk at all* without these moments of rest. Likewise, Aquinas's claim is not only that we would be lost in our own train of reasoning if we had no fixed points that guided our reasoning, but that it would be impossible *to reason at all* without fixed principles.

This is clearly expressed by Aquinas where he tells us that the understanding of the main principles is both the beginning and the end of the process of reasoning:

> [...] human reasoning, being a movement, has understanding as its point of *departure*, the understanding, namely, of some few things known naturally prior to rational analysis, which are its unfailing source. And it also has understanding as its point of *arrival*, when we *judge* what we have *discovered* by analysis in the light of those naturally obvious principles [my emphasis].[8]

This passage not only reinforces the analogy with walking, but also refers to the two important functions of style I pointed out in I.3. As I said, style has a twofold function: by its inherent constraints it is a source of creativity and at the same time it serves as a general evaluative criterion. In Aquinas's words, *synderesis* as the understanding of the first principle helps us to discover truths as well as to judge what

---

[7] ST I, II, 14, 2. The Pegis edition is used here, since the Blackfriars edition translates *supponere* as 'to take for granted'.

[8] ST I, 79, 12.

we discovered. In the terminology employed by contemporary philosophers of science one could say that the principle grasped by *synderesis* serves *both* as a regulative principle in the 'context of discovery' and at the same time as a principle that informs our judgement on what has been performed in the 'context of justification'. The first principle indeed serves as both 'departure' and 'arrival', in Aquinas's more imaginative terminology.

The comparison with modern philosophy of science enables us to determine the status Aquinas accorded to the divine style grasped by *synderesis*. We might say that Aquinas's conception of practical reasoning is comparable to what Thomas Kuhn called 'normal science'.[9] In periods of normal science—as opposed to periods of revolutionary science—scientific investigation consists mainly of puzzle-solving within a paradigm or framework which itself is unquestioned. During periods of normal science there is no debate about the main principles and parameters which constitute the scientific paradigm within which scientists work. Normal science is marked by the application of a style of scientific reasoning that itself remains unquestioned.

The similarities between Kuhn's concept of normal science and Aquinas's account of practical reasoning are remarkable. Firstly, they both share the idea that reasoning is not possible without the existence of a style, framework or paradigm that provides the principles in the light of which we can discover and judge. Secondly, both share the idea that really fruitful reasoning can only take place if these principles themselves are unquestioned.

This is not to say that there are not any huge differences between Kuhn and Aquinas either. Kuhn did not regard a scientific paradigm as God-given. And Aquinas could not conceive of the possibility that periods of normal science alternate with periods of revolutionary science, in which the parameters are challenged and overthrown, as Kuhn asserted. It was inconceivable to Aquinas that people would start questioning the first principles, perceived by *synderesis*. Since there is only one style available, the divine style, human beings can neither choose nor change their style. It is the *sine qua non* for all moral reasoning, and, as such, a prerequisite for our fundamental freedom in shaping our own world. By questioning the divine style,

---

[9] Kuhn, 1962.

people would jeopardise the only link they have with the angels and God.

3. *The scope of certainty*

Until now, we have described *synderesis* as the immediate grasp of the divine style. But what does this exactly mean? What exactly is 'grasped'? Aquinas tells us that *synderesis* grasps principles. But sometimes he refers to *a* single principle; sometimes he refers to the plural form: principle*s*. In the former case, he clearly refers to the first principle of natural law that good is to be done and pursued, and evil avoided. In the latter case, he seems to refer to the principles that correspond to the natural inclinations in creatures: self-preservation, procreation, sociability and knowledge of God. It seems then that *synderesis* grasps the divine style, both by the general principle that all things do and should move upwards on the scales of being and goodness, as well as by the particular inclinations of the various creatures.

This view can be reconciled with the way we grasp any style, either artistic or divine. As I remarked in I.4, general stylistic requirements are always accompanied by examples in which a style is expressed. But what does this view imply if we take seriously Aquinas's view that the principles grasped by *synderesis* are unquestionable parameters? How can we make sense of Aquinas's claim that not only the first principle is unquestioned, but *also* the particular examples in which the style is expressed? Does that imply that Aquinas's concept of *synderesis* boils down to the assumption that we are not allowed to deviate from the particular inclinations, detectable in the various creatures?

In order to answer that question, we should note that here a comparison with science has its dangers. Aquinas himself noted that there is an important difference between practical and theoretical reason. Practical reason is, as Grisez emphasises, active. It seeks to realise certain *ends*. In Aquinas's words:

> Now in matters of practice then end stands like a principle, not a conclusion, as Aristotle observes.[10]

---

[10] ST I, II, 13, 3.

Principles are ends, in the sense that the beginning (*principium*) of our reasoning on practical affairs is always informed by the end we want to achieve. To use a formulation of Aquinas, *synderesis* 'proposes to us' the ends to be pursued. This is the starting-point for any practical reasoning. But *which* ends does it propose to us?

The use of the plural form *principia* suggests that ends such as self-preservation, procreation and knowledge of God are *all* appreciated as natural ends that form the *principia* of our reasoning. And indeed they are. But I argued in I.5 that the various ends are not just various 'basic goods' all figuring at one and the same level. In the Thomist system, ends are ordered in a hierarchical way. Except for the ultimate end, which is truly an end in itself and desired for its own sake, all the other ends can *equally* be regarded as sub-ends,[11] conducive to the attainment of a further aim.

Whether one views a certain aim as end or as sub-end depends on the particular perspective and the particular situation in which one reasons. This implies that the practical reasoner may consider any end as a subordinate end, except for the ultimate end which of course is an end in itself. But as soon as something is regarded as a subordinate end which is conducive to another end it is an object for deliberation and choice.

Aquinas is quite clear on this point:

> For instance, medical health is the end for a doctor, and as such this for him is a settled principle, not an open question. Medical health, however, is subordinate to spiritual health, and consequently for one charged with the cure of souls health or sickness may be a matter of choice.[12]

Whether something should be regarded as a sub-end or as an ultimate end depends on the field of operation. We should keep in mind, however, that the job of the practical reasoner is not a restricted one, like that of the physician. He is concerned with moral behaviour in the widest possible sense. His actions should aim at the most com-

---

[11] I deliberately prefer the term 'sub-ends' to 'means' in order to avoid the misunderstanding that self-preservation and procreation are 'merely' instrumental for Aquinas. These ends have a value in themselves, but nevertheless they are conducive to a further aim (cf. I.5).

[12] ST I, II, 13, 3.

plete end, which according to Aquinas consists in contemplation of
the truth of God.[13]

If we take seriously what Aquinas tells us about the hierarchical
ordering of sub-ends and ends, we should admit that this ordering has
important implications for how *synderesis* should be perceived. The
role of *synderesis* is then a limited one: it enables us to see that it is
the general tendency of creatures, including ourselves, to move upwards on the scales of being and goodness and that there are several
ends, which are hierarchically ordered.

If we say that it is not for humans to decide on their own style,
this is merely a big word for saying that there is no discussion possible about this teleological and hierarchical ordering of the universe
and about our duty to prefer a more complete end to a less complete
end. If we do so, all ends that are subordinate to the ultimate end can
in principle be regarded as sub-ends, to be pursued in order to attain
the ultimate end. And if they are regarded as such sub-ends, they are
open for discussion and deliberation. The whole idea that the unquestionable principles are not open for debate, doubt or choice does not
involve an uncritical endorsement of *all* the ends perceptible in
nature.

This insight enables us to reply to the criticism of the legal positivist. He is right in the general sense that the moral principle that we
should strive for perfection is inferred from the observation that all
things do seek perfection. He is also right as regards the ultimate aim
for mankind. Aquinas's hierarchical world-view entails the view that
there *is* an ultimate aim for mankind, which we therefore *should* pursue. But he is certainly not right in thinking that all our moral norms
are inferred from the observations of nature. That animals do procreate does not entail the obligation for human beings to procreate. It
merely points to the fact that procreation is *a* value. But that value
can be outweighed by considerations concerning higher values, as is
the case of the monk who prefers celibacy. Subordinated values are
subject-matter of deliberation.

---

[13] Cf. ST I, II, 3, 5.

4. *The movement of reason*

It is not enough to perceive the divine style; we should also apply that style in the way we deliberate about the moral problems that present themselves in everyday life. In order to do that, we should be able to specify the general principles provided by *synderesis* to requirements that are applicable to particular circumstances. This activity of application is referred to by the term *conscientia*.

To the modern reader who is unacquainted with Aquinas's terminology this may sound strange. If we translate *conscientia* by the term 'conscience', we are tempted not to consider it an activity at all. It is rather associated with some 'inner voice', innate or acquired, that informs us about the moral rectitude of our actions. But to Aquinas, *conscientia* is essentially an activity, the operation through which general rules are translated or processed into more specific rules and eventually into conclusions, which refer to particular cases or circumstances.[14]

This operation is framed in the model of the Aristotelian syllogism, which is the model for both theoretical and practical reasoning. The general truths, grasped by *synderesis*, form the major premiss. The minor premiss provides us with an assessment of the particular situation we find ourselves in, a particular deed to be done or a particular social institution to be evaluated. It tells us how the end, presented in the major, can be achieved in these particular circumstances. In the conclusion a more specific rule is generated. Of course, unlike theoretical reason, practical reason does not rest at drawing conclusions only; these conclusions give rise to a particular action in that particular situation.

The act of combining the major and the minor premiss and of inferring the conclusion is, of course, exactly that process of reasoning Aquinas referred to as 'running from one point to another'. It is subject to error. Aquinas provides us with the—rather trivial—example in which the major 'God should be obeyed' is combined with the minor premiss 'taking oaths is forbidden by God'. The inevitable conclusion is reached that we should not take oaths. Aquinas remarks that although the process of reasoning is sound, the minor premiss is false. But it is also possible that one commits a logical error in the

---

[14] ST I, 79, 13.

process of reasoning itself. Only the major premiss is safe from such fallacies, for that is the product of angelic perception.

If we draw up an example for ourselves, it is easy to see that 'running from one point to another' is a hazardous undertaking. The dangers are not only brought about by the fact that reason is regarded as movement, but also that this 'running' takes place in a contingent field, where one is constantly asked to assess a certain empirical state of affairs. Consider the situation of a woman who is asked to deliver her husband to the police of a state which considers itself the true representative of God. She can go astray in her reasoning in a large number of ways. Firstly, she might wrongly assess the nature of the government. Secondly, she might be mistaken about the degree of piety of her husband. Finally, even if she correctly assesses both state and husband, she might be mistaken about which end is the more complete one. She might decide that the collective good is a more complete end than the well-being of her husband. Or she believes that the more complete good consists in procreation rather than the welfare of the state and decides to hide the husband in the attic. We see that the list of potential errors is long. This risk is inevitable, for we need to draw particular conclusions. Without these, it would be impossible to act at all in a given situation.

It is important to note that the function of *conscientia* is comparable to that of *synderesis*. Like the general principles grasped by *synderesis*, the conclusions drawn by *conscientia* help us to discover and to judge at the same time. Aquinas distinguishes two functions of the specific rules and conclusions generated by *conscientia*. The first is to indicate what should be done or avoided: 'In this case *conscientia* is said to incite or bind'.[15] The second function is to inform us about the moral value of things that have already been done: 'In this case we speak of *conscientia* excusing or accusing or tormenting'.[16] The conclusions drawn by *conscientia*, just like the principles perceived by *synderesis*, play a role in both the context of discovery and the context of justification. Both *orient* us in seeking the good and *evaluate* our choice of the good.

The fact that both *synderesis* and *conscientia* play the same twofold role, however, does not imply that they have the same object. In order to avoid confusion it is important to keep in mind that the task

---

[15] ST I, 79, 13.
[16] Ibid.

of *synderesis* is to grasp the major. On the basis of the major, it is possible to discover/assess the validity of the deductions carried out by *conscientia*. The job of *conscientia*, on the other hand, is to draw particular conclusions, and to guide/assess our moral behaviour in the light of these conclusions. The relationship can be pictured as follows:

FIRST PRINCIPLE (grasped by *synderesis*)
↓ discover ↑ judge
CONCLUSIONS (drawn by *conscientia*)
↓ discover ↑ judge ↑ witness
ACTIONS

That is why Aquinas speaks of *conscientia* not only as an act by which conclusions are generated, but also as an activity which itself is guided by a principle.[17] It is governed by the first principle grasped by *synderesis*.

Finally, *conscientia* has a third function, which is formulated as *testificari*: to witness. According to Aquinas, *conscientia* is said to witness or to acknowledge what we have done or not done.[18] This third function has led Potts to assert that *conscientia* should not be equated with 'conscience' alone, but also performs the function of 'consciousness'.[19] If we insist on pursuing the analogy with science further, we might say that the paradigmatic rules (of *synderesis*) that constitute the framework within which scientists work generate more specific methodological rules, which in their turn devise new experiments to be done, or evaluate experiments that have been carried out. Their third function is indeed that they provide for a kind of awareness that *monitors* the actual conduct of an experiment. Likewise the rules and conclusions, provided by *conscientia*, monitor our daily moral behaviour.

As I said, the specific rules and conclusions generated by *conscientia* are not the conclusions of faultless inferences from indubitable first premisses. All sorts of error might creep in. This implies that those specific rules that monitor our daily actions can be wrong and if so, should be revised. In this sense, *conscientia* is the reverse of

---

[17] *De Ver.* 17.2, 7.
[18] Ibid.
[19] Potts, 1980, p. 2.

synderesis. Whereas the indubitable truths grasped by *synderesis* do not allow for revision or discussion, the fallacious and hazardous character of inferential reasoning even obliges us to revise the specific rules whenever we see that the assessment of the particular situation or of the hierarchy of ends to be pursued could be improved.

In this respect, Aquinas warns us against exaggerated confidence in the conclusions we reach on practical matters. This is expressed in a passage where Aquinas speaks about the question to what extent people *agree* about principles and conclusions provided by practical reason. It is here that he makes an important distinction between the degree of unanimity that can be reached in theoretical reason and that which can be reached by practical reason:

> The business of the *theoretic reason* is with natural truths that cannot be otherwise, and so without mistake it finds truth in the particular conclusions it draws as in the premises it starts from. Whereas the business of *practical reason* is with contingent matters which are the domain of human acts, and although there is some necessity in general principles the more we get down to particular cases the more we can be mistaken [my emphasis].[20]

It is precisely because we are dealing with human affairs that we can be mistaken. And because we can be mistaken, Aquinas allows for an amount of flexibility in order to revise the specific rules and conclusions generated by practical reasoning.

It is important to stress this point, because it is here that Aquinas dramatically differs from his successors, as we shall see in the following chapters. We see that Aquinas, far more than subsequent natural lawyers, allowed for a certain degree of flexibility in moral decisions. The reason for this is that Aquinas perceived that human relations are variable and contingent, for which no standard recipes can be supplied. I think that Aquinas deplores this fact, since he considered it as a symptom of human imperfection. If he could have chosen between flexibility or certainty, he would probably have opted for the latter. But he was realistic enough to see that the kind of certainty attainable by theoretical reason cannot be achieved in the practical domain.

---

[20] ST I, II, 94, 4.

5. Prudentia: *undemonstrable wisdom*

Complete certainty cannot be reached in our conclusions concerning practical affairs, because man's nature, though essentially striving to fulfil its natural inclinations, is—accidentally—variable.[21] Human affairs are contingent, variable, and prone to exceptions. That is why, according to Aquinas, we should not completely rely on demonstrations when it comes to practical reasoning:

> Hence Aristotle says that in such matters we ought to pay as much attention to the undemonstrated sayings of those who surpass us in experience, seniority, and practical wisdom, as to their demonstrations.[22]

Here, Aquinas is referring to the kind of undemonstrable wisdom of the virtuous man. We have seen in I.6 that the virtuous man plays an important part in Aquinas's theory. In order to decide which is the more complete good we should be guided by the kind of reasoning carried out by the virtuous man with 'well-tempered affections'. I asserted in that section that Aquinas's definition of the good resembles Mill's, but that he was more precise about how we can recognise the virtuous man. It is time to substantiate that claim and to investigate Aquinas's views on the main virtue of the virtuous man: *prudentia*.

According to Aquinas, *prudentia* is:

> [...] applying general moral principles to particular conclusions regarding human conduct.[23]

At first sight this activity looks surprisingly similar to what is done by *conscientia*. Both *prudentia* and *conscientia* seem to perform the same task: that of translating general principles into more specific rules and conclusions that are applicable to our daily moral behaviour.

That Aquinas omitted to point out the relationship between the two concepts is all the more surprising if we look at the thoroughness with which the analysis of *prudentia* is carried out in the *Summa*,[24] where

---

[21] Lottin, 1931, pp. 83-5.
[22] ST I, II, 95, 2, ad 4.
[23] ST II, II, 47, 6.
[24] ST II, II, 51.

Aquinas distinguishes a vast array of concomitant virtues, the so-called 'allies' of *prudentia*, such as well-advisedness, sound judgement and wit (*gnome*), which enables people to decide what we nowadays would call 'hard cases' (those cases not unequivocally covered by any rule or law). *Conscientia* is absent from the list; apparently it does not accompany prudentia.

Apart from 'allies', Aquinas mentions a host of 'component parts' or, as we now would say, 'features' of *prudentia*. He mentions memory, insight, teachability, acumen, prevision, circumspection and caution. Even 'reasoning' is mentioned here, because

> [...] the ability to reason well is most important for *prudentia*, in order that general principles may be rightly applied to particular issues which are variable and uncertain.[25]

But again, Aquinas does not mention *conscientia*.

Several attempts have been made to solve this riddle and to establish the relationship between *conscientia* and *prudentia*. Pieper[26] suggests that both notions are essentially the same. But in that case we should account for the strange overlapping of the two terms. McInerny[27] points to the fact that *conscientia* in itself is a purely cognitive affair, whereas *prudentia* enables us not only to *know* the moral ideal but also to acquire the appetite to follow it.

Interesting as these attempts may be in themselves, I do not think we have to seek as far as that for an explanation. For if we examine the description of 'reasoning' as the component part of *prudentia* mentioned above, it catches the eye that the term here refers to the ability to reason *well*. Reasoning in this sense is taken to be successful. This applies to all the other parts mentioned: they are all abilities. They are features of an able and virtuous man. This is the main difference with *conscientia*, for we have seen that that is only the term for a specific operation or act, which may or may not succeed. It is an act that everybody has to perform in order to guide their behaviour, but it can be carried out in a wrong way. So *conscientia* is as different from *prudentia* as 'speaking' is from 'eloquence'.

---

[25] ST II, II, 49, 5, ad 2.
[26] Pieper, 1964, p. 25.
[27] McInerny, 1982, p. 109.

That is why *prudentia* is more extensively dealt with than *conscientia*: the latter is an isolated act, whereas the former is an integrated whole of good qualities.[28] And just as eloquence can only be valued in respect to the degree in which the public is actually convinced, *prudentia* can only be accorded to those who actually carry out the decisions which are the fruits of their deliberation. This explains that *prudentia* is not only cognitive, but has a link to action as well. The prudent man first 'takes counsel', then forms a judgement, and finally commands himself to execute his decision.[29]

About what then does the prudent man 'take counsel'? About the various ways which present themselves in order to achieve the aim he has in mind. As we have seen in section 3, that aim depends on the particular perspective adopted. For a physician it is physical health. For him that end is the final one and is therefore excluded from reasoning. The physician prudently deliberates upon the means that are to his disposal to achieve health. But for a priest, physical health is a subordinated aim and, according to Aquinas, therefore a 'matter of choice'. This implies that for a priest physical health is a subject for deliberation.[30] Someone who deliberates well is prudent.

If we think of the dilemma of the woman who is asked to surrender her husband to the police, we see at once where *prudentia* should come in.[31] The prudent woman has to have a good *memory*: she should for instance remember that a few years back a government with a similar behaviour turned out to consist of cunning bandits, skilful only in propaganda. She has to have *insight* (*intellectus*), which consists in the understanding of the general premisses, but also in the correct assessment of particular or individual ends. She should appreciate correctly the value of procreation against the good of the state. The fact that a correct assessment of individual ends is required does not contradict Aquinas's assertion that *prudentia* is about means and not about ends. We have seen that particular ends are to be regarded as subordinate to a further reaching end. Furthermore, *prudentia* can and should be *taught* since it depends on experience. The woman should therefore listen to sagacious and experienced elders in order to make up her mind. She has to have *acumen* as well:

---

[28] Cf. ST, Blackfriars edition, vol. 36, app. 3.
[29] ST II, II, 47, 8.
[30] ST II, II, 47, 2.
[31] Cf. ST II, II, 49.

if the police is at her door, she is required to make up her mind quickly. That she should *reason* in a sound manner is evident, all the more if the police is not yet at her door. She needs *prevision*, in order to assess the future of her jailed husband or the consequences of her disobedience. In her case *circumspection* is probably one of the more important qualities. It may well be that, considered in the abstract, disobedience is the best means in order to pursue the good she has opted for, but that this particular moment (the police is at her door) is highly unsuitable for such a course of action. And finally she needs *caution*, in particular if she has opted for civil disobedience.

This example clarifies the importance of all the features of *prudentia*, as well as why Aquinas reverts to a long descriptive list of these features. It is the only thing he can do. We can have no certainty about whether someone opts for the right course of action:

> [...] human deeds are multiform; rights are often entangled with wrongs, and wrongs wear the air of good.[32]

Since human affairs are contingent and variable, there are no unequivocal answers. Each answer should be appropriate to the particular circumstances and times. Aquinas acknowledges this problem and asserts that we can only know what the best option is in the majority of cases 'knowing which is enough for human prudence'.[33] *Prudentia* consists of indemonstrable wisdom of experienced people, whose knowledge is inductive rather than deductive. One needs practice in order to become prudent. *Prudentia* cannot be taught from a textbook. So the only way to come round this important virtue is by *describing* instead of demonstrating. And that is why we are presented with a long list of concomitant and component virtues.

We may find such an exposition unsatisfactory. Is the whole treatise on *prudentia* to be considered as a lengthy exposition of the thesis that morally good behaviour is morally good behaviour? It certainly is, in a sense. But one might wonder whether there is anything more to say. Precisely because *prudentia* qualifies people to determine their actions in a fleeting world, there is no room for theorising here. It all depends on the amount of 'Fingerspitzengefühl' someone has acquired over time.

---

[32] ST II, II, 49, 8.
[33] ST II, II, 47, 3, ad 2.

In this sense, *prudentia* can be compared to the virtue of a skilful and talented artist. *Synderesis* enables us to grasp the divine style. *Conscientia* specifies this style into stylistic requirements and prescriptions, adapted to the particular circumstances. But these are not enough. One cannot become a great artist by following the recipes in textbooks on 'how to paint'. One needs an additional, undefinable quality, that goes beyond prescriptions and guidelines. In moral affairs, things are no different. Experience, tacit knowledge and good taste are all required to adopt the divine style in a successful way. What taste is in the arts, *prudentia* is in moral affairs. There has never been a recipe for either of these qualities.

Of course, people did not stop looking for such recipes. But it seems as if only negative recipes could be found, not positive ones. That is probably one of the reasons why '*prudentia*' gradually disappeared from Roman Catholic doctrine as a major topic. As Pieper pointed out, it was replaced by casuistry: doctrines concerning *sins* instead of *virtues*.[34] Casuistry, Pieper remarks, can be understood as the attempt to mould the rich and ever changing reality into a few models according to which the degree of sin could be measured. A vain attempt, comparable to the mistake of the young physician who thinks that real diseases can be treated according to the models presented to him in the lecture-room.

Aquinas's philosophy did not suffer from the illusion that a book of recipes could be written. The treatise on *prudentia* testifies to Aquinas's awareness that humans are imperfect and that they therefore should be allowed a certain space for free deliberation about what should be done in contingent circumstances.

6. *Deduction and determination*

Our analysis of the difference between *conscientia* and *prudentia* enables us to assess Aquinas's views on legislation. The legislator confronts the same task as the deliberating individual. He should translate the general ends and principles grasped by *synderesis* into specific rules and conclusions applicable to the particular situation and society for which these rules are designed.

---

[34] Pieper, 1964, pp. 46-7.

Aquinas does not describe legislation in terms of *conscientia* and *prudentia*, because these terms have a personal flavour, which is hard to reconcile with the collective nature of the enterprise, but I believe that his analysis of legislation runs parallel to his views on practical reasoning.

In fact, Aquinas maintains that human laws are drafted by means of two mechanisms. The first is deduction. Deduction is conceived of as the result of syllogistic inferences, very much like the inferences drawn by *conscientia*. In fact two syllogisms are needed, the first syllogism consisting in the derivation of 'secondary precepts'. For instance, the precepts that one should not harm one another, or that deposits should be restored. These precepts are the conclusion of a major expressing the ends for mankind, in combination with a minor expressing the particular condition mankind is in.

As these secondary precepts are partly derived from a minor in which an assessment is made of particular situations and conditions, the secondary precepts are liable to error. In general it may be true that conditions are such that returning deposits help furthering the end of sociability, but there are exceptions:

> [...] a case can crop up when to return the deposit would be injurious, and consequently unreasonable, as for instance were it to be required in order to attack one's country.[35]

Apart from that, it is possible not only that there are exceptions to the general assessment expressed in the minor, but that the general assessment in itself is wrong and ill-informed. In that case, the secondary precepts, resulting from the combination of the infallible major and the wrong minor, are wrong, 'either by wrong persuasions [...] or by perverse customs and corrupt habits'.[36]

These (fallible) secondary precepts in their turn serve as major premises for the second syllogism, by means of which conclusions are drawn which specify the human laws that should be enacted. If we take, for instance, as secondary precept that man is entitled to use material things to his own benefit, we can couple this precept with a minor, informing us about the fact that man is always more careful with his own belongings than with property held in common. The

---

[35] ST I, II, 94, 4.
[36] ST I, II, 94, 6.

conclusion can be obtained that some form of private property should be instituted.[37] It is obvious that such an inference can be wrong in two ways. Firstly, the truth expressed in the major is not beyond dispute; secondly we might be mistaken about the minor. The second syllogism is therefore even less reliable than the first.

But deduction is not the only method by which general principles of natural law are processed into human laws. In the *quaestio* on human law Aquinas distinguishes two ways in which human laws can be derived from natural law:

> [...] one, drawn deductively like conclusions from premises; two, grounded on it like constructional implementations of general direc- tives.[38] The first process is like that of the sciences where inferences are demonstratively drawn from principles. The second process is like that of the arts where a special shape is given to a general idea, as when an architect determines that a house should be in this or that style.[39]

This second method does not consist of—syllogistic—deduction, but of *determinatio*. What Aquinas tells us in this passage is that natural law supplies the human lawgiver with *formae communes*, general forms, which the lawgiver then determines *ad aliquid speciale*, into something more specific.

It is not coincidental that Aquinas here uses the metaphor of the artist. It points to the fact that more is required than merely following the specific requirements generated by deductive inferences. Since Aquinas conceives of human nature as variable, law must be the product of a free adoption of God's style. As it is expressed by Aquinas:

> Owing to the great variety of human affairs the common principles of natural law do not apply stiffly to every case. One outcome is the diversity of positive laws among different peoples.[40]

---

[37] The example is an adaptation of ST I, II, 66, 2. Aquinas seldom actually carries out the kind of syllogistic reasoning he had in mind.

[38] '[...] determinationes quaedam aliquorum communium'.

[39] ST I, II, 95, 2.

[40] ST I, II, 95, 2, ad 3.

In dealing with human affairs, people are required to shape the general truths into certain specific forms. These forms should be appropriate to the times and circumstances for which they are designed. But again, these circumstances and situations are variable and contingent. That implies that the legislator is faced with the same uncertainties as the individual who deliberates on the desirable course of action. He can but partly rely on the stylistic requirements deduced from the main principles of natural law. Like the individual, he needs some Fingerspitzengefühl, coupled with insight, memory, acumen, sagacity, prevision, circumspection and caution, in order to adapt his laws to the particular exigencies of his time. In short, like the individual who deliberates on moral affairs, the legislator should possess the virtue of prudence. Natural law furnishes only the necessary information. Prudence is required in order to make human laws successful products of the divine style.

7. *The separation of law and morals*

Although one may wonder whether the distinction between *deductio* and *determinatio* is always a clear-cut one,[41] it enables Aquinas to clarify the relationship between natural law and human law in three important respects.

In the first place, it enables Aquinas to distinguish between those human laws that have their force from natural law and those laws which have their force 'from the fact of their enactment'.[42] In order to understand Aquinas's position, we should recall that, according to Aquinas, we do not have to rely on an additional obligatory force of natural law. The promulgation of the only available style entails the obligation to adopt that style (cf. I.3). It is clear then that the more particular stylistic requirements which are *deduced* from natural law (the secondary precepts) merely specify the general stylistic requirements, perceived by *synderesis*, and therefore have the same obligatory status as natural law itself. Although one may doubt whether the secondary precepts specify the divine style in an adequate way, they derive their obligatory force from the fact that they are regarded as specifications of the only style available.

---

[41] Cf. also Finnis's criticism in NLNR p. 289.
[42] ST I, II, 94, 2.

But the particular precepts which are the result of human determination are not obligatory in the same way. They are not mere specifications of general stylistic requirements, but they should be regarded as the products of the human artist, working in God's style. It may turn out to be the case that the human legislator so imperfectly adopted God's style, that his laws are corruptions rather than successful adoptions of the divine style. That is why we cannot assert that his products are backed by the force of natural law. Human laws which are the outcome of *determinatio*, and not of deductions, are not morally but merely legally obligatory.

In the second place, the distinction enables Aquinas to solve that pernicious question which haunts any philosophy of law: are acts evil because they are forbidden, or are certain acts forbidden because they are evil? Aquinas ingeniously remarks that those laws which are generated by deduction forbid or enjoin things because they are evil or good in themselves. They merely specify the ends and values to be realised by man in view of the circumstances he is in. Those laws however that are the product of determination can be seen in a more voluntarist perspective: the things forbidden or enjoined by those laws which derive their validity from their enactment are called bad or evil not because they are evil or good in themselves, but because they are enjoined or prohibited.[43]

It is important to note that Aquinas is *not* defending the position that positive law is only valid law if it is derived from or backed by the moral force of natural law. On the contrary, for the third distinction that Aquinas is able to draw on the basis of his distinction between deduction and determination is the distinction between the *ius gentium* and the *ius civile*. According to Aquinas, the precepts of the *ius gentium* are generated by deduction. These generally refer to what is needed for men to live sociably. They include precepts about selling and buying and so forth. They derive their validity from the fact that they are backed by the moral force of natural law. The *ius civile* consists of laws that are the product of determination. Aquinas tells us that '[...] here each political community decides for itself what is fitting'.[44]

The view that the law of a particular community or state is the outcome of determination has important consequences for Aquinas's

---

[43] ST II, II, 57, 2, ad 3.
[44] ST I, II, 95, 4.

views on the relation between law and morals. In the worst case, legal systems may be regarded as imperfect or even corrupt adoptions of the divine style; as very unsuccessful products of fallible and imprudent legislators. But that does not imply that these legal systems are not legal systems. Bad systems of law are nevertheless to be regarded as legal systems, just as a bad impressionist painting is still an impressionist painting.

I think therefore that Finnis is right in his criticism of what he thinks is the standard interpretation of Aquinas's theory, according to which Aquinas is alleged to have maintained the view that unjust law is not law at all.[45] The whole notion that the laws of the Nazi regime should not be regarded as 'law' because they lacked the force of natural law would indeed have been alien to Aquinas's thought. He would probably have agreed that these laws should be regarded as 'spoilt' or 'corrupt' law[46] but they are nevertheless law: the product of free determination. They are lacking in moral force but not in legal validity, which is derived from the 'fact of their enactment'. Aquinas would have subscribed to Hart's view that it is no good practice to apply the term 'law' only to those legal systems which are morally defensible.[47]

8. *Conclusion*

In this chapter we have discerned three stages of practical reasoning. The first step is not strictly 'reasoning': it is the immediate and infallible perception of the main principles of the divine style, expressed by the term *synderesis*.

The second step consists of syllogistic reasoning, by means of which particular conclusions are inferred from the general principles. When applied to individuals, this activity is termed *conscientia*, whereas in the case of legislation Aquinas speaks of *deductio*. Both *conscientia* and deduction generate more precise requirements and principles needed for a successful adoption of the divine style. The correctness of these inferences is necessary for any successful adoption of the divine style, but not a sufficient condition.

---

[45] NLNR pp. 363-4.
[46] ST I, II, 95, 2.
[47] Hart, 1961, ch. IX.

The third step refers to the additional qualities needed in order to reason *well* on private as well as collective morals. The virtue of *prudentia* refers to the kind of indemonstrable wisdom required in order to arrive at virtuous behaviour. On the level of legislation the term *determinatio* is used in order to describe the task of a legislator to shape a legal system that is best suited to the society for which it is designed. A successful legislator should therefore be prudent as well.

Aquinas was deeply aware of the risks attending the second and third step. Man can go astray in deduction and he can lack the additional qualities required for a successful adoption of God's style. The main principles perceived by *synderesis* cannot prevent us from mistakes.

Aquinas's sketch of practical reasoning both on the part of the individual and on the part of the legislator reveals that natural law has only limited significance. It merely shows us that the general tendency is and should be towards perfection, it furnishes us with some insight in how the various ends and aims are hierarchically ranked and it tells us that we should prefer the more complete to the less complete end.

On the basis of that scarce information, one can go wrong in a number of ways. Firstly, one can be mistaken about the more precise requirements that can be deduced from the first principle. It is possible to deduce some—secondary—precepts such as that deposits should be returned or that it is an offence to harm one another. But these secondary precepts are liable to error, if they are the conclusions of a syllogism where the minor is mistaken. The more specific precepts that are derived from those secondary precepts are even further removed from certainty and self-evidence.

But even if we were certain about the correctness of secondary precepts, even if were certain about the more particular precepts that are derived from these secondary precepts, then we are still not certain about the correctness of the specific laws human beings decide upon. Whether these are justified depends to a large extent on the prudence of the legislator. There are no guarantees, no precise criteria according to which we can judge the moral merits of a legal system. There are no recipes to be found in Aquinas's theory for the good legislator.

In view of the limited role of natural law as providing some general guidelines only, it is understandable that Aquinas allows for what may seem at first sight to be deviations from natural law. This is illustrated by his treatment of private property. Although Aquinas asserts that according to natural law all material things should be owned in common, Aquinas nevertheless maintains that natural law does not prohibit us to act contrary to that precept. If it is for the sake of human convenience to institute private property, we are free to do so, just as natural law does not prohibit people to make clothes although they are born naked.[48] The institution of private property is therefore regarded as a useful addition to natural law: man's own product. It is only to be condemned if, in times of scarcity, private property undermined the chances of self-preservation of the poor. It is only when one of the (sub-)ends are threatened that private property should be abolished.[49]

The amount of freedom allowed to human intervention in drafting his own laws and institutions as he sees fit, as long as the great ends for man are not undermined, enables us to attenuate the four assumptions with which I set out to analyse Aquinas's theory of natural law (cf. introduction).

It is true indeed that to Aquinas there are eternal and universally valid principles, grounded in nature and to be discovered by reason (assumptions b and c). It is by means of *synderesis* that we can immediately discern God's order. But we should not overemphasise the scope of man's reason. It can only discover the *main* principles, the general style of God. It cannot safely be attributed to man that he infers certain and indubitable rules from those general principles. Neither can man be trusted in his own adoption of God's style.

It is also clear that Aquinas thinks that these eternally valid principles serve as criteria by means of which positive law can be justified and/or criticised (assumption a). But again, we should not make too much of this. Aquinas's criteria and principles only concern the ends discernible in nature: self-preservation, procreation, sociability and knowledge of God. Positive law should ensure that these aims can be realised. And where it fails to do so, it can be criticised. But on the basis of these general criteria it is impossible to assess legal systems in a more detailed manner. For instance, it is not possible to decide whether a system of private property is to be preferred to a system of communal property. These are matters on which natural law is 'silent'.

---

[48] ST I, II, 94, 5, ad 3.
[49] ST II, II, 66, 2, concl.

The same applies to assumption d) that for positive law to be morally obligatory, it should be justified in terms of these principles and criteria. We have seen that it is Aquinas's view that only those laws that are the product of deduction can be said to be morally obligatory: only these are backed by the force of natural law. The laws that result from determination are merely legally obligatory,[50] in the sense that they derive their force exclusively from their enactment.

That is why Aquinas does not enter into a discussion of the moral obligatory character of each and every law. Most of these laws are merely legally obligatory. He confines his analysis to the legitimacy of—different types of—government. On the basis of the general principle that a king should not govern only for his own private benefit, there is room for critical evaluation. Consequently, Aquinas does not forbid an overthrow of tyrannical government in cases where the continuance of tyranny would cause greater misery than the rebellion itself.[51] He does not inform us that we have a moral obligation, derived from natural law, to obey each and every law, even if they are instituted by a rightful or prudent king.

The conclusion then seems to be justified that Aquinas's theory of natural law is of limited practical significance. To maintain that positive law is in agreement with natural law does not guarantee that it is a just system of law. It merely means that at least *some* general rules and laws are backed by the force of natural law. The principles of natural law are too general to give such guarantees. One may deplore this limited significance. But we should be aware that Aquinas nowhere *pretends* that natural law can do more. He was too much aware of man's imperfection to allow for the kind of confidence in man's reason, by which subsequent theories are marked.

Finally, this modesty concerning man's ability to partake in the eternal law has some practical advantages as well. Aquinas's theory does not compel us to infer from a legal obligation to follow the rules of a society that we have a moral obligation to obedience as well. As we shall see, Aquinas allows for more freedom in this respect than his 20th century successors.

---

[50] Cf. also ST I, II, 100, 9.

[51] ST II, II, 42, 2.

PART II

CHAPTER III

SUÁREZ'S DISTINCTION BETWEEN CREATION AND LEGIS-
LATION

In the preceding chapters we have seen that Aquinas's theory of natural law is based on the notion of eternal law as the ordering principle which regulates God's creation. It is on the basis of our understanding of that principle, as well as of our observation of how that principle is expressed in creation, that we are able to reason on moral affairs. I pointed out that the contemporary natural lawyers tend to overlook these metaphysical assumptions in their plea for a rehabilitation of Aquinas's theory.

The same applies to Finnis's and Grisez's analysis of the 16th century Spanish theologians and jurists. Finnis and Grisez maintain that these Thomists, well-known and celebrated for their innovations in political theory and international law on the basis of their reappraisal of Aquinas's writings simply misinterpreted Aquinas's theory:

> The substantive differences between the theory of natural law espoused by Vázquez and Suárez (and most Catholic manuals until the other day) and the theory espoused by Aquinas are scarcely less significant and extensive than the better-known differences between Aristotelian and Stoic ethics. But ecclesiastical deference to a misread Aquinas obscured the former differences until well into this century.[1]

The Spanish theorists are held responsible for the distorting lens through which Aquinas is commonly regarded. According to Grisez and Finnis, the basic mistake of the Spanish theorists, particularly of Suárez, was to understand the first principle of natural law as a moral precept, instead of a methodological requirement, as Aquinas had intended it to be. It is a misunderstanding which is caused by Suárez's failure to acknowledge the particular features of practical reason, as distinct from theoretical reason. On the basis of a concept of reason as theoretical reason, norms can only arise from an act of will. In Grisez's words:

---

[1] NLNR p. 47.

> The theory of law is permanently in danger of falling into the illusion
> that practical knowledge is merely theoretical knowledge plus force of
> will. This is exactly the mistake Suárez makes when he explains natural
> law as the natural goodness or badness of actions plus preceptive divine
> will.[2]

I tend to agree with Grisez here. In this chapter I shall confine my
analysis to the writings on law by Francisco Suárez (1548-1617),[3]
and I shall argue that he indeed drastically deviates from Aquinas's
teachings in the way described by Grisez. The question arises why he
did this. Why did Suárez understand natural law as a set of moral
precepts, why did he conceive of reason as theoretical reason? And
why did he feel the need to supply natural law with additional divine
obligatory force?

One might point to the different function natural law theory was
supposed to perform. The Spanish theorists sought inspiration in
Aquinas's writing in order to come to terms with two pressing problems. The first is the Reformation. Aquinas's rationalist theory
seemed to provide a useful weapon against Protestant theories which
assumed that God's will is impenetrable to the human mind, and that
all depends on God's grace.[4] The second issue concerns the legitimacy of the Spanish Crown, in particular in its dealings with the
subjects of the newly acquired colonies in the New World.[5] Aquinas's theory promised to furnish arguments for the kind of universal
legitimation required by an empire in which the sun never sets. It is
no wonder, then, that the theory had to be modified and adapted in
order to meet these new demands.

But there are theoretical reasons as well, which have to do exactly
with those underlying metaphysical assumptions that tend to be
underestimated by Finnis and Grisez. As I shall argue in the following chapters, Suárez's deviations and 'misinterpretations' can be
accounted for by the fact that the Spaniard was dissatisfied with some
important foundations of Aquinas's edifice. Suárez did not conceive
of God's creation in the same way as Aquinas did, nor did he adopt

---

[2] Grisez, 1965, p. 378.

[3] Francisco Suárez, 1612, *Tractatus de Legibus ac Deo Legislatore* (to be abbrevi-
ated as DL).

[4] Cf. Hamilton, 1963; Skinner, 1978.

[5] Cf. Chiappelli, 1976; Fernández-Santamaria, 1977; Pagden, 1986, 1990, 1991;
Parry, 1940; Scott, 1934; Truyol Serra, 1988; Koeck, 1987; Soder, 1973.

Aquinas's conception of law and neither did he share Aquinas's conception of nature as purposeful. On the basis of these different assumptions, it is difficult, if not impossible, to remain faithful to Aquinas's teachings. Rather than blaming Suárez for having misread Aquinas, we might understand Suárez's theory as an attempt to rescue as much as possible of Aquinas's theory on the basis of altered metaphysical assumptions.

Such an understanding is not only historically instructive, but sheds some light on the position of 20th century natural lawyers as well. If we succeed in understanding the link between practical reason and metaphysical assumptions concerning nature and God's role, we might gain insight in the kind of theoretical problems any modern lawyer has to face who, like Suárez, wants to remain true to Aquinas's teachings, but no longer shares some of Aquinas's basic assumptions.

As my analysis focuses mainly on the relationship between Suárez and Aquinas, I shall not deal with Suárez as a forerunner.[6] He is not studied as the 'founder of international law', nor as the initiator of contract theory, but merely as a Thomist. The question to what extent Suárez has been faithful to Aquinas's heritage has been one of the main concerns in the disputes between Dominicans and Jesuits. Whereas Jesuits tend to interpret Suárez as a worthy successor of Aquinas,[7] Dominicans are much more critical of Suárez. Eager to defend 'their' Aquinas rather than Suárez, they are more inclined to differentiate between 'Suárezians' and 'Thomists'.[8] It goes without saying that since I am not motivated by such considerations, my attempt to delineate the differences between Aquinas and Suárez should not be seen as a defense of the Dominican position.

Finally, it should be noted that Suárez's writings are at times tortuous and difficult to follow. Suárez's writings are scholastic, in the sense that they are evidently intended to cover as many authors and opposing views as possible, between which Suárez tries to steer a middle-course. But since he does not organise his treatise according to the scholastic method of presenting opposite opinions before

---

[6] Chroust, 1981, treats Suárez as a forerunner of Grotius; Wilenius, 1963, regards him even as a forerunner of Marx; whereas Skinner, 1978, analyses Suárez's views as early formulations of Locke and Rousseau (vol. II, pp. 158-9).

[7] The most amazing example is Fichter's biography of Suárez, 1940, in which the thesis is put forward that Suárez suddenly turned from a rather dull schoolboy into a brilliant scholar by the help of the Holy Virgin Herself.

[8] Mullaney, 1950; Farrell, 1930.

reaching a conclusion, it is not always clear which middle-course he opts for, or whether he endorses or rejects certain views.[9] Much reconstruction is therefore needed in order to present his views in a systematical manner. This may result in a more coherent picture than is realistic.

My analysis of the distance between Suárez and Aquinas will follow the same structure as the chapters on Aquinas. In this first chapter I shall mainly deal with the assumptions underlying Suárez's *foundation* of natural law. Attention will be paid to his concept of law (section 1) as well as to his view of eternal law (section 2), of creation (section 3), and of natural law (section 4), after which Suárez's proposal for the foundation of natural law will be explored (sections 5-9). In the following chapter, attention will be paid to Suárez's views on the *application* of natural law, in particular to the question how the precepts of natural law can play a role in the *ius civile* as well as in the *ius gentium*.

1. *A narrower concept of law*

The first conspicuous difference with Aquinas is revealed, immediately at the beginning of the DL, where Suárez comes to speak of law (*lex*) in general. Here, Suárez openly engages in a critique of Aquinas's concept of law. According to Suárez, Aquinas defined law as 'a certain rule and measure in accordance with which one is induced to act or is restrained from acting'. In I.3 we have seen that this is indeed Aquinas's definition. The definition of *lex* as *regula* (ensuring harmonious proportions) and *mensura* (ensuring the suitability to a further end) are seen as component parts of 'law', taken in the sense of an ordering principle. On the basis of this definition, I argued that Aquinas conceived of law as style.

Suárez thinks that this definition is too general and too broad, because it comprises three elements that should be excluded from the concept of law. He therefore proposes to give law a narrower and more precise meaning. The *first* limitation he proposes is that law should only be regarded as prescribing morally good behaviour. As such, the term 'law' should not be used in order to refer to the rules

---

[9] Nevertheless, among the many commentators, only Villey, 1968, acknowledges the troubles he had in reading a chapter by Suárez from beginning to end.

pertaining to so-called 'artificial matters'. According to Suárez, the Thomistic concept of law

> [...] would relate not only to moral matters, but also to artificial matters;[10] not only to what is good and upright, but also to what is evil; since the arts, too, whether licit or illicit, have their own rules and measures, according to which their operation is promoted or restrained.[11]

Suárez does not deny that there are rules pertaining to the proper production of 'artificial matters', but he considers the term 'law' to be inappropriate, because 'artificial matters' are morally neutral. The rules regulating 'artifical matters' not only guide the production of morally good things, but also of morally indifferent things (a beautiful table) or even of morally bad products (a well-designed gun).

Suárez's reading of Aquinas confirms my—and Grisez's—view that indeed Aquinas conceived of law as 'style' as merely an ordering principle which does not ensure a morally correct application of this principle. Suárez does not agree with that view and in fact distinguishes 'law' from 'style'. Law is not only an ordering principle, but a principle directing us to a morally good life.

The *second* limitation Suárez proposes concerns the binding force of law. As we have seen, Aquinas's concept of law as style comprises both precepts and counsels; it not only forbids certain actions, but it equally functions as a source for creativity. It is not surprising, therefore, that after having declined the view that law pertains to 'artificial matters', Suárez *also* rejects the view that law contains 'counsels'. According to Suárez, counsels have no place in 'law' in the proper sense of the term. Counsels are mere recommendations that lack the binding force which is characteristic of 'law' in the proper sense of the word.

The *third* objection of Suárez against Aquinas's broad definition of law is that it also includes irrational creatures as subject to law. According to Suárez, the term 'law' should be reserved for precepts that are promulgated to and understood by rational beings. Again, this specification is consistent with the other two limitations. As we have

---

[10] The Latin text gives: 'Lex ite non solum in moralibus, sed etiam in artificialibus [...]'.

[11] DL I, I, 1.

seen (I.3), it is Aquinas's view that law, as rule and measure, can be present as the ruling and measuring principle, as well as the principle expressed in the subject rul*ed* and measur*ed* by that principle. The first sense refers to what we nowadays would call a normative law, the second sense refers to descriptive laws, as the expressions of the divine style in His products.

In Suárez's view, this two-fold definition of the term 'law' is too unspecific. We should distinguish creatures who *follow* rules from creatures who merely *conform* to rules. The term 'law' is only applicable to those who can understand it and to whom it is explicitly promulgated. Only rational creatures can be said to follow rules. If we include irrational creatures, the use of the term 'law' can only be a metaphorical one

> [...] since things which lack reason are not, strictly speaking, susceptible to law, just as they are not capable of obedience.[12]

And:

> [...] the subordination and subjection of irrational creatures to God is but loosely and metaphorically called obedience, since it is more properly a kind of natural necessity; while, on the other hand, the eternal law, in so far as rational beings are thereby governed as moral beings and as members of society, has the true nature of law, and obedience in the true sense is paid to it.[13]

In short, according to Suárez, the term 'law' should be confined to binding precepts, promulgated to rational creatures only, who are directed to a morally good life. Henceforth, I shall call this narrower definition of law 'law-as-precept', in contrast to Aquinas's conception of 'law-as-style'.

2. *Eternal law*

It is understandable that this narrower concept of law seriously affects Suárez's concept of eternal law as well. Aquinas used that term in order to refer to God's style in creating the universe. If 'law' is no

---

[12] DL I, I, 2.
[13] DL II, II, 13.

longer understood as style but as a set of precepts, it is clear that Suárez has difficulty in integrating the concept of eternal law in his theory.

Suárez's first objection to the concept of eternal law is that it lacks any subjects:

> [...] from eternity there was no one upon whom law could be imposed.[14]

If we are to take the word 'eternal' literally, Suárez seems to say that we should suppose that there have been subjects from eternity to whom it was promulgated. But there are no such eternal subjects.The created is temporal.[15] As far as 'eternal law' is concerned, we only know that the superior has lived from eternity. Suárez therefore thinks that it is therefore not possible to speak of 'law' here in the proper sense of the term.

Probably, Suárez would have left it at that, had he not been confronted with the weight of tradition, in which the existence of eternal law had been assumed. Instead of discarding the whole notion altogether, Suárez looks for a compromise. The solution Suárez proposes is indicative for his search for a *media via*. He argues that there are two stages: in the *first* stage the law only exists in the mind of God; in the *second* stage it is 'externally established and promulgated for the subjects'.[16] It is because of this second stage, Suárez concludes, that we can call it 'law'. As long as the eternal law only dwells in the mind of God, it is not a proper law.

This attempt to rescue the notion of eternal law is not supported by Aquinas' teachings. According to Aquinas, eternal law is the divine order. Even if it had not been promulgated, it is still a law in the sense that it is an ordering principle regulating God's creation. This order is promulgated by means of the channels of divine and natural law. Had Aquinas shared Suárez's view that in order for the divine order to be a true law, promulgation is essential, he would have contented himself with saying that only natural and divine law deserve the title of 'law'. The eternal law refers merely to the assumption that

---

[14] DL II, I, 1.
[15] Cf. DL I, III, 6.
[16] DL II, I, 5.

there is an ontological substratum (the divine *exemplar*), to which we have access by means of natural and divine law.

It seems to me that Suárez is well aware of this difficulty. For he immediately adds:

> Ordinarily, however, God does not bind men by the eternal law, save through the medium of a law which is external and which constitutes a participation in and manifestation of the eternal law. [...] Accordingly, in the case of this law, in so far as it is eternal, its promulgation, properly speaking, has no place.[17]

So it seems that Suárez faces a problem here. On the one hand, he can only defend the use of the term 'eternal *law*' by referring to a second stage in which it is promulgated. On the other hand, he knows that this was not Aquinas's view, for whom promulgation of the divine order was not a prerequisite for the existence of that order. The conclusion seems to be justified that the term 'eternal law' is misleading. And this is indeed the conclusion at which Suárez arrives:

> We may, indeed, distinguish two aspects[18] of the eternal law. In one aspect, it is eternal, and being so, is independent of external promulgation, neither has it relation to creatures existing for the moment. In the other aspect, this law is promulgated and binding at the present time, and consequently has a temporal relation to creatures existing at the time. *In this sense, it may be called divine* [my emphasis].[19]

As regards the first stage, there is no need to talk of 'law' in the proper sense of the word, whereas in its second stage or aspect, eternal law can be identified with divine law without more ado.

This passage clearly reveals that on the basis of a conception of law-as-precept, 'eternal law' has lost its function. If it is eternal, it can only be located in the mind of God and is therefore no true 'law'. If it is a law, it must be established, promulgated and imposed on subjects, in which case it cannot be 'eternal'. The two cannot go

---

[17] DL II, I, 11.

[18] The translation correctly reveals Suárez's ambiguity in terms: whereas in DL II, I, 5 Suárez refers to 'stage' or 'phase' using the term *status*, in DL II, IV, 7 he proposes to distinguish not phases but *denominationes* of eternal law.

[19] DL II, IV, 7.

together. On the basis of Suárez's concept of law-as-precept, eternal law is properly speaking a contradiction in terms.

The concept of law-as-precept is also responsible for the second objection Suárez raises against the notion of eternal law. To speak of an eternal law, regulating God's creation, would imply that God Himself was subject to law. Such a view would deny God any freedom whatsoever. And of course we cannot allow the notion of a God who is not free to do what He pleases. Suárez emphasises this point several times:

> [...] no law can exist save in the relation to what must be ruled thereby; and the eternal law [...] is not imposed upon God or upon the Divine persons [...].[20]

According to Suárez, God's freedom cannot be limited. It would be downright blasphemous to suppose that God should be compelled to obey law.

This consequence only ensues if law is understood in the sense of Suárez. If we understand by law a set of binding precepts, imposed on rational beings, we cannot very well imagine that God is 'guided' by such precepts without supposing—blasphemously—that He lost His divine freedom. As I noted in chapter I, Aquinas did not run this risk at all, precisely because he did not share Suárez's concept of law, and conceived of law-as-style. And being guided by a style is, of course, very much different from being guided by a binding precept. On the basis of the notion of law-as-style, one can assume an order in God's mind without restraining God's freedom, whereas eternal law-as-precept entails the view that God is not sovereign.

This might shed some light on the debates between intellectualists and voluntarists as they were conducted until well into the 17th century and which revolved around the question whether good and evil exist prior to God's law, in which case God's law merely indicates good and evil (*lex indicans*), or whether good and evil should be seen as the result of God's law, in which case God's law is regarded as *lex imperans*. In these debates the theme of God's freedom constantly recurred: is God free to have legislated as He sees fit, or is He Himself bound by a higher law?

---

[20] DL II, III, 3.

I think that this debate can only arise on the basis of a fundamental shift of the notion of law itself. As long as one thinks of law-as-style, as a principle of order in God's mind, it is no use asking oneself whether God is guided by the ideas in His mind or whether He is free to change the ideas in His mind. This would be an absurd discussion. But as soon as 'law' is conceived of as essentially consisting of commands or precepts that are imposed, the urgent question arises whether God Himself is constrained by His own laws. The fact that intellectualists constantly felt obliged to deny the charge of blasphemy, implies that apparently they had already adopted the (originally voluntaristic) concept of law-as-precept. One might even say that the intellectualist already lost the battle by adopting the concept of law-as-precept. He needs to come to terms with the problem of God's limited freedom.

3. *First fissures*

We have seen that on the basis of the notion of law-as-precept, the concept of eternal law is incomprehensible, self-contradictory and blasphemous. Apart from that, the concept is superfluous. If we regard promulgation as essential for the existence of law, divine law and natural law as the promulgations of God's precepts suffice.

At this stage we might wonder why Suárez, who wants to remain faithful to Aquinas's teachings, adopts a notion of law which is apparently so hard to reconcile with Aquinas's theory. Why does he, as well as many other intellectualists of the period, adopt a notion of law-as-precept, which causes considerable problems for any Thomist? Is it desire for precision that motivates Suárez to specify the notion of law? Is it due to his professional legal training that Suárez looks for more precise definitions? These factors may certainly have contributed to his decisive step, but I think there are more fundamental reasons as well.

In order to gain insight into these reasons it is worthwhile to make a short excursion to the work of Marsiglio of Padua. Although Suárez naturally regarded this 14th century philosopher as a dangerous enemy of the Church, he was well-acquainted with his work. And Marsiglio made an interesting remark concerning the various meanings of 'law':

[...] it is well to distinguish the meanings or senses of the word 'law'. For this word means in one sense a natural sensitive inclination to any action or passion [...]. But in another sense this word 'law' is used of some operative quality, and generally of every form of an operable thing existing in the mind, from which as type or measure the forms of artifacts proceed [...]. But in a third sense law means a rule containing admonitions to prescribed human actions, according to which they are ordained to glory or punishment in the world to come [...].[21]

Marsiglio opted for—a secularised version of—the third sense as the one most suited for his political theory: without a 'coercive command' law was no genuine law, he declared.[22]

Whether Suárez obtained the idea directly from him or not, it seems that nearly three centuries before Suárez wrote his book, the unified concept of law (as used by Aquinas) was already deemed ambiguous. For if one examines the three senses distinguished by Marsiglio, it is clear that Aquinas thought of eternal law exactly as a *combination* of these three senses. According to Aquinas, God, in constructing and ordering the universe (sense 2), had implanted various inclinations (sense 1) which were accompanied (as far as mankind is concerned) by explicit admonitions (sense 3) to be known through revelation and natural reason. It seems as if this unity had been broken down within 50 years after Aquinas' death. Then, suddenly, this wide conception of law appears to be an inherently ambiguous one.

In a similar vein, Suárez distinguishes 'idea' (Marsiglio's sense 2) from 'law' (sense 3). Suárez writes:

[...] the true difference [...] [is] that an idea has only the character of an *exemplar* in relation to God Himself, so that He works in accordance with it, while it serves (so to speak) *merely* as a concrete pattern for the works of God; whereas the divine law *as law* has rather a *dynamic* character, giving rise to an inclination or obligation to action; and these diverse characteristics are entirely sufficient to constitute a conceptual distinction [my emphasis].[23]

---

[21] *Defensor Pacis* I, X, 3.
[22] *Defensor Pacis* I, X, 5.
[23] DL II, III ,10.

This passage is instructive, for it clearly reveals how Suárez understands the term *exemplar*: it is a pattern for the works of God which
only regulates God's *production*, but does not direct God's *products*.
Unlike Aquinas's assertion that law, as a rule and measure, is present
in *both* the ruling and measuring principles *and* in that which is 'ruled
and measured' thereby, Suárez confines the relevance of an *exemplar*
only to God's activity and does not extend its force to that which *is*
measured and ruled: the creatures.

We might be able to understand Suárez's different view as a
reflection of artistic developments and to keep in mind that Suárez
was a contemporary of Caravaggio (1573-1610), the great 'naturalist',
whose main aim was to represent nature, as well as biblical figures,
as realistically as possible. Probably, Suárez shared Caravaggio's
view that the main function of art is to represent faithfully. It is
significant that Suárez refers to God's creation as *representation*.[24]
Suárez defends his distinction between 'law' and 'idea' by saying that
ideas are represented, whereas laws are imposed. In Suárez's view,
God merely represents the idea which is 'rather fixed formally in the
mind of the artificer'.[25]

The conception of art as representation necessarily undervalues the
importance of style. Of course, realism (or naturalism) is itself a
particular style, but one of its main requirements is precisely to deny
that it is. It pretends to represent reality 'as it really is'. As such, it
tends to play down the amount of intervention on the part of the artist. If a realist talks about an *exemplar*, he pretends that it is no more
than an example to be copied.

However, the conception of *exemplar* as that which is represented
reduces the scope of such an *exemplar*. The real still-life can at best
serve as a criterion for judging the likeness of the picture. If the
representation is successful (and in the case of God, it certainly is!),
the still-life has no longer any function once the painting is completed. In this sense, Suárez's conception of *exemplar* is indeed only
relevant for God's creation. It ceases to have directive force after the
work is completed.

On the basis of this limited role of an *exemplar*, it is indeed not
possible to see why Aquinas couples the concepts *exemplar* and *idea*
with *ratio* and *lex*, as I noted in I.2. Whereas *exemplar* as style de-

---

[24] DL II, III, 10.
[25] DL II, III, 10.

notes an ordering principle which remains active after creation, *exemplar* as concrete example has no relevance for finished products. To put it in somewhat exaggerated terms: creatures are conceived as dummies, faithfully and successfully copied according to the fixed ideas in God's mind. These fixed ideas, once represented, lose their directive force in guiding creatures to a further end.

That is why Suárez no longer speaks about the natural inclinations of animals. Instead he refers to them as mere instincts (*instinctus*).[26] They are merely 'programmed', to use an anachronistic term. The actions of irrational creatures merely conform to the stereotypes God had in mind. These are no longer thought to be purposive. This implies that these faithful copies of God's stereotypes *also* fail to direct rational creatures. The natural instincts of animals have no moral relevance for rational beings. Non-rational nature is a mere product of God's design that does not inform us about morally correct behaviour. It is here that the first fissures in the teleological world-view begin to surface.

4. *The script of natural law*

If we regard the desires, needs and inclinations as features of finished products which have no relevance for our moral reasoning, it is clear that Aquinas's first principle ('do and pursue the good and avoid evil') acquires a different meaning. It is no longer based on the definition of good as 'that which all things seek'. This statement has become meaningless and provides no clues on the basis of which rational beings can take informed decisions in order to act freely and rationally.

But nor do *our* natural inclinations have any relevance as starting-points for moral reasoning. Suárez's division between rational crea-tures who follow rules and irrational creatures who merely conform to rules, also entails a division in human nature itself between its rational and its irrational part. It is only on the basis of our rational understanding of our inclinations that these inclinations can be brought to 'a higher level':

---

[26] DL I, III, 8.

Hence, the natural law brings man to perfection, with regard to every one of his tendencies [...]. For all these propensities in man, must be viewed as being in some way determined and *elevated by a process of rational gradation*.[27] For, if these propensities are considered merely in their natural aspect, or as animal propensities, they must be bridled, that virtue may be attained [...]; and on the other hand, if the same propensities are considered with respect to their capacity for being regulated by right reason, then proper and suitable precepts apply to each of them [my emphasis].[28]

A dichotomy is introduced here, which is absent in Aquinas's writings. As we have seen, Aquinas[29] mentioned a threefold ranking of inclinations: self-preservation, an inclination man shares with all animate creatures; procreation, an inclination man shares with animals, and finally the search for truth about God and social life, which are inclinations proper to mankind only. Aquinas conceives of rationality as an *additional* quality which distinguishes human beings from the rest of the creation. Self-preservation and procreation are 'subends', conducive to the ultimate end for mankind, but having value in themselves.

According to Suárez, however, self-preservation *as such* is no subend at all. The urge to self-preservation is mere instinct, if it is not coupled with rationality. Rationality is not only an additional property, it *changes* the natural propensities as well. Rationality pervades man's biological inclinations and turns these into more than 'mere' instincts. That is clearly visible in Suárez's account of Aquinas's hierarchy of inclinations. They are no longer inclinations we *share* with the rest of the creation but are humanized from the start. Suárez mentions the various aspects of the human condition only: individuality, mortality and rationality. As an 'individual entity' man is bound to preserve himself; as a mortal being, he is inclined to preserve his species, and as a rational being he inclines to communication with God and other rational creatures.

The dichotomy between rationality and nature, absent in Aquinas's writings, but pervading Suárez's entire theory, excludes the possibility that man might find his starting-point for practical reasoning in desires. There is such a gap between that which is naturally 'desired'

---

[27] '[...] eleuate per gradum rationalé'.
[28] DL II, VIII, 4.
[29] ST I, II, 94, 2.

and that which is morally and rationally 'desirable', that man cannot
be expected to reason from the desired to the desirable. He cannot
rely on his own natural inclinations, nor can he find any heuristical
clues in the tendencies of other, irrational creatures. That is why
Suárez assumes that in order to direct rational creatures to their due
ends, God needs to promulgate an additional law in the strict sense of
that term.

That law is the natural law. It is clear that only rational beings can
understand such an explicit law. Or, in Suárez's words: whereas God
commands irrational creatures 'by acts', (i.e. implanted instincts), He
commands rational creatures 'by words'.[30] Without natural law, men
would be no more than animals, motivated by blind instinct. These
ideas form the background of the plays of the famous playwright
Pedro Calderón de la Barca, himself a pupil of the Jesuits at the
School of Salamanca. In his didactic play 'El gran teatro del mundo'
God Himself is represented as 'El Autor', the dramatist of the play.
He literally puts words in the mouth of actors. The actors are
endowed with natural reason, which enables them to understand the
words they are supposed to utter, but of course it cannot be denied
that their reasoning, as well as the natural freedom Calderón's God
provides them with, are merely means to play out—in the best possible way—their roles as they were designed by El Autor.[31] God as
the dramatist of this theatre of the world is the figure we can best
keep in mind if we are to understand the views of Suárez on natural
law. Natural law is the *script* of that play, so to speak. That is why
rational beings are the only actors on the scene. Irrational animals are
no more than stage-properties, being 'moved' by the stage-director at
will.

5. *The silence of rational nature*

Since Suárez discards the notion that irrational nature might have any
moral relevance, natural law as God's promulgated law plays a much
more important role than in the theory of Aquinas, who could have

---

[30] DL II, III, 7.

[31] Fiore, 1975, made an interesting attempt to interpret the works of Calderón in
the light of natural law ethics. Unfortunately, however, Fiore bases his account of
natural law entirely on a reading of Aquinas, instead of Suárez of whom Calderón was
a pupil.

certain confidence in man's natural inclinations as well. But at the same time it is much more difficult for Suárez to ascertain the precise status of natural law.

Like Aquinas, Suárez conceives of natural law as an epistemological gateway. But *what* do we exactly know by means of natural law? To Aquinas, natural law denotes the possibility of man's knowledge of the eternal law; God's ordering principle and style. That answer is not available to Suárez. We have seen that, understood in the narrow sense of the term 'law', 'eternal law' is a contradiction in terms and a somewhat superfluous notion. So what is it, then, to which we have access by means of natural law?

This question is at the basis of the debate between voluntarists and intellectualists. As we have seen, both parties no longer conceive of law as style, but as a set of precepts. On the basis of that conception, God is no longer conceived to be 'regulated' by law as an artist can be said to be 'regulated' by a style. On the basis of law-as-precept, the question has to be answered whether God is legislator or subject.

It is clear, then, that the conception of natural law is entirely dependent on that answer. If God is subject to the eternal law, natural law is transmitted to us as a lesson. By means of natural law, God teaches us the law He Himself is bound to. The intellectualists conceive of God as a teacher and of natural law as based on reason (*lex indicans*). But if God is the ultimate Lawgiver of eternal law, He is also regarded as the legislator of natural law. Voluntarists therefore regard God as legislator of natural law and believe that natural law is based on God's will (*lex imperans*).

Suárez—correctly—thinks that these rival solutions both fail to do justice to Aquinas's opinions. According to Suárez, Aquinas's view can be described as follows:

> Not only does the natural law indicate what is good or evil, but furthermore, it contains its own prohibition of evil and command of the good.[32]

Indication and prohibition are not separated. Natural law is both *imperans* and *indicans*. As I argued in I.3, since we have no other alternative than to adopt God's style, the promulgation of that style entails its obligation.

---

[32] DL II, VI, 5.

Thus, on the one hand Suárez sets out to reconcile the rival foundations that present themselves, since he thinks such reconciliation would be more faithful to Aquinas's views; on the other hand, he did not himself share Aquinas's concept of law-as-style. How does he proceed? By answering three rival foundations. The first we might call an extreme intellectualist position, the second is a moderate form of intellectualism, and the third is voluntarism.

The extreme intellectualist view is represented by Gabriel Vázquez (d. 1604). He views natural law as nothing other than 'rational nature' as such. Since we can no longer be guided by nature, we should consult not nature itself, but 'rational nature'. The term 'rational nature' itself reflects the decline of Aquinas's view that, of course, all nature is rational. Aquinas was able to maintain that view on the basis of his assumption that nature is God's manifest reason.

Vázquez reverses that order. He assumes that there is a rational order, pointing out what good and evil is, *prior* to God's activity. We should understand 'God's activity' in the widest possible sense. It is not only Vázquez's view that evil is evil before God prohibits evil; he also maintains that something is even evil before God *judges* it as evil. Rational nature is assumed to exist not only prior to a *lex imperans*, but also prior to a *lex indicans*. In terms of my metaphor, we might say that it is Vázquez's view that natural law, as God's script, merely expresses the rational order. It does not construct that order.

That is why Vázquez considers God's script of secondary importance; it merely reaffirms the eternal truths.[33] Even without natural law, we might have had access to rational nature, for rational nature is expressed in *human* rational nature. We should consult (our) rational nature to know what is expected from us. This is not to say that God is bound by human rational nature. Of course, He is not: created human nature does not exist prior to God's creation. But it is Vázquez's view that God could not fail to create human rational nature as it is, since He was bound to create human beings according to rational nature.

Suárez describes Vázquez's view as follows:

---

[33] Cf. Welzel, 1951, pp. 95-7.

> [...] natural law is prior to the divine judgement and the divine will of God; and, therefore, natural law does not have God for its author, but necessarily dwells within rational nature [...].[34]

This view is not acceptable to Suárez, who, in fact, rejects it on the same grounds as he had rejected the concept of eternal law. Vázquez's view would entail serious blasphemy: God would have been constrained by a rational order not of His own making. He would have been subject, not sovereign.

But Suárez has a second objection as well. According to Suárez, good and evil do not 'exist' as such, neither in nature, nor in a supposed 'rational nature'. One can only speak of good and evil on the basis of a *judgement*. It is therefore absurd to maintain the view that there 'is' a good of evil, independent of and prior to God's judgement. In Suárez's words:

> [...] the rational nature itself [...] neither gives commands, nor makes evident the rectitude or turpitude of anything; neither does it direct or illuminate, or produce any of the other proper effects of law.[35]

What Suárez objects to is what we would call nowadays 'moral realism'. There are no values independent of value-judgements. In the first place, God's value-judgement is required, but *our* value-judgements are also required. Good and evil 'exist' only on the basis of a rational judgement. Suárez does not deny that there is something called 'rational nature' to which our actions can be compared. Rather, what he objects to is that rational nature in itself would immediately reveal the turpitude or the rectitude of actions. According to Suárez, it is only in the *act of comparing* our actions to rational nature that we might assess the degree of turpitude or rectitude of our actions.

In fact, he objects to Vázquez's views on the same grounds as he had criticised Aquinas's view that nature can provide us information on good and evil. Whether one speaks about nature, or about 'rational nature', both are silent if our judgement does not intervene.

---

[34] DL II, V, 8.
[35] DL II, V, 5.

6. *The ineffectiveness of rational judgement*

The second option is to say that the basis of natural law is rational nature *coupled* with divine judgement. According to this moderate form of intellectualism, natural law is not rational nature itself (as Vázquez would have it) but rational nature as it is indicated by God. God should teach us 'the upright character or turpitude of actions'. How does God teach us that? By pointing out which actions agree with rational nature and which actions disagree with it. Note here, that God does not evaluate actions according to the criterion whether they serve to *realise* natural inclinations. It is merely 'conformity' and 'lack of conformity' to rational nature which decides the moral merits of actions.

The difference between Aquinas's criterion of 'realisation' and the intellectualist criterion of 'conformity' testifies to the dominance of the conception of creation as representation (cf. III.3). God has faithfully *copied* the fixed patterns in His mind. The rational order which informed His creation is a fixed state of affairs. Consequently, our actions can only be compared to that fixed order by assessing the degree of their conformity, just as realist pictures can only be judged by their likeness. According to moderate intellectualism, then, natural law is based on divine reason, conceived as the ability to discern (lack of) conformity between actions and rational nature.

According to Suárez, this option is not sufficient either. In the first place, this view does not solve the problem that had haunted Vázquez's account: the blasphemy involved in the assertion that God Himself is bound by the rational order. His role as teacher may be less passive than Vázquez's theory allowed for, but still does not give Him the required scope of freedom. God cannot change natural law as He sees fit. He can merely point out which actions agree with rational nature. As such, He is still not the omnipotent Sovereign.

In the second place, even this more moderate version of intellectualism suffers from a misunderstanding of what 'law' is about. Law is not merely a judgement. Such a judgement, according to Suárez:

> has not the character of a law or a prohibition, but is merely a recognition of some fact already assumed to be true.[36]

---

[36] DL II, VI, 6.

In modern terminology, it is Suárez's objection that the intellectualist position treats natural law as a set of factual statements, not as norms. Judgements (as comparisons between 'actions' and 'rational nature') do not have the necessary binding force. The mere *indication* of good and evil does not *oblige* people to act accordingly and therefore does not establish genuine 'law'.

In this respect, Suárez's qualms are similar to Hume's criticism. Completely in line with Suárez, Hume criticises natural law for two reasons. First, natural law suffers from the mistaken idea that 'there are eternal fitnesses and unfitnesses of things', 'a real right and wrong [...] independent of [...] judgements'.[37] This criticism is formulated by Suárez in his discussion of extreme intellectualism. Hume's second reason for criticising natural law is that it mistakenly presupposes that these rational judgements alone suffice to act accordingly:

> Since morals, therefore, have an influence on the actions and affections, it follows, that they cannot be deriv'd from reason; and that because reason alone, [...] can never have any such influence.[38]

It is true that Hume deplores here the lack of motivating force ('influence'), whereas Suárez's deplores the lack of obligatory force. A difference which is understandable in view of the fact that Hume intended to explain human behaviour, whereas Suárez intends to justify/criticise human actions.[39] But it is remarkable that both writers share the view that *neither* (rational) nature by itself, *nor* judgements concerning good and evil have the power to induce people to follow moral principles. This is a surprising similarity in view of the fact that, whereas Suárez is commonly praised as the one who resuscitated natural law from the grave, Hume is celebrated for having dug its grave. Yet, although their therapy is different, they both share the diagnosis of the weaknesses of natural law if it is founded on reason and nature alone. Both nature and reason are felt to be inert and inactive and therefore not suited as foundations of natural law, taken in the sense of law-as-precept.

---

[37] Hume, 1739, p. 456, 460.
[38] Hume, 1739, p. 457.
[39] Cf. introduction to chapter IX, as well as my 1994 publication.

It is obvious that this inability of reason to give rise to moral obligations is the result of the limited view of reason as merely judging likenesses. Finnis and Grisez have criticised this view on the grounds that Suárez narrows down the scope of reason to that of theoretical reason only. He is blamed for having overlooked the importance of practical reason as distinct from theoretical reason, guided by its own self-evident principle.

However, on the basis of the important shifts we witnessed in Suárez's work, we can see that these are no mere 'mistakes'. Suárez's removal of practical reason is not only entirely consistent with his metaphysical assumptions; it can even be argued that he has no need for practical reason.

According to Aquinas, the first principle of natural law ('good is to be done and pursued, and evil avoided') is the starting-point for our reasoning on moral affairs. It is by means of this unquestionable and self-evident principle, grasped by *synderesis*, that we are able to reason at all. By means of *synderesis* we see that there is a general tendency to seek the good, as well as how this tendency is expressed in the various creatures.

Suárez has no room for *synderesis*. Although he knows the term, he hardly uses it and where he does it is mainly in order to refer to the fact that rationality is the same in all men.[40] This is understandable, since Suárez does not conceive of the *exemplar* as something which has to do with the way *we* deal with moral problems. God's *exemplar* only regulates His own creation (as representation), it does not direct God's subjects.

We have seen that on the basis of his altered view of God's creation, Suárez divides the universe in an irrational and a rational part. Since the natural inclinations in irrational creatures are seen as mechanisms and instincts, we can safely rely on theoretical reason in order to observe and understand that natural world. It is perfectly possible to understand the way these creatures conform to God's rules in descriptive terms, consonant with theoretical reason. There is no need for 'practical reason' here, since the expressions of God's style in irrational creatures have no *moral* relevance to rational beings.

As for rational creatures, they are supposed to follow God's explicit laws. All they have to do is to rely on God's commands. Here, there is no room for practical reason either in Aquinas's sense

---

[40] Cf. DL II, VIII, 5, where Suárez also identifies *synderesis* with *conscientia*.

of the word, as the kind of reasoning that starts from the perception of 'ends'. It is sufficient that rational creatures understand the moral precepts issued by God.

Therefore, on the basis of Suárez's view of creation and the division between irrational and rational beings, there is no need for practical reason. Since there are no 'ends' which have moral relevance, there is no need to grasp these ends. Instead, we should introduce a distinction between descriptive and normative statements. The former describe the mechanisms implanted by God in nature; the latter explicate God's moral precepts for rational beings. This implies that within the framework of Suárez's theory, there is no room for the first principle of practical reason as a general stylistic requirement. If the principle has a function at all, it is as a general moral *precept*.

7. Suárez's middle-course

The third available candidate for the foundation of natural law is the voluntarist option, according to which natural law is solely founded in the will of God. Why God wills what He wills, there is no further ground for it, except that the will is God's will, so said Duns Scotus. And William Occam, stretching this voluntarism further, remarked that if God had ordered us to steal, theft would have been a virtuous activity.

Voluntarism has some definite theoretical advantages. Adopting a narrow definition of law-as-command, voluntarists can hardly be accused of metaphorical use of language. Nor can they be accused of blasphemy. In no way God is subject to laws. He is the Sovereign, from whom all laws spring. But the problem with a concept of natural law as *lex imperans* is that such a law risks becoming incomprehensible to the human mind. If we follow Occam in supposing that indeed God might have ordered us to hate Him, or to commit adultery, how can we *know* these commands? We might push aside this question as academic trifle; yet, this knowledge is what natural law is about. Natural law as the key to knowledge of morality by means of unaided reason inherently conflicts with the notion of *lex imperans*. And we see indeed that writers like Occam tend to identify natural law with the Scriptures,[41] which of course marks the end of the notion of natural law.

Suárez does not want to draw that consequence.[42] His reappraisal of Aquinas was partly inspired by the desire to provide an adequate reasonable response to Lutheran and Calvinist theories concerning God's impenetrable mind, and I think he was well-aware that a voluntarist reading of natural law as *lex imperans* would inevitably bring him dangerously close to that detested position.

So we see that although Suárez is clearly unhappy with intellectualism, he hesitates to draw the consequences of full-blown voluntarism as well. The intrinsic rectitude or turpitude of rational nature may not be the only foundation for natural law, but nor is the divine will. Both should *go together*:

> [...] this divine volition, in the form of a prohibition or in that of an [affirmative] command, is not the whole reason for the good or evil involved in the observance or transgression of the natural law; on the contrary, it necessarily presupposes the existence of a certain righteousness or turpitude in these actions, and *attaches to them a special obligation derived from divine law* [my emphasis].[43]

And again, in a slightly different formulation:

> For the natural law prohibits those things which are bad in themselves; and this law is true divine law and a true prohibition; hence it must necessarily result in some sort of *additional obligation* to avoid an evil which is already evil of itself and by its very nature [my emphasis].[44]

This argument appears to be subtle, but in fact contains a *petitio principii*. Instead of providing arguments for the claim that natural law contains true prohibitions, the prescriptive character of natural law is already presupposed and in turn serves as an argument for the existence of an additional obligation. Apart from that, we might wonder whether Suárez can escape here from the charge of blasphemy. Although God's role is not limited to reaffirming or teaching

---

[41] Cf. Welzel, 1951, p. 87.

[42] Villey, 1968, p. 391; and Farrell, 1930, p. 55, interpret Suárez too much as a voluntarist.

[43] DL II, VI, 11.

[44] DL II, VI, 12.

eternal truths, He is still not free to command whatever He pleases. He can only attach an obligation to avoid things which are 'bad in themselves'.

Yet, Suárez believes that he found a satisfactory middle-course, which is truly faithful to Aquinas's position, in which natural law indicates and prohibits at the same time. Of course, it is not. It could not be, since he did not share Aquinas's view of creation, according to which God not only created the universe to be but also to become. On the basis of a concept of eternal law as the only available style, it is possible to discern purposiveness in the creation as such for which no additional obligation is needed.

That view is completely different from Suárez's 'middle-course'. Since he regards God's creation as representation, lacking the 'dynamic' qualities required to direct creatures after creation, he was confronted with three rival foundations of natural law: nature, reason, and will. Although Suárez thinks that all three foundations are necessary ingredients of a foundation of natural law, he does not think that each of these, taken by itself, would suffice. And he can only bring the rival foundations together by *adding them up*. To him, the natural law does not indicate and prescribe at the same time, but consists of three elements, added to each other.

The basis of natural law is rational nature itself. In this, Suárez agrees with Vázquez. But this nature cannot acquire any moral relevance to us, if it is not accompanied by promulgation, brought about by reasonable judgement. So, God's judgement is required in order to pronounce certain things as 'good or bad in themselves'. And since this judgement is not sufficient to oblige us to act accordingly, the binding force of natural law calls for additional divine volition.

Metaphorically speaking, we see that whereas Aquinas's concept of natural law was supported by one great pillar, the eternal law, this pillar is supplanted by three smaller columns, nature, reason and will, in Suárez's concept of natural law. This solution is necessitated by the fact that the notion of eternal law as style was found ambiguous and unsatisfactory, long before Suárez wrote his treatise. It is only by reconciling the three competing foundations that Aquinas's natural law theory can be rescued from imbalance and collapse. Rather than blaming Suárez for having perverted Aquinas's teachings, we should, I think, be impressed by the perseverance with which Suárez seeks to bridge the gaps that result from the dismissal of Aquinas's unified teleological view.

8. *Human nature*

The replacement of Aquinas's teleological foundation of natural law by three elements (nature, reason, and will) raises the question to what extent all these three foundations are necessary. Why is it necessary to suppose that nature forms the basis of natural law, and reason its promulgation? Would it not be possible to dispense with nature and reason and to endorse without further ado the voluntarist position that natural law is founded on God's will alone? Would that not be a more elegant position? Why should one introduce three elements where one would suffice?

We have already seen that Suárez recoiled at the danger such a solution would involve: it would amount to the collapse of the notion that we have access to God's will by means of reason. It would amount to a denial of the existence of natural law. But this is, of course, merely an ideological consideration, which cannot serve as a philosophical argument that underpins his threefold foundation. Suárez therefore needs to argue why he thinks that God's commands are reasonable, in accordance with rational nature, and laid down in the reasonable form of natural law.

He finds that argument in human nature:

> For, absolutely speaking, God could have refrained from laying down any command or prohibition; yet, assuming that He had willed to have subjects endowed with the use of reason, He could not have failed to be their lawgiver [...].[45]

God laid down His commands in natural law, because He willed His subjects to be reasonable. Although God is free to choose whether or not He would declare His will, it would have been very unwise to refrain from reasonable promulgation.

> [...] it may further be stated that this very faculty of judgement which is contained in right reason and bestowed by nature upon men, is of itself a sufficient sign of such divine volition, no other notification being necessary.[46]

---

[45] DL II, VI, 23.
[46] DL II, VI, 24.

This passage is instructive. In order to defend the existence of natural law, Suárez sees no other way than to provide us with an *a posteriori* argument; the argument from human nature itself. Because we human beings are created as rational, it is logical that God should have established and promulgated laws that we human beings are able to know and to follow. Otherwise there would have been *no point* in creating us as rational beings. Human nature provides us with the ultimate argument for the existence of natural law.

This may look similar to Aquinas's point of view, but we should not be misled here. Aquinas's starting-point is God and the ideas in His mind. Human nature is seen as the product of God's exemplars. Suárez, however, reverses that argument. It is only from the fact that human beings can be considered as rational beings that the existence of natural law can be inferred. Not God, but human nature is the starting-point. The human mind is the only proof that natural law is based on rationality and not on God's arbitrary decisions. It seems then that the voluntarist position can only be avoided by maintaining that God's commands are reasonable because *we* are reasonable. However, Suárez's remarks here are scattered. He did not provide us with a systematical argument concerning human nature as a starting-point for natural law. But we might interpret these remarks as hesitant beginnings of Grotius's theory of natural law.

9. *Conclusion*

In this chapter we have seen that Suárez raises two important objections against Aquinas's theory of natural law. The first concerns Aquinas's concept of law-as-style. The second regards Aquinas's concept of eternal law. Both criticisms result from a different view of creation, which is regarded as representation of a fixed 'pattern'.

This conception of creation implies a division of the universe between rational and irrational creatures. Irrational creatures should be seen as the finished products of God's creation, which have no other option than to conform to naturally implanted instincts and desires. Rational beings, on the other hand, are capable of following God's rules, but in order to do so, they should rely on God's explicit commands. Natural desires are irrelevant to moral reasoning.

This division in turn is responsible for the decline of the notion of practical reason as distinct from theoretical reason. Theoretical reason suffices for the observation of the natural world, whereas the ability to understand precepts suffices in order to understand God's promulgated law. The decline of the unified notion of eternal law results in the decline of the notion of practical reason.

On the basis of the model of theoretical reasoning, God can be supposed to discern (dis)agreement of actions with nature, but such a judgement does not entail any norms. These comparisons only result in factual statements, from which no norms can be derived. That is why Suárez struggles to find a foundation for natural law. Nature itself is silent, nature plus reason indicate good and evil but do not oblige. If we are to understand natural law as genuine 'law' we should assume God's binding will. It is by adding up reason, nature and will as component parts of the foundation of natural law that Suárez tries to be faithful to Aquinas's unified vision of natural law. Since this necessarily raises the question why God's will would not have sufficed, Suárez sees no other alternative than to provide an *a posteriori* argument, which starts from man's rational nature.

Although we have seen that Suárez's 'misinterpretations' can be understood as theoretically defensible moves within a changed conceptual framework, this analysis does not point out *why* that framework had changed. Although we might point to changed political conditions in order to explain his altered view of 'law', it is unclear why Suárez started from a different view of creation, and why he did not endorse Aquinas's conception of eternal law. Suárez's work only allows us an occasional glimpse of these deeper shifts. The only certainty is that these concepts were deemed ambiguous long before Suárez and that Suárez's theory can be seen as a heroic attempt to fasten together the elements that tended to drift apart.

Therefore, I tend to disagree with the opinion of Finnis and Grisez that Suárez should be blamed for having rendered natural law theory vulnerable to Hume's fatal attack. Instead, Suárez's theory should be understood as the attempt to rescue natural law from the charge that it infers norms from facts. The three pillars that together form the foundation of natural law, are designed in order to avoid the impression that it is only nature (facts), or only nature plus reason (ought-statements) which give rise to moral obligations. In order to turn normative statements into real obligatory norms, additional divine obligation is needed.

CHAPTER IV

THE LIMITS OF SUAREZ'S NATURAL LAW THEORY

According to Suárez, God has willed human beings to act according
to the law that has been promulgated to them and to which they have
access by their rationality. What is more, rational beings can *only* be
guided by that promulgated law. Without such a law to direct them
they would be no more than copies of God's plan. Nature as such
does not give any directions concerning good and evil.

This view implies that Suárez no longer conceives of practical
reasoning in the sense of Aquinas. Natural law is not just an ordering
style or principle on the basis of which people can reason for themselves at the best of their abilities. Natural law is a real 'law'; it
consists of binding precepts. Our rationality does not denote a general
capacity to apply the divine style, but refers more specifically to our
ability to understand God's promulgated precepts.

The question arises what these precepts look like. Are they just
general directions, or precise instructions? If we compare natural law
to a—compelling—script, is there any room for the actors to interpret
that script? Or should they stick to the literal text? This is the question that will be addressed in this chapter. In answering this question,
a number of issues will appear to be relevant. After having dealt with
the way conclusions can be derived from natural law (sections 1-2),
the status of political government vis-à-vis natural law will be examined (sections 3-5). Sections 6 and 7 are devoted to the field for
which Suárez has become famous: international law. Attention is paid
to the role of custom as a source for the *ius gentium*, which enables
us to assess more precisely the role of natural law in Suárez's theory
(section 8).

1. *The certainty of conclusions*

In chapter II, I pointed out that Aquinas made a sharp distinction
between the first principles of natural law and the conclusions that are
derived from them. The first principles are perceived by that angelic
power of immediate vision, which he called *synderesis*. These first

principles he held to be necessarily true, self-evident and indubitable.
They cannot be changed. But, Aquinas remarked, the conclusions that
are derived from these principles are variable and uncertain. These
conclusions are marked by a high degree of ambiguity and 'lack of
unanimity', due to the inherent contingency of human affairs.[1]

Suárez discards this distinction. In his view there is no fundamental difference in certainty between the general precepts of natural law
and the particular conclusions that are derived from these precepts.
Suárez distinguishes three groups of precepts: the first, most evident
of all, contains precepts such as: 'one must do good, and shun evil'
and 'do not to another that which you would not wish done to yourself'. The second group contains—slightly—more specific precepts
like: 'God must be worshipped' and 'Justice must be observed'.
Suárez remarks that these are self-evident 'by their very terminology'.
The third group, finally, contains precepts that are deduced from the
first and second group and which are even more specific, referring to
theft, adultery and the like.[2]

This threefold division is not new. Aquinas also allowed for a
continuum of precepts, more specific and less evident ones at the
bottom, and less specific ones with a higher degree of self-evidence at
the top. Therefore I do not think it is correct to think that Suárez
differed from Aquinas in extending natural law to the specific conclusions.[3] Aquinas equally included these conclusions.[4] But unlike
Aquinas, Suárez thinks that we can know the more specific precepts
with the same degree of certainty as the more general ones. Suárez
believes that not only the primary principles but also the conclusions,
however remote, are necessarily true. This also implies that specific
precepts have the same binding force as the general ones.

> [...] no one is doubtful as to the primary and general principles; hence,
> neither can there be doubt as to the specific principles, since these,
> also, in themselves and by virtue of their very terminology, harmonize
> with rational nature as such; and, therefore, there should be no doubt
> with respect to the conclusions clearly derived from these principles,
> inasmuch as the truth of the principle is contained in the conclusion,
> and he who prescribes or forbids the one, necessarily prescribes or

---

[1] Cf. ST I, II, 94, 4.
[2] Cf. DL II, VII, 5.
[3] This is Welzel's view, 1951, p. 98.
[4] ST I, II, 94, 4.

forbids that which is bound up in it, or without which it could not exist.[5]

Suárez repeats this argument when he comes to speak of the immutability of natural law.[6] So we see that whereas Aquinas doubted the possibility of precise moral instructions because of the contingent and variable nature of human affairs, Suárez is convinced that natural law comprises specific rules, which are just as certain as the major premisses they are derived from.

In fact, contrary to Aquinas, who held the first principles to be the most important part of natural law, Suárez thinks that the conclusions form the most vital part of natural law. In Suárez's words:

> Indeed, strictly speaking, the natural law works more through these proximate principles or conclusions than through universal principles; for a law is a proximate rule of operation, and the general principles mentioned above are not rules save in so far as they are definitely applied by specific rules to the individual sorts of acts or virtues.[7]

Here again, Suárez is consistently applying his notion of law-as-precept. Natural law is based on rational nature and apprehended by rational reason, but it operates as a set of binding precepts. As such, it should be as explicit and as detailed as possible in order to have some effect on our doings. Natural law is no longer, as Aquinas thought, a set of general guidelines that should be applied to everyday life with prudence and awareness of the ambiguity of human affairs, but consists of specific and detailed rules. To Suárez, the importance of natural law lies in its effectiveness. And obviously, the more specified its precepts are, the more effective it is. That is why the conclusions are more important than the more general principles from which these conclusions are derived.

2. Implied conditions

In chapter II, we have seen that Aquinas distinguished theoretical reason from practical reason. One of the major differences between

---

[5] DL II, VII, 7.
[6] DL II, XIII, 3.
[7] DL II, VII, 7.

the two kinds of reason is, according to Aquinas, the degree of certainty that can be achieved in the conclusions deduced from the general principles. Whereas theoretical reason 'without mistake finds truth in the particular conclusions it draws as in the premises it starts from', this cannot be achieved by practical reason, because 'the more we get down to particular cases the more we can be mistaken'.[8] This is due to the inherent contingency of human affairs.

Suárez considerably deviates from this view. Whether one reasons about theoretical or practical matters, this makes no difference in the degree of certainty with which one can arrive at particular conclusions. Suárez's view is understandable in view of the fact that he did not conceive of practical reason as distinct from theoretical reason. In the preceding chapter (III.7) we have seen that Suárez thinks that the main task of reason is to compare actions with rational nature. The task of reason is to formulate propositions of the type: 'action x agrees/disagrees with rational nature'. Reason does not exhort us to refrain from stealing (such an exhortation is the effect of the additional will of God); it only asserts that theft is not in conformity with rational nature. On the basis of such a conception of reason it is only consistent to think that the conclusions have the same degree of certainty as the premises they are derived from: if action x lacks conformity with rational nature, this *equally* applies to all the specifications of x. If theft in general disagrees with rational nature, theft of a shoe, of food, or of money all disagree with rational nature.

Aquinas would criticise this view as too simple. Even if he had endorsed Suárez's view that reason's job is to compare actions with rational nature, he would still have argued that our assessment of particular conditions, expressed in the minor, can lead us astray:

Major: Theft disagrees with rational nature.
Minor: Stealing food is theft.
Conclusion: Stealing food disagrees with rational nature.

Aquinas would argue—in fact, he *did* argue—, that it depends on the circumstances whether the minor is true that stealing food is to be counted as 'theft'. If someone's life is at stake and there is no alternative available, 'he may take what is necessary from another's goods

---

[8] ST I, II, 94, 4.

[...]. Nor is this, strictly speaking, fraud or robbery'.[9] Since these circumstances are contingent and variable, we might go wrong in the minor.

Suárez was aware of the importance of circumstances, but he believed that the general precepts of natural law indicate precisely the conditions and circumstances in which they should be applied:

> [...] natural reason itself dictates that a given act shall be performed in such and such a way, and not otherwise, or under specific concurrent circumstances, and not unless those circumstances exist.[10]

Therefore, there is no need to change the precept itself if we apply it to everyday life. A moral precept tells us that a certain act is in accordance with rational nature 'assuming that the proper circumstances exist'.[11] As an example he mentions the natural precept 'Thou shalt not kill'. This precept, according to Suárez,

> includes [...] many conditions, [so that it means,] for example, 'Thou shalt not kill upon thine own authority, and as an aggressor'.[12]

Because Suárez thinks that the general precepts contain—implicitly—a list of appropriate or normal conditions, he no longer shares Aquinas's view that the conclusions of natural law lack certainty because of the variable, contingent nature of human affairs. In his own words:

> Therefore, neither is any objection to our view involved in the fact that the subject-matter is changeable. For the natural law discerns the mutability in the subject-matter itself, and adapts its own precepts to this mutability, prescribing in regard to such subject-matter a certain sort of conduct for one condition, and another sort of conduct for another condition; so that the law in itself remains at all times unchanged [...].[13]

---

[9] ST II, II, 66, 7, concl.
[10] DL II, XIII, 7.
[11] DL II, XIII, 9.
[12] DL II, XIII, 8.
[13] DL II, XIII, 9.

And he remarks that our reasoning, on both moral and 'scientific' matters, proceeds from general precepts which specify (implicitly or explicitly) the conditions under which they are applicable. Theoretical and practical reason proceed in the same way.[14]

Suárez's version of Aquinas's syllogism would be:

> Major: Theft disagrees with rational nature in normal conditions [i.e. if one's life is not in danger].
> Minor: In this case, normal conditions apply. Hence: stealing food is theft.
> Conclusion: Stealing food disagrees with rational nature.

Since Suárez argues that every general precept implies such conditions, he can maintain that there are never any exceptions to such precepts. If we take the example of the general precept that deposits should be returned, that precept clearly is meant to be applicable to normal conditions only. When we are confronted with the possibility that the creditor might launch a bloody war with the money returned, we can refuse to return the money. In doing so, we do not really violate the precept, since the general precept was never intended to cover that particular case.[15] Consequently, Suárez can argue that natural law does not admit of any change or exception.

It should be noted that for Suárez there are no 'general' precepts in Aquinas's sense of the term 'general'. Each and every precept is specified from the outset to be applicable to only such and such conditions. This implies that natural law is not thought to furnish just a few general precepts, but a multitude of precepts, each specifying the particular circumstances in which it is applicable. The only reason to regard some precepts as more 'general' than others is that general precepts refer to 'normal' conditions, whereas specific ones contain exceptional conditions. This means that in Suárez's account natural law has turned from an ordering principle with which we have to work as best as we can into an elaborate legal system.[16]

One might wonder, however, whether this solution solves the problems perceived by Aquinas. Even if we start from 'specified'

---

[14] DL II, XIII, 9.

[15] DL II, XIII, 8.

[16] I tend to disagree with Jonsen and Toulmin (1988), who assert that casuistry reached its pinnacle in the 16th century. Instead, I think that increasing legalism gradually undermined it.

precepts, i.e. precepts which apply to exceptional conditions, we might go astray, and mistakenly suppose that we are dealing with exceptional conditions, whereas in fact normal conditions apply. Even if we know that theft is only prohibited in normal conditions, we might be mistaken in thinking that in a particular case normal conditions do or do not apply. I do not think that Suárez sufficiently recognises that problem.

3. *Human power*

The main reason for Suárez's sketch of general precepts as implying conditions is that this seems to be the only way to maintain that natural law is unchangeable, and does not permit of exceptions. Suárez repeatedly emphasises that 'men cannot change that which is unchangeable'.[17] He adduces several arguments in favour of this claim, the first of which refers to human nature as the basis for natural law, a basis which human beings are obviously not free to change. We shall see that for the Protestant writers, this argument will be the most important one in favour of the inherent immutability of natural law. But for Suárez this is not the most crucial argument. Completely in tune with his notion of law-as-precept, the strongest argument in Suárez's view is that God is the lawgiver of natural law, and that inferiors cannot stand up against Him.

Suárez asserts that even the Pope, despite his position as the Vicar of Christ, is not allowed to grant dispensations from natural law. He adduces three arguments for this position. Firstly, Suárez maintains that it is already difficult for God Himself to change the law, since natural law is based upon rational nature.[18] Secondly, Suárez asserts that if we grant the Pope such powers, the same powers should also be given to secular rulers concerning those precepts of natural law that regulate temporal affairs, which is a form of equal treatment that would be highly undesirable. Thirdly, he thinks that changes should not be permitted because once we allow conclusions to be altered or changed we would be compelled to allow changes in the first prin-

---

[17] DL II, XIV, 8.

[18] Here, Suárez's 'middle-course' (cf. III. 8) is clearly unable to avoid the blasphemous implications of the intellectualist position.

ciples as well.[19] This argument is consistent with Suárez's view that conclusions and general precepts form part and parcel of the same legal system. Alterations in conclusions would lead to the gradual undermining of the entire system.

It seems then that Suárez conceives of natural law as an inflexible body of detailed precepts. The whole edifice is of a rigidity that not even the Pope himself can attenuate. That is why Suárez has been interpreted as a legalist who has no room for prudence, and lacks the flexibility required to do justice to the contingencies of human life. Villey, for example, sees Suárez's principles as 'figées dans l'immobilisme'; as the death of a living natural law.[20]

This, however, is a one-sided picture. Suárez makes an important distinction *within* natural law, between the so-called *ius naturale praeceptivum* and the *ius naturale dominativum*. His rigidity is only visible in the former part of natural law, but remarkably absent in the latter part. The preceptive part of natural law comprises

> [...] the positive precepts of religion in relation to God, of filial piety, of mercy, and of almsgiving to one's neighbour; and the negative precepts against killing, those against slander, and similar prohibitions.[21]

These precepts can never be changed, Suárez emphasises. Why not? Because these are

> rules and principles for right conduct which involve necessary truth, and are therefore immutable, since they are based upon the intrinsic rectitude or perversity of their objects [...].[22]

But not so with the *ius naturale dominativum*. This is that part of the natural law which has to do with man's *dominium*. And what is *dominium*? It is

---

[19] DL II, XIV, 10.
[20] Villey, 1968, p. 393.
[21] DL II, XIV, 7.
[22] DL II, XIV, 19.

moral power [*facultas*], which every man possesses with respect to his own property or with respect to a thing which in some way pertains to him [...].[23]

In order to understand Suárez's view on *dominium*, we should note that he abandons here the traditional Thomistic view of *ius* as 'giving everyone his due'. Rather, he identifies *ius* with *facultas*: the power people exercise over those things that belong to them.[24] Finnis remarks that in this sense Suárez and Grotius 'are on the same side of the watershed'. '*Ius* is essentially something someone *has*'.[25] *Ius* no longer refers to an overall regulative and distributive framework in which, but as something one is free to dispose of as one sees fit.

The *ius naturale dominativum* contains precepts concerning those things over which man has *dominium*. These precepts refer to what we would nowadays call 'subjective rights': notably property, liberty and the right to make contracts. Since this part of natural law deals with the *dominium* people have, Suárez maintains that these precepts allow for more flexibility than the preceptive part of natural law.

This does not imply that man is allowed to change that part of natural law as such, but its 'subject-matter' (*materia*) can be altered

> [...] through changing subject-matter; so that a given action is with-drawn from the obligation imposed by natural law, not because the law is abolished or diminished, since it always is and has been binding in this sense, but because the matter dealt with by the law is changed [...].[26]

For instance, the precept that theft is forbidden is in itself invariable and does not admit of change. But what we *understand* by 'theft' is, of course, dependent on the way we have organised property. It is dependent on human institutions. In this sense, its *materia* (theft) can be said to be liable to change by human beings. People have the right to change that *materia* by virtue of that *dominium*.

---

[23] DL I, II, 5. For an elaborate analysis of the development of the concept of rights, see Tuck, 1979.

[24] Cf. Villey, 1968, p. 381.

[25] NLNR p. 207.

[26] DL II, XIII, 6.

Welzel, sharing Villey's interpretation of Suárez as a rigid legalist, regards Suárez's permission to change the subject-matter as a pathetic, ill-fated attempt to rescue natural law from immanent fossilisation.[27] I think, however, that he underrates the importance of this attempt. In fact, Suárez's permission to change the subject-matter of the natural law concerning *dominium* allows for an unprecedentedly wide scope for human intervention, as we shall see in the next section.

4. *Liberty and property*

In order to examine the implications of Suárez's permission to change the *materia* of this part of natural law, it is worthwhile to take a brief look at those things that are said to belong to man's *dominium*. The first example is property. Suárez argues here that although nature gave all things in common ownership, natural law has not positively decreed that men should own things in common. We should understand that common ownership

> [...] falls negatively under the natural law because that law does not prohibit, but on the contrary permits, while not positively prescribing its performance. [...] Hence, a division of property is not contrary to positive natural law; for there was no natural precept to forbid the making of such a division.[28]

In Suárez's view, which is similar to Aquinas's (II.8), natural law is silent on how property should be organised and has granted human beings the *dominium* to organise property as they themselves see fit.[29] The establishment of the institution of private property should therefore be considered a purely human affair. That means that laws pertaining to private property have a *materia*, dependent on human agreement. This *materia* can therefore be changed by human power.

Since man has *dominium* about *all* things 'which in some way pertain to him', liberty itself also belongs to those things. But here natural law did not leave it to mankind to decide how to deal with

---

[27] Welzel, 1980, p. 98.

[28] DL II, XIV, 14.

[29] DL II, XIV, 17. This argument will later be repeated and elaborated by Samuel Pufendorf.

liberty. Suárez concedes that nature has not granted us liberty in a negative way, but in a positive sense. We are endowed with 'an intrinsic right to liberty'.[30] Yet, surprisingly enough, this difference does not make any difference as to the changeability of the natural law concerning liberty. Suárez leaves no doubt about his view that the *materia* of the laws dealing with liberty is just as liable to change as the laws concerning property. In a telling passage he writes:

> Accordingly, we say of liberty and of any similar lawful right, that even if such a right has been positively granted by nature, it may be changed by human agency, since it is dependent, in the individual persons, either upon their own wills, or upon the state, in so far as the latter has lawful power over all private individuals and over their property, to the extent necessary for right government.[31]

It is remarkable that Suárez allows for changes in exactly that part of natural law that in modern eyes should be considered sacrosanct: the part that regulates subjective rights. Whereas we would nowadays be inclined to regard liberty as one of those few 'natural' rights that should be protected from governmental intervention, Suárez draws the opposite conclusion. It is because liberty is given in the hands of mankind that it should be regulated and dealt with as human beings see fit. It is by virtue of the nature of liberty itself that it can be regulated according to the human, and not the divine, will. Suárez unequivocally tells us that:

> [...] although it [nature] granted liberty and dominion over that liberty, [it] has nevertheless not absolutely forbidden that it should be taken away. For, in the first place, for the very reason that man is lord over his own liberty, it is possible for him to sell or alienate the same. A commonwealth, too, acting through the higher power which it possesses for the government of men, may deprive a man of his liberty for a just cause [...]. For nature also gave to man the use and possession of his own life; yet he may sometimes justly be deprived of it through human agency.[32]

---

[30] DL II, XIV, 16.
[31] DL II, XIV, 19.
[32] DL II, XIV, 18.

Although Suárez repeatedly uses terms as 'justly' and 'for a just cause', it is hard to see how we can *determine* whether something is just or not. Aquinas had at least some principles at hand: the ends for mankind, self-preservation, procreation, sociability and knowledge of God served as minimal criteria for justice. Suárez, on the other hand, has to dispense with these principles. Natural ends are irrelevant to moral considerations. It is his view that rational beings can only rely on God's explicit and promulgated law. But exactly *that* law leaves these important subject-matters to be decided by mankind. That implies that we hardly have any independent criteria according to which we can decide on what is to be counted as 'just'. In fact, on the basis of the above-quoted passage it is not impossible to defend slavery. The inhabitants of West-Africa, enslaved by Portuguese traders, merely made use of their natural right to alienate and sell their own liberty.[33]

This interpretation may seem too strong. Would it not be possible to criticise the enslavement of Africans by means of a particular interpretation of natural law? However, these possibilities are limited within Suárez's theory.

It is here that we have to deal with Suárez's political philosophy, for it is his view that only those who have *legislative* power have the power to change the *materia* of natural law of *dominium*. Only those who are entrusted with the power to make laws, are allowed to exercise *dominium*.

Suárez did not conceive of legislative power as merely the sum-total of individual rights powers in a Lockean way. This may be judged from Suárez's distinction between two conceptions of society: one in which 'the multitude of mankind' is understood 'as a kind of aggregation, without any order or any physical or moral union', the other as 'a single mystical body' unifying men by a 'bond of fellowship'.[34] It is the latter conception Suárez considers to be a genuine political society, unified under one 'single head'. Suárez thought of man's *dominium* as entrusted to political government, which is the expression of this genuine moral union; *not* to individual subjects.[35]

---

[33] Cf. also Tuck, 1979, p. 49.
[34] DL III, II, 4.
[35] Cf. DL III, III, 6.

We should keep this in mind in order to understand his account of the establishment of political power.[36] He conceives of political power as the outcome of a gradual process in which small family-units gather into larger societies, a process which is made necessary by the fact that

> [...] each individual member has a care for its individual advantages, and these are often opposed to the common good.[37]

He therefore emphasises that political power does not reside in an individual man, such as a prince, but only 'in the whole body of mankind'.[38] It is by virtue of that collective power that the prince reigns.

Because of this emphasis on the collective will rather than the individual wills as constitutive for political power, I think that Skinner is right in his remark that we should not make too much of the notion of *consent* that Suárez introduces in his account of the establishment of political society. Suárez's account of how smaller units agree to gather into a larger political community indeed serves to *explain* the origins of political society, not to justify it. His account here is a historical, not a philosophical one. The justification of government is therefore not dependent on the consent of individuals. Instead, rather than stressing the importance of consent, Suárez emphasises that rulers should not rule 'in a way that fails to accord with God's will'.[39] This is, of course, entirely in agreement with Suárez's conception of natural law as precepts that are binding by the will of God.

But the fact that consent does not play a justificatory role does not imply that Skinner is right in asserting that the legitimacy of governments is decided by 'the question about whether the government's enactments are congruent with the law of nature'.[40] Too much is made of natural law here. This function can only be performed by what Suárez calls 'preceptive natural law'. If a government sets out to kill its subjects, it directly violates one of those immutable precepts, prohibiting an intrinsic evil: killing.

---

[36] Cf. Skinner, 1978, pp. 135-74.

[37] DL III, I, 5.

[38] DL III, II, 3.

[39] DL III, I, 11.

[40] Skinner, 1978, p. 162.

Many governmental decisions, however, concern exactly those
affairs that are left to man's *dominium*. But as we have seen, natural
law concerning *dominium* can be changed in its *materia*. Not by individuals, but by public authority. It is Suárez's view that all those
things that fall under man's *dominium* can and should only be regulated by public authority. This is something, which is

> [...] not contrary to but rather in harmony with nature itself; since
> nature itself is able (so to speak) to cede its right, for the sake of some
> greater good which will also redound to its own advantage.[41]

But if natural law entrusts the administration of those affairs to public
authority, it is hard to see how public authority itself can be criticised
by means of that part of natural law. If it is decided by public authority how property is to be organised, it 'changes' the *materia* of the
precept that theft is forbidden, in the sense that it defines what is to
count as 'theft'. On the basis of that definition, it is not possible to
say that the government itself is guilty of theft if it raises too much
tax, or if it confiscates property of unwilling subjects. If individual
citizens have no say at all in the definition of the *materia*, it is
difficult if not impossible to evaluate governmental interpretations and
changes of the natural law concerning *dominium*.

5. *Reason plus will*

It is clear that Suárez's permission to change the *materia* of that part
of natural law which regulates man's *dominium* is more than a vain
attempt to provide for more flexibility. By his division of natural law
into two parts (*ius naturale praeceptivum* and *ius naturale dominativum*), Suárez reduces the scope of natural law to a considerable
extent. Although Suárez stresses that a change in the *materia* of
natural law does not change that law itself, it is clear that in practice
the—natural—jurisdiction over those things pertaining to man's
dominium is handed over to public authority.

That means that we can only effectively judge and criticise positive
law according to preceptive natural law. Only that preceptive part is
regarded as absolutely binding and not admitting of any change in its

---

[41] DL II, XIV, 20.

subject-matter. That leaves us with a very meagre body of natural law which is essentially immutable. The commands to honour God, to keep Sabbath or not to abuse God's name are indeed immutable (for both man and God), but one already runs into trouble with the prohibition to kill. As we have seen, Suárez added to this latter prohibition the conditions 'on one's own accord' and 'aggressively'. But the very criterion whether the killing is aggressive or not (for example in a just war) is, of course, again dependent on human (read: governmental) interpretations of whether this particular war is justified or not.

It seems then that Suárez's theory presents us with a Janus-faced account of natural law. On the one hand, he claims that natural law is essentially immutable and universal. Its precepts are necessarily true, not only the general ones, but also its conclusions. The certainty that can be reached in its conclusions is comparable to the certainty we have concerning the conclusions of theoretical reason. The instructions of natural law are detailed and should be followed to the letter.

On the other hand, however, Suárez is aware that this view is not tenable when it comes to applying these detailed instructions to practical politics. In fact, Suárez is no less aware of the contingency of human affairs than Aquinas:

> [...] all created things [...] are characterized through nature by many conditions that are changeable and capable of being abolished by many causes.[42]

But in order to cope with contingency, Suárez sees no other option than to permit the *materia* of the precepts to be changed by an act of will. And this decision considerably diminishes the role of natural law in assessing positive law.

These two faces of Suárez's account of natural law mirror the situation I described in the preceding chapter. We have seen there that in speaking about the foundation of natural law Suárez ran into difficulty because he understood reason as purely theoretical reason. Theoretical reason alone cannot give rise to obligations. He therefore had to add the divine will as an extra pillar. Here, we see that the rigidity of the model of theoretical reason is not only problematical in providing natural law with a proper foundation, but that it also causes

---

[42] DL II, XIV, 19.

problems on the level of *application*. The problem here is that his
theoretical model of rigid deduction does not allow for the flexibility
required in contingent circumstances. And again Suárez sees no other
option than to introduce an extra element. Whereas the foundation of
natural law required the divine will, the application of natural law
requires the human will as an extra source.

In both the foundation and the application of natural law, we hit
upon a combination of pure (theoretical) reason and will. Will and
reason are not linked together in a comprehensive manner; they are
juxtaposed in an unmediated way. I think that is due to the fact that
Suárez does not assign an important role to interpretation. The
prudent and sagacious interpreter of natural law whom we encountered in Aquinas's writings has disappeared from the scene.[43] According to Suárez, there is no room for interpretation[44] of the laws of
nature, only of positive laws, where the intention of the legislator is
at stake. To Suárez, interpretation of natural law is no more than the
discovery and exposition of the *'true sense'* of the meaning of the
terms as well as the normal conditions that are comprised within the
formulation of the laws.[45] The only way any flexibility can be ensured is to allow for changes in the *materia* of (a part of) natural law.
These changes however, cannot be regarded as the result of interpretation. They arise on the basis of an act of will on the part of public
authority.

The account of the foundation as well as the application of natural
law in terms of—theoretical—reason and will introduces a dichotomy
that replaces Aquinas's gradual account. Aquinas distinguished
various stages of interpretation. *Determinatio* (by means of which the
ius civile is shaped) requires more interpretation than *deductio* (by
means of which the *ius gentium* is generated), but *deductio* cannot be
carried out either without any interpretation at all. Suárez on the other
hand allows for only two possibilities. Either one applies the instructions to the letter, or one changes its *materia* through an act of will.

---

[43] See also the interesting account of Virt, 1983, p. 231.

[44] Suárez conceives of *epieikeia* as that form of interpretation where the general law
'fails in particular instances', whereas the term *interpretatio* is reserved for explaining
ambiguities in the general laws (for an elaborate account see DL II, XVI).

[45] DL II, XVI, 6 and 7.

6. *The* ius gentium

There is one area left in which the role of natural law should be examined, the field for which Suárez has become most famous: his analysis of international law. Is there any role left for natural law here, or does he rely again on an additional will?

Suárez distinguishes two meanings of the term *ius gentium*. In the first place, it refers to

> [...] the law which all the various peoples and nations ought to observe in their relations with each other.[46]

This meaning of *ius gentium* refers to the norms pertaining to international relations, such as the laws of war, slavery (as punishment of the conquered nation), treaties of peace, the immunity of ambassadors and the like.

In the second place, it is

> [...] a body of laws which individual states or kingdoms observe within their own borders, but which is called *ius gentium* because the said laws are similar [in each instance] and commonly accepted.[47]

Here, Suárez alludes to the similarity of customs within various political communities. Suárez mentions, for instance, the institution of religion, the role of sacrifices, the existence of a class of priests, the invention of money, and the establishment of settlements.

One might be surprised to find both types of laws classified under the same heading of *ius gentium*. Would it not have been more appropriate to distinguish interstate relations (*ius inter gentes*) from the common elements to be found within the borders of political communities? Suárez, however, has important reasons for taking the two meanings together. Both types of rules have the same foundation. They neither belong to natural law, nor can they be classified as ordinary positive law. Let us first examine why Suárez discards the view that the *ius gentium* belongs to natural law. In the next section, we shall see why he does not regard it as positive law either.

---

[46] DL II, XIX, 8.
[47] DL II, XIX, 8.

As we have seen in II.7, Aquinas maintained that the rules of the *ius gentium* are conclusions deduced from natural law. This option was not open to Suárez. He thought that the conclusions arrived at by means of *deductio* have the same degree of certainty as the general precepts from which they are deduced. But if the conclusions are just as certain as the general precepts from which they are derived, there would be no substantial difference between *ius gentium* and natural law.[48] This view is not tenable. Natural law is God's promulgated law. It would be blasphemous to suppose that the laws pertaining to international relations can be identified with these divine precepts.

Suárez therefore firmly discards the view that the *ius gentium* belongs to natural law. The first argument Suárez adduces is that the precepts of the *ius gentium* deal with many things pertaining to man's *dominium*. In this respect he points to slavery and division of property. This is a somewhat astonishing remark after his lengthy exposition of the fact that the subject-matter of natural law can be changed if it refers to *dominium*. If there was no reason for Suárez to exclude the precepts on property and liberty from natural law, why would he suddenly do so when speaking about international law? But he immediately answers that objection[49] by writing that this is not the only reason to exclude the *ius gentium* from natural law. There is a second reason as well:

> Consequently, in order that the *ius gentium* may be distinguished from the natural law, it is necessary—after making the assumption with regard to the particular subject-matter [...]—that, in addition, these precepts should follow not as a manifest conclusion [from natural principles] but rather by an inference less certain, so that they are dependent upon the intervention of human free will and of moral expediency rather than that of necessity.[50]

The *ius gentium* does not belong to natural law because its subject-matter is man's *dominium and* because it arises from the free will of mankind. It has a completely different foundation. *Ius gentium* is not

---

[48] This conclusion is drawn by Francisco Vitoria (1495-1546), who writes: '[...] The *ius gentium* does not necessarily follow from the natural law, nor is it necessary simply for the conservation of natural law, for if it should follow necessarily from the natural law, now it would *be* the natural law' (Vitoria, 1532).

[49] DL II, XVII, 9.

[50] DL II, XVII, 9.

founded in rational nature, is not promulgated by God's judgement and is not binding by means of God's divine will. All three pillars that together made up the foundation of natural law, are lacking in the *ius gentium*:

> [...] the precepts of the *ius gentium* were introduced by the free will and consent of mankind, whether we refer to the whole community or to the major portion thereof; consequently, they cannot be said to be written upon the hearts of men by the Author of Nature; and therefore they are a part of the human, and not of the natural law.[51]

Suárez could not have been more outspoken. The *ius gentium* should not be regarded as belonging to natural law. As such, the *ius gentium* does not *indicate* what good and evil is, but *makes* something good or evil. The *ius gentium*

> is not so much indicative of what is [inherently] evil, as it is constitutive of evil. Thus it does not forbid evil acts on the ground that they are evil, but renders [certain] acts evil by prohibiting them.[52]

This is the reversal of Aquinas's position, who maintained that the *ius gentium*, like natural law, only forbids or enjoins that which is intrinsically evil or good.

7. *Custom*

To say that the *ius gentium* is not natural law does, however, *not* imply that it is positive law in the proper sense of the term. Although Suárez writes that it arises from the 'will of mankind', this does not imply that it is 'posited' in the true sense of the word: as arising from the will of a legislator. Suárez remarks that

> [...] it has grown, almost by a natural process, with the growth of the human race; and therefore it does not exist in a written form, since it was not dictated by a legislator, but has, on the contrary, waxed strong through usage.[53]

---

[51] DL II, XVII, 8.
[52] DL II, XIX, 2.
[53] DL II, XX, 1.

With this organic metaphor, Suárez breaks through the dichotomy of pure reason and pure will. Suárez conceives of the *ius gentium* as being located somewhere in the *middle* between the 'two extremes' of natural law and of civil law.[54] Whereas natural law is entirely based upon (rational) nature and positive civil law is based upon the decree and will of the legislator, the *ius gentium* is based upon—unwritten—custom.

It is important to note that Suárez did not conceive of customs as local peculiarities. The notion of custom did not serve him to point out the variety of morals as a result of widely varying local habits, as Montaigne did. On the contrary, he emphasised the similarity of customs in different societies. As such, the existence of customs testifies to the fundamental moral unity of mankind:

> [...] the human race, into howsoever many different peoples and kingdoms it may be divided, always preserves a certain unity, not only as a species, but also a moral and political unity (as it were) enjoined by the natural precepts of mutual love and mercy; a precept which applies to all, even to strangers of every nation.[55]

It should be noted that what is natural here is only the admonition to mutual love. But how we should shape that mutual love is not prescribed by natural law. That is left to human invention, in the form of customary practices, established over the ages and to be found all over the world.

It seems to me that Suárez's concept of custom fulfils the same function as Aquinas' virtuous interpreters of natural law. Suárez writes that customs serve to *interpret* natural law. Speaking of good customs, Suárez writes:

> Such custom is, of course, useful for adding strength [...] to the natural law, by keeping fresh its memory, and by facilitating its observance on the part of the whole community. Such a custom may at times—if it be approved by prudent, wise, and virtuous men—serve to interpret the law of nature.[56]

---

[54] Cf. DL II, XIX, 7.
[55] DL II, XIX, 9.
[56] DL VII, IV, 4.

Of course, this only applies to 'good' customs. A bad custom 'is not worthy of the name of custom'.[57] One might object to this view that Suárez argues in circles here. In order to interpret the natural law, we should rely on customs, but in order to assess the quality of customs we should rely on natural law. This objection is justified, but one should keep in mind that things are no different in Aquinas's concept of interpretation by the prudent man. In fact, every act of interpretation moves in hermeneutic circles.

I think that the important role of custom as interpreter of natural law is commonly underestimated by commentators on Suárez's theory of international law. Since Suárez is consistently regarded as one of the pioneers in this field, much more attention is given to (international) 'rights' than to custom,[58] despite Suárez's elaborate analysis of custom. One of the factors that probably contributed to this omission is the dominance of scepticism in the 17th century. The notion of 'custom' acquired particularistic overtones that seemed at odds with any form of natural law. And indeed, as we shall see in the following chapter, subsequent natural law theories are indeed partly meant as a response to scepticist emphasis on the particularity of customs. But Suárez did not conceive of a dichotomy between 'universal' natural law and 'particular' customs. For him, custom was the *mediator* between universal theoretical reason and the particular acts of will of monarchs. It is by the introduction and development of custom that Suárez tries to strike a balance between the two competing concepts of law: law as an instrument of power and law as the embodiment of justice.

8. *Conclusion*

In the preceding chapter we saw that the rational perception of nature was felt to be an inadequate foundation of natural law. The additional divine will had to ensure that the rational perception of rational nature can give rise to obligatory precepts.

In this chapter, I argued that Suárez is confronted with similar problems in his account of the application of natural law to positive law. The model of theoretical reason, according to which conclusions

---

[57] DL VII, IV, 4.
[58] Soder, 1973, is a good example in point.

are mechanically derived from general precepts, cannot adequately account for the inherent variability of human affairs. In order to ensure the required flexibility, Suárez allows for changes in the *materia* in that part of natural law that has to do with the natural right to *dominium*. This enables Suárez to maintain that the natural law itself is unchangeable.

In practice, his solution boils down to a drastic limitation of natural law. Its scope is reduced to the preceptive part of natural law alone (essentially consisting in the precepts of the Decalogue). The natural law concerning man's *dominium* (pertaining to liberty, property and contracts) is made highly dependent on how its *materia* is conceived by public authority. Again, we see that the rigidity of theoretical reason requires the introduction of an additional act of will; in this case not the divine will, but the will of public authority.

Suárez's treatment of the *ius gentium*, however, suggests that he does not merely juxtapose reason and will. Speaking about the rules that can universally be found within particular communities, as well as in international relations, Suárez asserts that these are founded in custom. And he regards these customary rules and practices as evidence for a universal community of mankind. Customary practices, gradually developing over time, are neither deduced from the precepts of natural law, nor are they instituted by an act of will on the part of legislators.

What does this analysis offer in terms of the four assumptions, I mentioned in the introduction as a preliminary understanding of natural law theory? As for the assumption a) that there are universally and eternally valid laws by means of which positive law can be criticised and/or justified, we see that Suárez indeed shares that assumption. He spends hundreds of pages of minute theorising on the eternally and universally binding character of natural law and its intrinsic and essential unchangeability. But when it comes to actually using these eternal laws in order to assess positive law, we are left with only the Decalogue (the preceptive part of natural law) to rely upon. All the other laws can be changed in their *materia* by governmental decisions. These governmental modifications cannot be criticised. Since Suárez does not share Aquinas's views that there are some guidelines directly accessible to us by an investigation of nature, we are left with empty hands.

The second assumption b) that the laws of nature are grounded in nature, is but partially endorsed by Suárez. In the first place, nature is narrowed down to 'rational nature' as it is manifest in rational beings. Irrational nature had no relevance at all for natural law. In the second place, (rational) nature is only one of the three pillars on which natural law rests, the others being natural reason and the divine will, as we saw in the preceding chapter.

Suárez unequivocally underscores assumption c) that human beings can discover the principles of natural law by means of reason. He takes reason in the sense of theoretical reason: comparing actions with rational nature. On the basis of that ability, it is possible to understand the precepts of natural law.

Finally, Suárez pretends that it is his view that indeed (assumption d) positive law is only morally obligatory if it is in agreement with natural law. But on the basis of our findings with respect to assumption a), we may safely conclude that since it is extremely difficult to tell whether positive law (dis)agrees with natural law (its *materia* being changeable), we should not make too much of this last assumption either. In fact, since it is his view that only public authority, entrusted with legislative power, can change the *materia* of natural law, it is impossible for an individual citizen to claim that positive law disagrees with natural law and therefore lacks morally obligatory force.

On the basis of these findings, we might conclude that the role of natural law as the judge of positive law is even less important in Suárez's theory than it was in Aquinas's theory. In II. 8, I noted that we should not exaggerate the potential of natural law in Aquinas's theory. At best it furnishes us with some minimal requirements for positive law. But Aquinas never pretended that natural law could do more. In Suárez's theory, this role is further reduced, notwithstanding his protestations to the contrary. There is a gap between Suárez's theoretical account of natural law and the function it can actually perform that had been absent in Aquinas's theory.

At the same time, we see that there is another programme carried out by Suárez. Both the treatment of natural law and the *ius gentium* testify to the importance of the concept of *dominium*. The view that man has a right (*facultas*) to dispose of property and liberty as he himself sees fit, absent in Aquinas's theory, results in a drastic change in both natural law theory and the concept of *ius gentium*. With respect to natural law, it leads to the special status of the *ius naturale dominativum*, with the corresponding permission to change its *materia*. As for the *ius gentium*, it results in the claim that it is grounded in the free will or consent of mankind. In fact, the only difference between the two bodies of law is Suárez's allegation that they have a different basis. But there are no substantial differences between the two concepts. Both the *ius gentium* and the natural law on *dominium* deal with the regulation of man's *dominium*.

In the preceding chapter, I compared Suárez's concept of natural law to the script of Calderón's play. In this chapter we have seen that it is indeed Suárez's view that the human actors should stick to the text of El Autor as literally as possible. But I think that Suárez was also aware of the fact that God's script has little to do with how human beings actually shape the world. It seems then that Suárez makes room for another play as well, written by human playwrights and acted out on a second stage. On this stage, man exercises his *dominium*.

CHAPTER V

GROTIUS'S HUMANISATION OF NATURAL LAW

In the preceding chapter I concluded that in Suárez's theory the scope of natural law is in fact a rather limited one. Despite extensive theorising about the nature, foundation and obligatory force of natural law, an important role is assigned to the way man's *dominium* is regulated by man-made conventions.

One would expect this development to continue and to evolve towards an orientation which focuses on human customs and conventions rather than on laws ordained by God or nature. This expectation would be all the more justified in the case of Hugo Grotius, a practically minded lawyer who sets out to find a *modus vivendi* in order to regulate the competing claims of the emergent nation-states and a Protestant thinker who did not feel bound by the teachings of Thomas Aquinas. One would expect such a man to minimise the significance of natural law and to give room to an autonomous sphere of international law, based on custom. Instead, Grotius became known as the one who rehabilitated natural law in the Protestant world as the proper basis for international law; he is even heralded as the founder of a new science of natural law.[1]

How can we account for the resilience of natural law theory? In Grotius's work it no longer serves as an instrument to refute the epistemological scepticism of the Reformists, who stressed the—impenetrable—will of God as the source of all morality. Yet, we see that it still performs the function of a bulwark, be it that this was no longer erected against epistemological scepticism, but against a new brand of scepticism, which we might label 'cultural scepticism'. In Grotius's famous Prolegomena of *De Jure Belli ac Pacis*,[2] references to natural law and to the universal nature of mankind figure in the context of a critique on the new scepticists. The main scape-goat is Carneades, the Greek philosopher and head of the Platonic Academy in the 2nd century B.C., who had maintained that law rested on no other foundation than mere expediency. In the texts of Grotius and

---

[1] Cf. e.g. Dufour, 1984; d'Entrèves, 1951, p. 71; Tuck, 1987, p. 104.
[2] Grotius, 1625.

later also of Pufendorf, the figure of Carneades seems to epitomise
the modern kind of scepticism represented by Michel de Montaigne
and Pierre Charron. According to Tuck, the attack on Carneades
might as well be read as criticism of these sceptics.[3]

In the face of this new brand of scepticism, it was indeed dangerous to follow Suárez in emphasising the importance of custom as the
basis of the *ius gentium*. For Montaigne not only stressed the tenacity
and power of custom as a force that shapes human institutions. Suárez
had also maintained that view. Montaigne's claim was stronger: he
reduced morality and law to the force of custom alone. What people
attribute to 'reason' or to 'nature', Montaigne wrote, is nothing else
than sheer custom: 'Les lois de la conscience, que nous disons naître
de nature, naissent de la coutume [...]'.[4] Montaigne persistently
treats 'nature' and 'custom' as opposing notions.

But there was another difference with Suárez's views on custom as
well. Whereas Suárez had confidently believed that the human race,
notwithstanding its division into peoples and kingdoms, had 'preserved a certain unity', Montaigne was deeply aware of the enormous
variety of beliefs, customs and laws. And Grotius agreed with this.
Indeed, as he had witnessed during his diplomatic career, the variety
of beliefs and opinions was one of the sources of conflict both within
and between the nations for the regulation of which he set out to
construct a body of law. Custom, as one of the sources for those
conflicts, could evidently not be used as a foundation for such a
system of law. He had to find his inspiration in a notion which
promised to provide for universal and eternal standards that could be
acceptable to anyone, irrespective of the customs and opinions people
happened to cherish. He found this in the notion of natural law.

In this sense we might say, paradoxically as it may sound, that the
revival of natural law can—indirectly—be attributed to the sceptics.
By 'contaminating' their emphasis on custom with ethical relativism,
the sceptics undermined the potentiality of 'custom' as a viable way
of explaining and justifying the *ius gentium*. Custom could no longer
play the honourable role that Suárez had assigned to it. In the writings of the sceptics 'custom' became 'mere custom'. It became identified with that which is particular and local. The sceptics set the terms
for a debate in which 'local customs' figure in opposition to 'univer-

---

[3] Tuck, 1987, p. 109.
[4] Montaigne, 1577-80, Essai I, 23.

sal laws', and in which 'opinion' is contrasted to 'reason'. It is in this context that natural law can be conceived as the pure opposite of 'custom' and as the only firm and universal pillar in the morass of ethical relativism.[5]

It was not easy to erect this pillar: natural law theory brought with it a number of problems. In the preceding chapter we witnessed some of the tensions that are inherent in a concept of natural law which is no longer supported by teleological metaphysics. Although it sometimes appears as if Grotius rather naively adopted a simple Aristotelian view which seemed to disregard these tensions between will and reason, and between reason and nature, it cannot be denied that to Grotius the teleological world was no longer accessible either. Besides, he was acquainted with the works of the Spaniards. There are striking similarities to be found between Suárez's and Grotius's treatment of natural law. These similarities might be ascribed to Grotius having read the Spaniards, but might equally be conceived as the logical outcome of having to deal with the same conceptual problems.

Although it never was Grotius's explicit aim to develop a theory of natural law, we can read his work as an attempt to unify once more the various competing elements into one coherent concept of natural law. In this respect Grotius's theory can be regarded as a thorough innovation, which succeeded in solving some of the problems Suárez had encountered, or to put it more precisely, which rendered these problems irrelevant to natural law theory. On the other hand, we shall see that some of the old tensions surface again in his new concept of natural law, be it on a different level. In that sense we might regard his theory as a continuation of natural law theory.

To regard Grotius's theory as a continuation of natural law theory as expounded by Suárez is not to deny the importance of Stoic influences in Grotius's theory. But as I noted in the introduction, I shall refrain from treating these influences as an *explanation* for theoretical modifications and innovations. Instead of explaining theoretical innovations by pointing to the popularity of Stoic sources, we can

---

[5] Today, the debate on the importance of human rights in non-Western cultures versus the desirability of legal pluralism is still framed in the parameters of these opposing notions, not only by Western but also by non-Western intellectuals. See, for example, the plea for a 'more universalist' interpretation of the Shari-ah (Islamic law) by An-Na'im, 1992.

understand that popularity by pointing to the conceptual problems the Stoics promised to solve.

In this chapter I shall mainly focus on the theoretical innovations in the internal structure of the concept of natural law. That implies that we are dealing here with only a tiny part of Grotius's work, which as a whole is dedicated to much more practical matters. It never was Grotius's aim to give a systematical and philosophical account of natural law, comparable to that of Suárez. Welzel therefore characterises Grotius's account of natural law in the Prolegomena of the *De Jure Belli ac Pacis* as mere 'incidental music' ('Begleitmusik').[6] But in order to understand the development of natural law, and in particular of the theory subsequently developed by Pufendorf, this incidental music is important.

In the next chapter we shall focus on 'the main theme' and inquire into Grotius's concepts of municipal law and international law. There, the full implications of his new theory of natural law can be assessed.

1. De Jure Praedae: *the formal structure of law*

In order to gain some insight into the way the new concept of natural law was construed, it is useful to compare Grotius's main oeuvre *De Jure Belli ac Pacis* (JBP)[7] with a very early work, called *De Jure Praedae Commentarius* (JP).[8] Most interpreters seem to regard the JP as merely a preparation for the more mature JBP: it would contain the nucleus of the theory that was to be developed more fully in the JBP.[9]

However, such an interpretation overlooks the fact that in the JP there is no room for a proper concept of natural law, whereas the JBP is centred around that concept as the basis for all law. A comparison between the JP and the JBP might give us some insight into the question why the original theoretical framework of the JP was later thought to be insufficient. On the basis of that insight it is possible to assess the importance of natural law in the JBP.

---

[6] Welzel, 1951, p. 125.
[7] Grotius, 1625.
[8] Grotius, 1604.
[9] These interpreters follow the analysis of the Dutch historian Fruin, 1868.

In 1604, at the age of 21, Grotius was commissioned by the Dutch East India Company (V.O.C.) to write a justification of the action of one of its admirals in seizing a Portuguese vessel. This action needed further justification; Holland was not at war with Portugal and many share-holders of the V.O.C. viewed the seizure as pure looting, in which they did not want to take part, despite the riches that could be obtained. As a result, some share-holders tried to set up their own company, which threatened to undermine the monopoly of the V.O.C. Grotius, bored at the time with his purely practical work as an advocate, complied enthusiastically. This resulted in the JP, which for unknown reasons was not published at the time and was only discovered as late as 1868.[10]

For someone who is acquainted only with the JBP, reading this early work comes as a surprise. It is not only that the work is pervaded by patriotic zest which makes it different—something which is comprehensible in view of both the purpose of the book and the youthful enthusiasm of a man who is at that time still honoured by his country—; but the whole theoretical setting of the work, expounded in the Prolegomena of the JP, is different from that of the JBP.

The theoretical framework of the JP is structured along the division between so-called 'rules' (*regulae*) and 'laws' (*leges*). The rules specify the various sources of laws. There are nine of such 'rules'. The laws on the other hand, thirteen in total, contain substantive normative principles. Each rule functions as a foundation for the laws, which according to Grotius are 'derived' from these rules. The relationship can be visualized as follows:

Rule I. What God has shown to be His Will, that is law.
→ Law I. It shall be permissible to defend one's own life and to shun that which threatens to prove injurious.
Law II. It shall be permissible to acquire for oneself, and to retain, those things which are useful for life.
Rule II. What the common consent of mankind has shown to be the will of all, that is law.
→ Law III. Let no one inflict injury upon his fellow.
Law IV. Let no one seize possession of that which has been taken into the possession of another.
Etc.

---

[10] The historical details around the JP can be found in Fruin, 1868.

In the same fashion this list can be continued.[11] It is true that Grotius thinks that in the last instance all laws are derived from rule I (the will of God) but they do so by the intermediate rules.

This causes some difficulties, which become apparent if we read Grotius's argument. Laws I and II enjoining us to self-preservation are directly derived from God's will, for He has willed His creation to last. But then Grotius goes on to argue that it is reasonable to expect God to have willed not only our own preservation, but the preservation of the whole species. He therefore willed that all people 'might be linked in mutual harmony as if by everlasting covenant'.[12] This harmony is at the basis of rule II, from which laws III and IV are derived, enjoining us to a social life.

The problem is that properly speaking there is no real need for rule II. For if the necessity of mutual harmony for the preservation of mankind can be derived directly from the will of God, as Grotius argues, what then is the need for introducing an *intermediate* source (i.e. rule II) for the laws ensuring such harmony? Why is it necessary to introduce 'common consent' as an extra source for those laws that prescribe social behaviour? Apparently, Grotius hesitates to link these social obligations directly to God, otherwise he would not have established 'the will of all' as an extra source for laws regulating human relations.

2. *The scepticism of the JP*

The fact that the laws pertaining to self-preservation and those enjoining us to sociability rest on two different proximate foundations causes another problem as well. This problem has to do with the question which rules should be given priority in case the various laws conflict. Grotius would not have been a true lawyer, had he not answered that question. At the end of the Prolegomena he formulates 'the law of all laws' as he calls it, which runs: 'In cases where [the laws] can be observed simultaneously, let them [all] be observed; when this is impossible, the law of superior rank shall prevail'.[13]

---

[11] For a complete list of all rules and laws, see Appendix A in the above-mentioned edition of the JP.

[12] JP Prol., p. 11.

[13] JP Prol., p. 29.

As far as the source is concerned, there is no doubt about the superiority of the laws generated by rule I over rule II. Laws springing from God's will are superior to the laws arising from the common consent of mankind (rule II). But there is a problem regarding the substance (or in Grotius's words: the 'purpose') of these rules, expressed in the laws that are derived from the rules. We have seen that the laws emanating from rule I exhort us to seek our self-preservation. The laws enjoining us to further the preservation of others are not derived from rule I, but from rule II, which locates the source of these laws in the common consent of mankind. If we are to follow the 'law of all laws', we should give priority to those laws which stress self-preservation rather than social behaviour. This means that in case of conflict we should think of our own interests first.

And this is indeed the consequence Grotius explicitly draws: '[...] that which concerns one's own good is preferred to that which concerns another's good'.[14] But apparently Grotius feels uneasy with his own consistency. For a few pages earlier he stated that:

> [...] although the order of presentation [...] has indicated that one's own good takes precedence over the good of another person [...] the more general concept should take precedence on the ground that it includes the good of individuals as well.[15]

The whole problem arises, of course, in the plurality of sources Grotius adduces. Had he merely stated that God wills us to preserve ourselves *and* the lives of our fellowmen, he would not have encountered these problems. As it is now, God commands us only to live by proverbs like 'I myself am my closest neighbour' and 'my tunic is closer than my cloak'.[16] The truly altruistic and more 'noble' ends find their origin only in the common consent of mankind.[17]

Why does Grotius refrain from grounding all laws in the will of God? Two reasons seem to present themselves. In the first place it is tempting to compare Grotius's solution to that of Suárez. Grotius had not yet read Suárez by that time, but his hesitation to ground all laws in the will of God and his tendency to regard the will of mankind as

---

[14] JP Prol., p. 29.

[15] JP Prol., p. 21.

[16] JP Prol., p. 21.

[17] Tuck, however, reads Grotius's solution as an unequivocal plea for the superiority of self-preservation. Cf. Tuck, 1993, p. 174.

an additional source are comparable to Suárez's opinion in which the laws regulating man's *dominium* do not belong to God's preceptive natural law either. Both theories reflect a new and keen awareness of the man-made character of those moral principles that pertain to human matters.

In the second place, we should refer to a truly un-Suárezian element in Grotius's theory: the sudden re-emergence of the notion of eternal law. The will of God as the source for the laws that enjoin us to seek self-preservation is described in a way that recalls Aristotle's and Aquinas's description of eternal law.[18] The young Grotius writes:

> [...] Since God fashioned creation and willed its existence, every individual part thereof has received from Him certain natural properties whereby that existence may be preserved and each part may be guided for its own good, in conformity [...] with the fundamental law inherent in its origin. From this fact the old poets and philosophers have rightly deduced that love, whose primary force and action are directed to self-interest, is the first principle of the whole natural order.[19]

In the JP, the Aristotelian metaphysical framework seems to have remained intact.[20] Grotius writes explicitly that natural properties serve to *guide* created beings to their own good. Once more, nature is conceived as purposive.

But although eternal law as a metaphysical assumption is revived, its substance is curtailed. According to Grotius, God's 'design'[21] reveals *only* the inclination to self-preservation. The inclinations to a social life and Aquinas's emphasis on the desire for knowledge of God are left out. Apparently, Hobbes was not the first who found it difficult to conceive of natural inclinations which transcend self-interest.

The primacy of self-preservation as the only really natural inclination, its priority in case of conflict with sociability, as well as its fortified position, being directly grounded in God's will, all indicate

---

[18] Cf. Besselink, 1988, p. 16.

[19] JP Prol., p. 9.

[20] This Aristotelianism is not surprising. Kossmann characterised the Dutch intellectual climate in the first half of the 17th century as pervaded by a blend of Aristotelianism, Calvinism and humanism. Cf. Kossmann, 1960, p. 9.

[21] JP Prol., p. 8.

that here the young Grotius is not very far removed from the sceptics who claimed that the mother of all justice is expediency. And indeed, Grotius did not hesitate to endorse the sceptical claim. In unequivocal terms he asserts:

> [...] Horace should not be censured for saying, in imitation of the Academics, that expediency might perhaps be called the mother of justice and equity. For all things in nature, as Cicero repeatedly insists, are tenderly regardful of self, and seek their own happiness and security. This phenomenon can be observed not only in the human race, but among the beasts also and even in connexion with inanimate objects, being a manifestation of that true and divinely inspired self-love which is laudable in every phase of creation.[22]

Apparently, if one restricts the inclinations which God implanted in nature to that toward self-preservation alone, the Aristotelian concept of eternal law can easily lead to the kind of scepticism according to which all morality is founded in 'expediency'.

3. *The inadequacy of the JP*

This sceptical form of Aristotelianism might be convenient for a man who tries to justify the looting of Portuguese ships, but it is not for the man who sets out to write a comprehensive study of law. Apart from that, it is probable that private as well as political experiences had taught Grotius the inadequacy of 'the will of mankind' as a reliable source of law.

The Prolegomena of the JBP is written in a fierce mood. It contains unambiguous criticism of the view he had inclined to in the JP:

> Carneades, then, having undertaken to hold a brief against justice [...] was able to muster no argument stronger than this, that, for reasons of expediency, men imposed upon themselves laws, which vary according to customs, and among the same peoples often undergo changes as times change; moreover that there is no law of nature, because all creatures, men as well as animals, are impelled by nature towards ends advantageous to themselves [...]. What the philosopher here says [...] must not for one moment be admitted. Man is, to be sure, an animal,

---

[22] JP Prol., p. 9.

but an animal of superior kind [...]. But among the traits characteristic
of man is an impelling desire for society [...]. Stated as a universal
truth, therefore, the assertion that every animal is impelled by nature to
seek only its own good cannot be conceded.[23]

In one breath, this passage criticises scepticism as well as the restricted version of eternal law he had endorsed himself in the JP. In
fact, his criticism resembles very closely the way Suárez had criticised the concept of eternal law. Like Suárez, Grotius points out that
for an inclination to be morally just, it is no longer sufficient to show
that it is natural. Like Suárez, Grotius now maintains that reason
should intervene in order to 'elevate' the natural propensities in order
to turn them into law:

> [...] it is meet for the nature of man, within the limits of human
> intelligence, to follow the direction of a well-tempered judgement,
> being neither led astray by fear or the allurement of immediate pleas-
> ure, nor carried away by rash impulse.[24]

This emphasis on rationality implies a fundamental distinction
between man and animal. Again, like Suárez, Grotius emphasises that
only intelligent beings can be subject to law.

> The distinction, which appears in the books of Roman law, between an
> unchangeable law common to animals and man, which the Roman legal
> writers call the law of nature in a more restricted sense, and a law
> peculiar to man, which they frequently call the law of nations, is of
> hardly any value. For, strictly speaking, only a being that applies
> general principles is capable of law [...].[25]

His position in the JBP comes closer to that of Suárez than to his own
former views he had developed in the JP.[26] One can only speak of
law in the proper sense of the word if it directs intelligent beings.

---

[23] JBP Prol. 5-6.
[24] JBP Prol. 9.
[25] JBP I, I, XI, 1.
[26] Whether this change can be ascribed to Grotius' reading of Suárez's DL, which
had appeared in 1612 (so after the JP and before the JBP), has been and still is a
matter for debate. In view of other similarities between the JBP and Suárez's work,
which had been absent in the JP, I tend to think Grotius was thoroughly influenced by
Suárez.

But this emphasis on the link between human rationality and law does not induce him to exalt Rule II (the common consent of mankind) as the true source for morality and law. He does not share Suárez's optimism concerning the moral union of all mankind. Grotius no longer regards common consent as the foundation for the laws enjoining us to a social life, as he had done in the JP. That union seems to have fallen apart in competing 'sects'. This can be judged from Grotius's description of the 'testimony of philosophers, historians, poets and orators':

> Not that confidence is to be reposed in them without discrimination; for they were accustomed to serve the interests of their sect, their subject, or their cause.[27]

The only role he allows 'common consent' to play is an epistemological one. It may play a role in the *post hoc* justification of acts. Although not with 'absolute assurance', common consent, at least 'among those that are more advanced in civilization', may indicate a common sense of mankind.[28] The emphasis on the limited reliability of common consent illustrates how far the older Grotius is removed from the beliefs he had cherished in the JP. The added qualification 'more advanced in civilization' is accompanied by extensive quotes regarding the occurrence of 'habits of doing wrong' and 'distorted mentalities'.

4. *Human nature*

So neither the will of God, nor common consent seemed to be suitable candidates for the foundation of a comprehensive system of law. Consequently, we see that in the JBP the whole complex structure of rules and laws of the JP has been abandoned in favour of a simple distinction between positive and natural law. Natural law contains those precepts which can be deduced from nature. Positive law contains all those laws which have their source in the will of the various authorities, including the will of God. One might say that in

---

[27] JBP Prol. 40.
[28] JBP I, I, XII, 1.

the eyes of the mature Grotius the JP had only dealt with positive law.

Time and again Grotius stresses this distinction, and it is as if he speaks to his own younger self when he writes that it is not possible to give 'a well-ordered presentation' of law 'unless [...] those elements which come from positive law are properly separated from those which arise from nature'.[29] Those who consecrate themselves 'to true justice', Grotius writes, 'should undertake to treat the parts of the natural and unchangeable philosophy of law, after having removed all that has its origin in the free will of man'.[30]

What then is the basis of the natural law? Grotius asserts that the sole foundation of the law of nature is *human nature*. According to Grotius:

> [...] the very nature of man, which even if we had no lack of anything would lead us into the mutual relations of society, is the mother of the law of nature.[31]

Different traits are distinguishable in human nature: an inclination to self-preservation, a desire for society, knowledge, the faculty of reasoning and of speech. Here, sociability and reason acquire a position that is thought to be just as firmly rooted in nature as self-preservation. It is from all those traits together that we can derive some immutable precepts of natural law.

The foundation of natural law in human nature is, as I noted in III.8, foreshadowed by Suárez. Suárez writes that the very fact that we are rational beings 'is of itself a sufficient sign of such divine voliton, no other notification being necessary'.[32] I concluded there that this solution implies that human nature serves as the starting-point for any proof of the existence of natural law; a reversal of the traditional Thomistic point of view.

However, Suárez does not draw the full implications of that view. He does not conceive of human nature as the sole foundation of natural law. His solution consisted in combining the several competing foundations that presented themselves. According to Suárez, none of these foundations, taken by itself, suffice. The middle-course Suárez

---

[29] JBP Prol. 30.
[30] JBP Prol. 31.
[31] JBP Prol. 16.
[32] DL II, VI, 24.

decides upon was inspired by his wish to avoid both extremes of voluntarism and intellectualism. By *adding* God's will to reason and nature, he hoped to avoid the charge of blasphemy, and at the same time to preserve the notion that God's law was accessible to human reason.

The question arises to what extent Grotius's foundation of natural law in human nature alone can avoid these pitfalls as successfully as Suárez's solution. The issue whether Grotius should be regarded as an intellectualist or as a voluntarist has been the subject of an extended debate,[33] revolving around a famous passage in the Prolegomena to the JBP, the so-called 'impious hypothesis':

> What we have been saying would have a degree of validity even if we should concede that which cannot be conceded without the utmost wickedness, that there is no God, or that the affairs of men are of no concern to Him.[34]

This passage is commonly regarded as the purest expression of Grotius's intellectualism and it has been observed that Grotius was not the first to have maintained such a view. Indeed, 'the hypothesis no longer protrudes like an intellectual good deed in the naughty world of nominalism',[35] because it had its forerunners, even among nominalists. This is all very plausible and indeed we saw (III.5) how Suárez quoted this very passage almost in the same wording, as the motto of the intellectualist.[36] So Grotius is indeed not very original here. He did not invent the 'impious hypothesis'. The phrase had a long history.

Yet, what is overlooked, is that Grotius does not seem to engage in the debate between voluntarists and intellectualists at all here. It is a loose remark in a context in which he is only eager to stress the immutability of natural law. In fact, if we fully realise the implications of Grotius's move, that the sole foundation of natural law is in human nature, it transpires that the question whether God's will or God's reason was at the basis of law, which is in fact the issue at stake in any debate between voluntarists and intellectualists, was

---

[33] Cf. Hervada, 1983; Besselink, 1988; Crowe, 1976; Haggenmacher, 1983; d'Entrèves, 1951, p. 71.

[34] JBP Prol. 11.

[35] Crowe, 1976, p. 405.

[36] DL II, VI, 14.

irrelevant to Grotius. The only thing that matters to him is that human nature is the source of natural law. God's will or reason only come into play as soon as the question is raised about the origin of human nature. But that question is not addressed by Grotius, rightly so. Whether human nature is the product of God's intellect or of Gods will is not important for the status of natural law. Natural law is not directly grounded in God, but only indirectly and by means of human nature.[37]

The intermediate link of human nature enables him to stress both God's freedom *and* the intelligibility of natural law. The one does not exclude the other. It is with confidence that he asserts in his correspondence:

> God was free not to create man. But man having been created, that is, a nature using reason and being eminently sociable, he necessarily approves of actions in harmony with such a nature and disapproves of the opposite.[38]

In order to change natural law, God should change human nature first. Since nobody would deny the possibility that God can change human nature as He sees fit, His freedom is not endangered. But this freedom does not turn natural law into an arbitrary affair, inaccessible to the human intellect. If He changes human nature, we human beings are the first to know. The construction excludes both blasphemy and arbitrariness on God's part and thus solves the dilemma Suárez had faced.

5. *Divine law*

This reading of Grotius makes the debate concerning Grotius's intellectualism or voluntarism rather superfluous. Once we realise the full implications of Grotius's move, we can account for those passages (such as the impious hypothesis) in which he seems to take an intellectualist turn, as well as the passages with a more voluntarist flavour, such as:

---

[37] Cf. Röd, 1970, p. 74.
[38] Briefw. IX, no. 3586, 21 May 1638. Quoted in Besselink, 1988, p. 38.

Herein, then, is another source of law besides the source in nature, that is, the free will of God, to which beyond all cavil our reason tells us we must render obedience. But the law of nature of which we have spoken, comprising alike that which relates to the social life of man and that which is so called in a larger sense, proceeding as it does from the essential traits implanted in man, can nevertheless rightly be attributed to God, because of *His having willed that such traits exist in us* [my emphasis].[39]

This passage is not inconsistent with 'the impious hypothesis'. It merely reveals that the impious hypothesis is not impious at all. The 'impious hypothesis' asserts that if we take human nature as our starting-point for a derivation of natural law, the validity of this derivation in itself is independent from any belief in God. But that does not imply that Grotius did not believe in God. On the contrary, he believes that God is the ultimate source of human nature. Grotius's secularisation of natural law does not remove God from the scene; it merely provides for an extra link in the chain that connects God with His law. This extra link is human nature.

It is this extra link that marks the difference between divine volitional law and natural law. Grotius is very clear on this difference. Natural law, he writes,

points out that an act, according as it is or is not in conformity with rational nature, has in it a quality of moral baseness or moral necessity; and that, *in consequence*, such an act is either forbidden or enjoined by the author of nature, God [my emphasis;][40]

whereas

[...] volitional divine law does not enjoin or forbid those things which in themselves and by their own nature are obligatory or not permissible, but by forbidding things it *makes* them unlawful, and by commanding things it *makes* them obligatory [my emphasis].[41]

Judging from the terminology that is used here, it looks as if the intellectualist position is neatly summed up in the definition of natural

---

[39] JBP Prol. p. 12.
[40] JBP I, I, X, 1.
[41] JBP I, I, X, 2.

law, whereas the voluntarist position is described in the definition of divine positive law. But appearances mislead. The debate between voluntarists and intellectualists revolved around the status of *natural* law and asked whether that law proceeds from Gods will or intellect. Here the question is at stake which role God performs in both natural and positive divine law. Grotius remarks that in natural law God's role is limited to *re-affirming* the truths He had Himself created by creating mankind, whereas in divine law God can be regarded as the direct Legislator. Divine positive and natural law are logically distinct. Those who maintain that 'the Old Testament can be used as a source of the law of nature' are therefore criticised. 'Without doubt they are in error', Grotius writes, 'for many of its rules [i.e. of the Old Testament] come from the free will of God'.[42]

Not only, however, is their status a different one, they also differ in content. In the first place, Grotius remarks that divine law strives for a 'greater degree of moral perfection'[43] so that it may contain explicit precepts on things that are permissible by natural law.[44] Secondly, according to Grotius, natural law only contains precepts that regulate the relations of men among themselves, whereas divine law regulates our conduct towards God as well.[45]

These substantial differences between divine positive law and natural law strongly remind us of the distinction Suárez had drawn between the two parts of natural law: preceptive natural law and that part of natural law which concerns man's *dominium*. Suárez had maintained that preceptive natural law concerned our relation towards God as well as the duties mentioned in the Decalogue. It is distinguished from that part of natural law which pertains to human affairs and entrusts these affairs to human authority. It seems as if Grotius has a similar division in mind, but takes a step further. Preceptive natural law is identified with positive divine law. There, God's explicit decree is indeed needed to turn it into binding law. 'Natural law' is confined to Suárez's concept of natural law concerning man's *dominium*. It permits many things that are regulated by the divine law. It exclusively deals with the 'relations of men among them-

---

[42] JBP Prol. 48.
[43] JBP Prol. 50.
[44] JBP I, II, V, 1.
[45] JBP Prol. 48.

selves'. By thus restricting the scope of natural law, we might say that indeed natural law is thoroughly 'humanised'.[46]

6. *A comparison with Aquinas and Vázquez*

In section 4, I argued that for Grotius the old dilemma between voluntarism and intellectualism had become irrelevant. By taking human nature as the foundation of natural law, he simply short-circuited the discussion. But is this solution really a new one? First, one may wonder whether there is any real difference between Grotius's account and the traditional one by Aquinas. Both seem to derive natural principles from nature, so what is the novelty of Grotius's approach? Second, one may object that Grotius's approach comes very close to that of Vázquez, who had maintained that 'rational nature' is the true basis of natural law, a position that had been criticised by Suárez (III.5).

As for the first objection, it is true that Aquinas thought that the principles of natural law could be deduced from the natural inclinations implanted in man. But there are important differences as well. To Aquinas the inclinations and traits of mankind had been implanted in human nature according to God's style: the eternal law. Natural law served only as an epistemological gateway to eternal law. It is by the use of natural reason that man participates in God's intellect (*synderesis*).

I think that this view was partially endorsed by Grotius in the JP, but was discarded in the JBP. We have seen that in the JP the description of rule I reminds one of the notion of eternal law. But in the JBP the eternal law is discarded in a way similar to that of Suárez. Its function is taken over by human nature. Reason, as one of the traits constituting human nature, has therefore acquired a more important role. It is no longer merely a *gateway* to God's design, but also—an important element of—the *foundation* of natural law.[47]

This difference with Aquinas would seem to give more credit to the second objection that Grotius's solution comes very close to the

---

. [46] Cf. Tuck, 1983, pp. 56-7.

[47] Besselink rightly points out the existence of eternal law and *analogia entis* in Grotius's work, but I think he does not sufficiently recognise the differences between the JP and the JBP (Besselink, 1988, p. 21).

one attributed to Vázquez, that natural law is grounded in 'rational nature'. There is indeed evidence to be found for this comparison. According to Suárez, Vázquez had maintained that the upright character of actions is to be found in their conformity or lack of conformity with rational nature itself. If we read Grotius's definition of the law of nature, he seems to agree with this view:

> The law of nature is a dictate of right reason, which points out that an act, according as it is or is not in conformity with rational nature, has in it a quality of moral baseness or moral necessity [...].[48]

At first sight, it looks as if Grotius is merely repeating Vázquez here. As I argued above, the disappearance of eternal law left the natural lawyers with three rival foundations for natural law: God's will, God's intellect, and rational nature. We have already seen that Grotius did not opt for the first two options as a proximate or direct source for natural law. He short-circuited the dilemma. Can it be then that Grotius opted for the third alternative, rational nature?

In a sense, Grotius's solution is indeed similar to Vázquez's. We have seen (III.5) that Vázquez thought that God's promulgated law was only of secondary importance. Rational nature is first and foremost expressed in human rational nature. In order to know the eternal order that directs God's creation, we should consult human nature. That is why Crowe identifies the expression 'rational nature' with 'human rational nature'.[49] And on the basis of that reading Grotius and Vázquez share the same view.

Yet, this interpretation oversimplifies matters. According to both Suárez's and Welzel's interpretation,[50] Vázquez maintained that rational nature is independent from and even *prior to* God's will or even God's judgement. That means that Vázquez can hardly be said to have identified rational nature with human rational nature. For how can human nature be thought to be prior to God's will or judgement? Rather, it seems to have been Vázquez's view that God was bound to rational nature (in the sense of an eternal rational order) and therefore could not fail to create human beings accordingly. But that does not turn human rational nature into a foundation. Vázquez conceives of

---

[48] JBP I, I, X, 1.
[49] Crowe, 1976, pp. 390-1.
[50] Welzel, 1951, pp. 95-6.

human nature as an *expression* of rational nature. It is the latter that forms the foundation of natural law, not the former. It seems to me that if there is a connection between Vázquez and Grotius at all, Grotius radicalises Vázquez's view. If we should consult our nature in order to know rational nature, why then should we refrain from turning human nature itself into a foundation? Whether God Himself was bound to rational nature or not, we do not know. Nor need we know. We have access to human nature, and that is sufficient for any concept of natural law, which is about the *human* capacity to discover moral principles. Therefore, we can safely regard that as the proximate foundation of natural law.

This humanisation of Vázquez's concept of 'rational nature' also solves the problem of obligation. We have seen that Suárez had rejected both 'rational nature' and 'God's intellect' as sufficient foundations for natural law, because he thought these notions lacked the necessary obligatory force and threatened to make natural law ineffective. Although both concepts ensured the intelligibility of natural law, they did not seem to give rise to an obligation to *act* according to rational insight. Suárez maintained therefore that God's will was needed as an additional foundation, because only God's will could provide for obligatory force (III.7).

Grotius, however, can dispense with the notion of an *additional* divine volition. The mere fact that God has *willed* some traits to exist in human nature is already sufficient argument for the claim that we should act in conformity to our nature. We do not need any extra commands from God, because God's will is already manifest in human nature.[51] God has willed us to be sociable, and therefore we should abstain from another's property and fulfil promises.

In order to turn *ius* into a truly binding *lex*, Grotius does not have to become a voluntarist. Nor, however, does he turn to intellectualism for that reason, as Finnis maintains.[52] Here again, the persistent attempt to read Grotius in terms of voluntarism versus intellectualism obscures the novelty of Grotius's approach, or, more precisely, the

---

[51] Röd, who asserts that the conformity of an act with human nature does not by itself constitute an obligation to perform that act, overlooks the fact that Grotius stressed God's creation of human nature. Cf. Röd, 1970, p. 73.

[52] Finnis thinks that Grotius can be regarded as a forerunner of Clarke, who 'tried to treat obligation as just one more of the set of relations of consistency'. Cf. NLNR pp. 44-5.

fact that Grotius had drawn the full consequences of the solution already hinted at by Suárez.

7. *The idealisation of human nature*

Although Grotius's step towards a humanisation of natural law solves some traditional dilemmas, it creates a new problem as well. We might summarise this as 'the problem of overload'. The concept of human nature had to fulfil too many tasks.

In III.7 we saw that Suárez needed three elements in order to account for the foundation of natural law. He had located the *basis* for natural law in (Vázquez's concept of) 'rational nature'; he had assigned the *promulgation* of natural law to natural reason; and he had derived the *binding force* of natural law from God's will. I characterised his solution as a somewhat desperate attempt to hold together the component elements of natural law, (reason, nature, and will) which had been drifting apart as a result of the decline of teleological metaphysics.

Grotius's move can be understood as an attempt to unify natural law once more into one coherent concept. Human nature serves as the *basis* of natural law. The *promulgation* of natural law is understood in terms of human reason: it is by consulting human nature that we might understand which actions (dis)agree with our nature. The *binding force* he derives from human nature as the manifestation of God's will.

'Human nature' is therefore turned into a multi-purpose device, which accounts for the problematic status of this concept. First of all, this is apparent in Grotius's opinion on how natural law is promulgated. Like his predecessors, Grotius takes theoretical reasoning as the model for all reasoning, according to which right and wrong can be discovered by comparing actions to rational nature. If actions agree with rational nature, they are morally good; if they disagree with rational nature they are wrong. We have seen that this view was equally expressed by Vázquez. In Vázquez's theory, however, rational nature was regarded as an eternal, rational order prior to God's creation. It is clear that a comparison between human actions and this rational order can give us insight in what should and should not be done.

But as I pointed out Grotius understands by rational nature '*human rational nature*'. Now the problem is that *all* human actions can be said to 'conform to human nature'; otherwise we cannot even label them as 'human' actions.[53] If people break promises, we should conclude that human nature is apparently such that it can manifest itself in acts like breaking promises.

How then can human nature itself be the criterion by means of which we can assess the moral value of these acts? Only by presenting human nature as inherently 'good'. This, of course, is highly unrealistic. Grotius, more than anyone else, was aware of the evil side of human nature. The only solution that presents itself is therefore to abstract from reality. In order to serve as a reliable standard, human nature should be presented in an idealised form. 'Essential' traits in human nature should be distinguished from 'accidental' or 'unessential' characteristics.

One might object that this distinction is not new and was also drawn by Aquinas. Aquinas also starts from 'essential' inclinations: he does not deal with all the inclinations by which people are actually moved. However, Grotius's account has to dispense with a notion that had been important in Aquinas's account, the notion of practical reason. This causes two problems in Grotius's account which had been absent in Aquinas's theory.

In the first place, Aquinas did not need to differentiate between natural inclinations which are morally defensible and those which are not. He assumed that the general tendency of things is to seek the good. But what exactly that good consists in and whether we are right or wrong in this assessment of an aim as *morally* good is for practical reason to decide (which is based on *synderesis*). Nature only provides information about that which is desired, not about that which is morally desirable. We might use natural information as a heuristical device in order to arrive at moral judgements, but it does not by itself generate such judgements. This option is not available to Grotius. Human nature is the sole foundation of natural law. We cannot hope to find criteria for right and wrong outside human nature, and therefore we have no means to decide whether the desired is desirable.

In the second place, if one adopts the view that reason's job mainly consists in comparing actions to nature, this task can only be carried out by means of immutable standards. This had caused no problem for Vázquez and Suárez, who compared actions with a rational and eternal order. But it is difficult for Grotius, who takes

---

[53] Cf. Röd, 1970, p. 73.

human nature as a criterion. He cannot take human nature as striving
to fulfil its inclinations. How can we measure the size of an object
along a yardstick which 'strives to be' a meter? Whereas Aquinas's
concept of practical reason could take man's natural inclinations as
orientations for our practical thinking, Grotius's concept of theoretical
reason has to dispense with that possibility. This implies that wher-
ever Grotius writes about 'inclinations' he regards these as *dispositions*. They are conceived of as essential and invariable traits.

The need for an idealised concept of man's invariable and 'essential' nature is reflected in Grotius's writings. He simply asserts that
human nature seeks self-interest, that it is sociable, reasonable and
capable of speech. No further arguments are adduced, except, of
course, massive quotations of classical authors, in particular the
Stoics. From this description of essential characteristics he immediately 'deduces' four laws of nature, i.e. abstaining from that which is
another's, restoration to another of anything of his which we may
have, the obligation to fulfil promises, the making good of a loss
incurred through our fault, and the inflicting of penalties upon men
according to their deserts.[54]

Any real discussion of the starting-point of analysis, human nature,
is left out. The characteristics are taken as self-evident:

> [...] I have made it my concern to refer the proofs of things touching
> the law of nature to certain fundamental conceptions which are beyond
> question, so that no one can deny them without doing violence to
> himself. For the principles of that law, if only you pay strict heed to
> them, are in themselves manifest and clear, almost as evident as are
> those things which we perceive by the external senses [...].[55]

The self-evidence of human nature as a starting-point for the deduction of fundamental principles has led interpreters to believe that
Grotius advocated the 'geometrical method'.[56] In favour of such a
view also Prol. 58 could be adduced:

---

[54] JBP Prol. 8.
[55] JBP Prol. 39.
[56] Cf. Tuck, 1993, pp. 171-2; Van Eikema Hommes, 1972, pp. 74-5.

> With all truthfulness I aver that, just as mathematicians treat their
> figures as abstracted from bodies, so in treating law I have withdrawn
> my mind from every particular fact.[57]

The problem with this passage, however, is that he does not write
here about a mathematical treatment of human nature. He simply
asserts that he wants to abstract from existing political controversies
of his time.[58] In the JBP Grotius does not provide us with mathematical deductions at all.

What is apparent, however, is that human nature is taken as a
starting-point for the derivation of the four primary laws of nature. A
starting-point that remains unargued and is taken as self-evident, in
other words: as an 'axiom', although Grotius does not mention the
term. In this sense, human nature is indeed represented as a 'figure
abstracted from a body'.[59] And this analogy is subsequently taken
over by Pufendorf, Locke and countless more minor figures who
assert that from human nature alone certain immutable principles can
be deduced, in the same way that from the existence of a triangle
alone the indubitable proposition can be deduced that its three angles
are equal to two right angles.[60]

Such statements, although they are inspired by the ambition to
create a science of morals with the same degree of certainty as
mathematics, never led to full-scale deductions. But they do indicate
the need for a concept of human nature that could adequately perform
its function as the sole foundation of natural law. For indeed, a
triangle is a triangle if and only if its three angles can be equated to
two right angles. In a similar vein, man is human if and only if he is
social and rational. By leaving out 'accidental' traits and 'particular
facts', normative elements (that which is 'desirable') are smuggled
into the very definition of human nature itself. This is no 'mistake'
that can be corrected. It is indispensable for any concept of human
nature if it should serve as the touchstone for morally correct behaviour.

---

[57] JBP Prol. 58.

[58] Cf. Vermeulen, 1983. Vermeulen correctly points out that there is no textual
evidence for a mathematical method in the JBP. Cf. also Besselink, 1992, p. 389.

[59] Cf. d'Entrèves, 1951, p. 56.

[60] Pufendorf, 1688, I, II, 2, p. 23; Locke, 1954, p. 199. See also my discussion of
Grotius: Westerman, 1994, p. 86.

8. *Tensions in 'human nature'*

However, the definitions of the terms used in this highly idealised description of human nature are rather ambiguous. This is not surprising, for human nature was turned into the sole thread connecting will, reason and nature. These tensions surface again within the concept of human nature.

Firstly, there is the assertion that man seeks self-preservation. In the JP, Grotius had argued that God wills us to preserve ourselves and to further our interests (the laws generated by rule I). It is only by the 'will of mankind' (rule II) that the meaning of self-preservation was extended to the interests of others. We have seen, however, that in the JBP both rule I and rule II are supplanted by 'human nature'. Consequently, Grotius alternates here between different meanings of self-preservation: sometimes he understands it as the preservation of the individual, sometimes as that of the nation and sometimes as that of the species as a whole.

Secondly, there is the 'impelling desire for society'. Not any society, Grotius adds, but 'peaceful, and organised according to the measure of his intelligence'.[61] There are, however, different interpretations of that fundamental trait. Sometimes he refers to sociability as something which is implanted in man's nature. Grotius remarks that even some animals

> [...] do in a way restrain the appetency for that which is good for themselves alone, to the advantage, now of their offspring, now of other animals of the same species.[62]

Of course, this is at odds with his Suárezian statements concerning the fundamental distinction between man and animal. And indeed, a few pages further on Grotius no longer refers to sociability as a trait firmly rooted in nature and shared with other animals. Instead, he remarks:

> The law of nature nevertheless has the reinforcement of expediency; for the Author of nature willed that as individuals we should be weak, and

---

[61] JBP Prol. 6.
[62] JBP Prol. 7.

should lack many things needed in order to live properly, to the end
that we might be the more constrained to cultivate the social life.[63]

Apparently, here the natural inclination to sociability does not manifest itself spontaneously; it has to be triggered off by the experienced
hardships of unsocial life. These hardships make us reflect on how to
improve our life and how to ensure our self-preservation. And that is
why Grotius speaks of the social order as 'consonant with human
intelligence'.[64] It is by means of human intelligence that man discovers his proper interests.

One might object that there is no contradiction involved here, since
it is clearly Grotius's view that natural inclinations are *reinforced* by
our rational perception of human weakness. Reason only ensures that
the inclinations are fulfilled. Yet, we should keep in mind that the
inclinations are not taken in Aquinas's dynamical sense. In Grotius's
theory they take the form of invariable dispositions. And on the basis
of that view, it makes a difference whether one emphasises that sociability is one of those natural dispositions, or that it is ultimately
grounded in enlightened self-interest.

This brings us to the third characteristic trait of human nature,
reason. In passages such as the one quoted above, he seems to regard
reason as instrumental. Reason enables us to discern our proper
interests. But he adopts a broader concept of reason as well. When
Grotius writes that reason is the 'faculty of knowing and of acting in
accordance with general principles',[65] he uses the more traditional
conception of reason as the channel through which the natural law is
promulgated.

The ambiguity in the definitions of the traits of human nature is
echoed in the way the *relations* between these traits are perceived.
This is particularly clearly revealed in the relation between self-
preservation and sociability. If we take sociability as a trait firmly
rooted in nature, the argument closely resembles the one developed in
the JP that sociability is necessary for the preservation of the species.
God has willed us to preserve ourselves and *therefore* he made us
(and some other animals as well) sociable. But in the passage in
which he deals with sociability as the necessary outcome of mankind

---

[63] JBP Prol. 16.
[64] JBP Prol. 8.
[65] JBP Prol. 7.

being created as weak, he reverses the argument. If God's most important object had been the preservation of His creation, it is hard to understand that he has created us so weak. To judge from this passage, not preservation but sociability has been His primary goal. He created us weak *'to the end'* that we might be 'constrained to cultivate the social life'.

The relationship between reason and sociability also suffers from the confusion of terms. If reason is conceived as purely instrumental cunning, we would not need to assume sociability as a fundamental and independent characteristic. Reason would by itself reveal that in the long run self-preservation is best served by society. Such an argument, however, threatens to turn sociability into a contingent characteristic, dependent upon instrumental reasoning. If, for instance, we were able to devise another way of ensuring preservation of the species, we would not need to be sociable any more.

I think that these ambiguities are inevitable, both in respect to the relations between the various traits and in the definitions of these traits themselves. As the sole thread connecting will, reason and nature, human nature is bound to be in an uneasy position. If we once more turn our attention to the three important traits of mankind we can indeed see that they are torn up between the various centrifugal forces.

'Self-preservation' is divided between reason and nature. It can either mean preservation of the self or of the species and it is only in the latter case that it can be reconciled with sociability. In the first sense it is conceived as a natural instinct; in the latter case it is equally the product of reason.

'Reason' as one of the three competing forces itself cannot be torn apart between the three notions, but is thoroughly ambiguous in itself: it can be conceived as an instrument to further the goals of sociability and self-preservation, it can be regarded as an autonomous trait, having the same status as the other two, or it can be the *sine qua non* for any form of natural law.

Finally, *'sociability'* suffers the tension of all three competing notions. Where sociability is regarded as an instinct, it is ascribed to *nature*; where it is seen as God's primary goal in creating man weak, it is ascribed to God's *will*, and where it is seen as 'reinforced by expediency' it is conceived as the product of human *reason*.

9. *Conclusion*

In this chapter we witnessed both innovation and continuity. Innovation in the sense that Grotius drew the full implications of a solution already vaguely suggested by Suárez (see III.8). He took human nature as the proximate source for natural law and consequently as the starting-point for the derivation of natural law. By establishing human nature as the intermediate link between God and His law, he short-circuited the discussion about the kind of role God ·plays in a concept of natural law. Reason, will and nature are once more pulled together; they all converge in the concept of human nature.

This solution could have resulted in a humanisation of Aquinas's concept of natural law. However, Grotius does not conceive of reason as practical reason, but remains faithful to the views of the Spaniards, who focus on theoretical reason as the comparison between actions and rational nature. This necessarily leads to a static and idealised notion of human nature.

As a consequence, human nature itself has become subject to certain tensions. As an idealised construct, its essential traits do not fit together in a harmonious way. There is a profound ambiguity both in the definition of the various traits and in the relations between these essential traits of human nature. The traditional dilemmas concerning God's relation to natural law recur in the concept of human nature itself.

CHAPTER VI

GROTIUS'S SHIFT FROM NATURAL LAW TO NATURAL RIGHTS

As I noted in the preceding chapter, Grotius's new theory of human nature as the proper foundation of natural law is not his main theme. Grotius did not develop natural law theory for its own sake. He was above all a lawyer, who wanted to settle legal matters by means of natural law, although he used other sources as well, such as divine law, and the teachings of the early Christians and classical authors, notably the Stoics. It is therefore time to turn to Grotius's 'main theme'; the analysis of positive municipal and international law.

An examination of these views is surprising. Not only can we witness a gap between Grotius's theoretical programme and its implementation, but it seems as if his views on positive law should induce us to modify the interpretation at which we arrived in the preceding chapter. There, I noted that Grotius has difficulty in reconciling the various elements (will, reason, nature) within the concept of human nature. But as we shall see, these tensions are to a large extent resolved as soon as Grotius starts applying his insights to practice.

As I shall argue, human nature in fact does not serve him as a foundation of natural law, but as a foundation of natural *rights*. The primary laws of nature which Grotius derives from human nature make much more sense if we regard them as formulations of rights than of laws. Such a reading enables us to assess the relationship between the various essential traits of human nature more clearly. As soon as Grotius starts to apply natural law to positive law, the right to self-preservation turns out to be the most important one. The natural inclinations to sociability and man's natural reason are viewed as instrumental to that right.

This insight also enables us to account for the differences between Grotius's analysis of municipal law and of international law. The self-preservation of individuals can only be ensured by obedience to municipal law. Therefore, on the level of municipal law (sections 2-4), the justificatory function of natural law is dramatically reduced to the notion of consent only, and the attending obligation to abide by that

consent. States, on the other hand, have more means to their disposal
in order to preserve themselves. Consequently, natural law is much
more important on the level of international law, and it exercises its
task in the form of the inalienable natural rights of states (sections 5-
6).

After having examined Grotius's theories of municipal and international law, we shall pay attention to the notion of 'perfect right' that
pervades Grotius's theory of law, as well as the related decision on
Grotius's part to confine law to restorative justice only as dealing
with these perfect rights (sections 7-8). This decision has been
criticised by Finnis, who thought that the exclusive focus on rights
and correlative duties is partly responsible for the fact that modern
legal theory no longer refers to an overall common good as the basis
for moral evaluations of law.[1] I shall argue, instead, that Grotius's
move has two important advantages and is in fact a fruitful option for
anyone who attempts to rehabilitate natural law.

1. *The limited scope of natural law*

As we have seen in IV.3 and IV.4, Suárez, despite his claims to the
contrary, provided for an unprecedentedly wide scope of human
intervention within the boundaries of natural law. According to
Suárez, two parts of natural law can be distinguished: a 'preceptive'
part and a part which concerns the *dominium* of man over things (subjective rights). It is this latter part that is particularly prone to alterations, because it regulates human affairs. Man may therefore change
the *materia* of these laws. Such a change, Suárez had maintained,
does not change the law itself.

Grotius adopts this view, but its meaning is extended in the context
of his definition of natural law. As we have seen in V.5, Grotius
identifies Suárez's 'preceptive natural law' with positive divine law.
Grotius's concept of natural law is thereby restricted to that part
which Suárez called the natural law concerning *dominium*. That
means that Grotius allows for changes in the *materia* in the whole
body of natural law. Let us investigate his argument step by step.

The first step of his argument is to point out that there are many
things which are not explicitly regulated by natural law (although they

---

[1] NLNR ch. VIII.

are regulated by divine law). Thus, we see him repeating Suárez's views about natural law being silent on certain matters:

> For the understanding of the law of nature [...] we must note that certain things are said to be according to this law not in a proper sense but—as the Schoolmen love to say—by reduction, the law of nature not being in conflict with them [...].[2]

By pointing out that natural law does not contain regulations about certain matters, the discretionary powers of mankind are enhanced.

The second step is to argue that certain institutions are established by the free will of mankind. The famous example is, as it was for Suárez, ownership.

> Thus ownership, such as now obtains, was introduced by the will of man; but, once introduced, the law of nature points out that it is wrong for me, against your will, to take away that which is subject to your ownership.[3]

So although natural law is silent about the institutions themselves, its precepts are effective within the framework of these man-made institutions.

The third step is to point out that the *materia* of a law may be changed without affecting the validity of the law itself. Suárez had mentioned the example of the creditor who decides to change a debt into a gift. Grotius mentions the same example:

> Sometimes nevertheless it happens that in the acts in regard to which the law of nature has ordained something, an appearance of change deceives the unwary, although in fact the law of nature, being unchangeable, undergoes no change; but the thing, in regard to which the law of nature has ordained, undergoes change. For example, if a creditor gives a receipt for that which I owe him, I am no longer bound to pay him, not because the law of nature has ceased to enjoin upon me that I must pay what I owe, but because that which I was owing has ceased to be owed.[4]

---

[2] JBP I, I, X, 3.
[3] JBP I, I, X, 4.
[4] JBP I, I, X, 6.

I quote Grotius so extensively in order to indicate how much Grotius in fact took over from Suárez when it comes to widening the scope for human intervention.[5]

As I argued in IV.5, Suárez entrusts the task of regulating man's *dominium* to legislative authority. It is public authority which in the final instance changes the *materia* of natural law. This view is endorsed by Grotius as well:

> When, however, municipal law has laid down a different rule, *the law of nature itself prescribes that this must be obeyed.* For although municipal law cannot enjoin anything which the law of nature forbids, or forbid what the law of nature enjoins, it can nevertheless set limits to natural liberty, and forbid what by nature was permitted [...] [my emphasis].[6]

Although Grotius writes that municipal law cannot conflict with natural law, it is difficult to see how we can *know* whether they conflict or not. As I pointed out in IV.5, it was already difficult on the basis of Suárez's views on natural law to criticise public authority. If public authority determines what should be understood by 'liberty' or 'property', it is difficult if not impossible, to criticise positive laws on the basis of natural law. Its precepts are simply too general to be informative. In Suárez's theory, governments can only be effectively criticised by reference to preceptive law (of which the *materia* cannot be changed by public authority).

Grotius reinforces this tendency, since he discards preceptive law from natural law and identifies it with 'divine law' (see V.5). The only kind of natural law he allows for is natural law concerning *dominium*. But that law is silent on many matters and permits public authority to regulate affairs according to its own wishes. The emphasis in the passage quoted above on the natural obligation to obey public authority testifies to this confined role of natural law.

---

[5] This is not to say that Chroust is right in regarding Grotius as the last of the Scholastics. Cf. Chroust, 1943. As I pointed out in the preceding chapter, the fact that Grotius drew the full consequences of the points already hinted at by Suárez solved a number of traditional scholastic problems. Here again we see that Grotius not only endorses but also radicalises Suárez's position. If there is any 'watershed' at all between scholastics and 'moderns', we might as well say that both Suárez and Grotius stand on 'this side of the watershed', as indeed Finnis writes (NLNR p. 207).

[6] JBP II, II, V.

2. *The crucial role of consent*

According to Grotius, natural law itself prescribes that municipal law, even if it has laid down a different rule, should be obeyed. However, if we examine the four primary natural laws Grotius deduces from human nature, none of these four laws exhort us to civil obedience. Grotius formulates these laws as urging us

> a) to 'abstain from that which is another's and to restore to another of anything of his which we may have';
> b) to fulfil promises;
> c) to make good of a loss incurred through our fault;
> d) to inflict 'penalties upon men according to their deserts'.[7]

Natural law does not tell us to comply with positive law. So the only way in which natural law can be understood as enjoining us to obey the municipal law is to interpret this obedience as the fulfilment of a promise. That this is indeed what Grotius had in mind can be judged from the passage in which he asserts:

> [...] since it is a rule of the law of nature to abide by pacts (for it was necessary that among men there be some method of obligating themselves one to another, and no other natural method can be imagined), out of this source the bodies of municipal law have arisen.[8]

These pacts form the link connecting positive law to natural law. The natural precept that we should fulfil promises can only become effective after we have consented. In Grotius's words:

> For the very nature of man, which even if we had no lack of anything would lead us into the mutual relations of society, is the mother of the law of nature. But the mother of municipal law is that obligation which arises from mutual consent; and since this obligation derives its force from the law of nature, nature may be considered, so to say, the great-grandmother of municipal law.[9]

---

[7] JBP Prol. 8.

[8] JBP Prol. 15.

[9] JBP Prol. 16. Note that here, sociability is considered as a trait firmly rooted in nature and not dependent on reason.

This passage clearly defines the relationship between natural law and positive civil law. If human nature is the 'great-grandmother' of municipal law, natural law is the grandmother. But not the mother herself! It is only by means of the intermediate link of consent that positive law is related to natural law. The chain consists of four elements: 1) human nature; 2) natural law (= the obligation to keep promises); 3) consent as such a promise; and 4) municipal law.

The passage quoted above looks harmless enough, but it has important consequences. The implication seems to be that it is *only* by the notion of consent that positive municipal law can ultimately be justified by natural law. But how can that be, if human nature as a whole is the basis for natural law, and if Grotius distinguishes four primary laws instead of only one?

A closer look at the other three laws, however, makes clear that indeed they can serve at best as a marginal justification of positive law. Law a), urging us to abstain from another's property, can only be put into operation after public authority has decided how to organise property. The same applies to b), the precept regarding compensation. Again, what is to be counted as 'loss' has to be decided by positive law. It cannot serve as a standard according to which positive law itself can be evaluated. The precept d) that penalties may be inflicted on transgressors merely points out that one has a right to punish. But if one has consented to the establishment of society, it only informs us that states have a right to punish. As such, the precept can only serve as a global justification of penal law, but it does not inform us on how the right to punish should be executed.

Therefore, the conclusion drawn by Grotius, seems to be correct. On the basis of laws a), c) and d), natural law only comes into play in assessing the moral quality of actions *within* the framework of these human institutions. Whether the institutions themselves are justified or not according to the law of nature can only be decided by the question whether we consented to positive law. If that is the case, natural precept b) becomes effective; it tells us that we should fulfil that promise and obey.

This reduction of the function of natural law to the precept concerning promises has important implications. Since the other three laws of nature can only be put into operation within the framework of municipal law, they only marginally inform us about whether we are right to consent to municipal law. It tells us that we should not consent to a system of law in which no system of property is introduced. It informs us that we should not consent to a government that omits to punish offenders. But that is all natural law can do. Natural law does not furnish us with a standard according to which we can decide which kind of government we *ought* to consent to. It only tells us that *because* we have consented, we are bound to the natural obligation to keep promises.[10] Consent is the thin thread by means of which positive law is linked to natural law.[11]

In itself, this reduction of natural law is not an inevitable step. On the basis of the essential traits of human nature (self-preservation, sociability, reason) Grotius could have assigned to natural law a wider scope. Like Aquinas, he could have formulated several general criteria according to which positive law can be evaluated. Yet, his restriction of natural law to those precepts which refer to man's *dominium* renders natural law inadequate as a judge of positive law. His formulation of the four primary laws reveals that in practice natural law can only justify/criticise by means of the notion of consent. In the following section, we shall see why the scope of natural law is thus restricted.

3. *The artificial state*

On the basis of the four primary precepts of natural law, we are not able to judge which social arrangements deserve our consent or not. Yet, consent acquires an unprecedented importance in Grotius's political theory. It serves not only as a foundation for society, but also as the basis for positive law.

In order to understand how far Grotius is removed here from Aquinas and Suárez, we should keep in mind that both predecessors conceived of a political community as natural entities, slowly developed over time. No extra sign of will was needed in order to link the members of such a community together. Suárez did not use the notion of consent in order to justify the establishment of a society, but instead used it merely in order to explain historical developments (IV.4).

---

[10] I agree here with Scheltens, 1983, p. 50.

[11] Cf. Zwiebach, 1975, p. 42. Zwiebach's eloquent and convincing criticism of consent as the source of obligation overlooks that this reversal of roles between natural law and consent already took place before Locke.

Since Suárez and Aquinas took the existence of societies for granted, they instead focused on its 'products': the body of civil and municipal law. They did not need to justify society itself, but its laws. And that is why they inquired into the relationship between the principles of natural law and the positive laws of such a society. It is true that both acknowledged that the *ius civile* could not be conceived as the logical outcome of a mechanical deduction. We have seen that Aquinas viewed it as the product of free *determinatio* of these eternal principles (II.7). But both Suárez and Aquinas thought that positive law should somehow reflect or embody the eternal laws of nature, be it in an imperfect way. That is why Suárez kept stressing that positive law should accord to God's will (IV.4).

In Grotius we see a shift of focus. To him the primary question is no longer whether positive *law* is congruent with natural law, but whether *society as such* is congruent with natural law and ultimately with human nature. This question can arise because he no longer views society as a natural association, but as an *artificial* one. These artificial bodies may resemble natural ones,[12] but the fact that they are essentially man-made makes it necessary to justify them as an artifice that is congruent with human nature. Once it has been established that these artificial unions and their primary institutions are in harmony with natural law and consequently with human nature, there is no longer any need to justify the positive laws of society. In the words of Röd, the social contract is here not only the conceptual foundation of a concept of state, but it also makes its positive laws and norms obligatory and binding.[13]

In itself this shift could have implied an enhancement of the critical potentialities of natural law. Moral evaluation no longer confines itself to the legal system alone. From now on, society as a whole can be critically examined on the basis of natural law. Grotius's turn could have paved the way for systematic social criticism.

But it did not, at least not in Grotius's own theory. There are two reasons for this. The first reason was already mentioned above: consent itself cannot be evaluated according to the four primary laws of nature. The second reason is that Grotius combines his shift of

---

[12] JBP II, IX, III, 1.

[13] Cf. Röd, 1970, p. 75: 'Die Idee [...] des Sozialkontrakts ist daher nicht nur die begriffliche Grundlage der Staatskonzeption, sondern begründet auch die Verbindlichkeit positiver Normen'.

attention with Suárez's views concerning the alienability of man's *dominium*. People can trade away not only their possessions but also their liberties (cf. IV.4). Suárez had written that 'for the very reason that man is lord over his own liberty, it is possible for him to sell and alienate the same'.[14] In the JBP, Grotius endorses that view:[15]

> To every man it is permitted to enslave himself to any one he pleases for private ownership [...]. Why, then, would it not be permitted to a people having legal competence to submit itself to some one person, or to several persons, in such a way as plainly to transfer to him the legal right to govern, retaining no vestige of that right for itself?[16]

In the JBP, the dangers of the state of nature loom large. Grotius maintains that 'we ought to endure [unjust treatment] rather than resist by force'[17] because rebellion would undermine social and peaceful life and would turn the state into a 'non-social horde'.[18] In order to ensure self-preservation, individuals should transfer their rights to govern. After that alienation, no 'vestige' of that right remains. Apparently, Grotius thinks that only within society, no matter how that society is organised, self-preservation can be ensured.

The overriding importance of self-preservation may help answering the question why Grotius confines the scope of natural law to the fulfilment of promises alone, and why he does not refer to the other essential traits of human nature (reason, sociability) in order to criticise positive law. I concluded the preceding chapter by remarking that the concept of human nature suffers from tensions between the various features: sociability, self-preservation and reason. In practice, however, Grotius seems to adopt a much more unified concept. Sociability and reason are subordinated to the great aim of self-preservation. It is by means of reason that people can understand that their self-preservation is only guaranteed by living in society. That is why the law of nature, derived from human nature, merely admonishes the individual to keep his promise and to remain within society. The

---

[14] DL II, XIV, 18.
[15] Cf. Tuck, 1979, p. 71. Tuck correctly points out that especially in the *Inleiding tot de Hollandsche Rechtsgeleerdheid*, Grotius emphatically asserts the contrary: life, limbs and liberty are inalienable.
[16] JBP I, III, VIII, 1.
[17] JBP I, IV, 1, 3.
[18] JBP I, IV, II, 1.

overriding importance of self-preservation and the subordination of sociability and reason as instrumental to that goal explain why these latter traits cannot serve as a basis for natural precepts according to which positive law can be evaluated.

4. *Implied consent*

The notion of consent is, however, not only used as a key-concept in the justification of positive law. Grotius also uses it, as Suárez before him had done, in order to *explain* how the various human institutions had come into being. To offer such an explanation was important to him, for the sceptics had argued on the basis of history that morality and law were no more than the outcome of contingent and variable developments. If Grotius succeeded in showing that, despite historical contingencies, consent is always at the basis of all these institutions, he could hope to have established a truly universal foundation of morals. His description of historical developments was, as Tuck points out, an attempt to defeat the sceptics on their own battle-ground.[19]

Therefore 'consent' acquires a double function: it not only forms the single thread between natural law and positive law; it also figures prominently in historical descriptions, in particular in the description of the development towards the institution of private ownership. Here, Grotius is careful to emphasise that this development was gradual. Common ownership was abandoned, 'first of movable objects, later also of immovable property',[20] a development which he explained by the increasing desire for a more refined mode of life. Such an account, however, implies that 'consent' should be presented in a realistic manner.[21] Consequently, Grotius writes:

> At the same time we learn how things became subject to private owner-
> ship. This happened *not by a mere act of will*, for one could not know
> what things another wished to have, in order to abstain from them—and
> besides several might desire the same thing—but rather by a kind of

---

[19] Tuck, 1987, p. 115.
[20] JBP II, II, II, 4.
[21] Cf. Tuck, 1993, p. 179.

agreement, either expressed, as by a division, or implied, as by occupation [my emphasis].[22]

Here, Grotius is elaborating on the kind of historical accounts provided by Suárez[23] but he encounters a serious difficulty that had been absent in Suárez's work. As I pointed out, the notion of consent in Suárez's work only played a role in the explanation of the gradual development of societies. But in Grotius's theory, 'consent' performs a justificatory task as well. 'Consent' is the *only* 'natural method' by which individuals oblige themselves to one another. Unlike Suárez, Grotius does not conceive of society as a union, naturally grown over the ages, but as an artificial body of individuals, tied together by consent.

Viewed in this context, we should conceive of consent not as 'implied agreement' but as an explicit promise. People's lives depend on it! Their consent binds them and subsequent generations to obedience, as we have seen. The least one should expect of such a consent is that it has been given consciously and in the awareness of alternatives. Natural law exhorts us to keep promises; it does not admonish us to abide by implied agreements.

In his chapter on 'contracts'[24] Grotius himself enumerates the requirements for a contract in order to be valid and binding. It presupposes equality of the parties,[25] knowledge of facts,[26] and freedom of choice.[27] None of these requirements, however, are met by the individuals in the pre-contractual state; their 'implied' consent with occupation is not a contract at all; it is no more than the resignation to a *fait accompli*, in which there is no room for the equality of parties and their freedom of choice. The realistic account of consent as the origin of ownership and of society is in conflict with the justificatory notion of a 'contract' in the legally binding sense of the word. If the justificatory task is given priority, the notion discredits the historical descriptions as unrealistic; if its explanatory task is predominant, it seriously undermines the credibility of the notion as a true ground for obligation.

---

[22] JBP II, II, II, 5.
[23] Cf. e.g. DL III, II, 3.
[24] JBP II, XII.
[25] JBP II, XII, VIII.
[26] JBP II, XII, IX.
[27] JBP II, XII, X.

Some interpreters have welcomed the appearance of historical accounts in the work of natural lawyers such as Grotius as the birth of a 'new science of man', and in this sense Grotius has been heralded as a predecessor of David Hume.[28] What is generally overlooked, however, is the price that Grotius paid for this innovation. On the basis of a realistic notion of consent as implied agreement, the justificatory potential of his theory is undermined. Natural law exhorts us to keep promises. If these promises are understood as tacit agreements, natural law in fact admonishes us to abide by a state of affairs that we never consciously agreed to, but which have gradually been established over the ages.[29]

But such a theory was not at all what Grotius had intended. He had set out to *refute* the sceptical claim that the question of right and wrong is decided by customs that are culturally variable and contingent. However, the inner logic of his system of natural law in fact allowed scepticism to creep in. By restricting the scope of natural law, he had undermined its effectiveness as a weapon against the sceptics. When he resolved to choose their battleground, the battle was lost.

5. *International pacts*

These conclusions with respect to the role of natural law should not be generalised, however, to the field for which Grotius has become famous: that of international law. Here indeed there is an important task assigned to natural law; here 'consent' is no longer the sole thread connecting positive law with natural law. And it is in the field of international law that Grotius most markedly differs from Suárez.

There are two differences with Suárez. The first is that Grotius restricts Suárez's two meanings to only one.[30] The *ius gentium* no

---

[28] Cf. Forbes, 1975; Haakonssen, 1981; Buckle, 1991.

[29] This insight is useful for our interpretation of Hume as well. If Hume was influenced by Grotius at all, he took over only the historical part, not the justificatory intention of Grotius's work. Cf. my review of Buckle: Westerman, 1992, and Westerman, 1994.

[30] In the JP, Grotius did distinguish a primary from a secondary *ius gentium*, but this distinction does not run parallel to Suárez's distinction, as Kosters (1924, p. 78) thinks. Only Grotius's secondary *ius gentium* can be identified with Suárez's primary *ius gentium*.

longer includes the laws and practices which different cultures have in common. International law is confined to Suárez's second meaning of the term *ius gentium*: the *ius inter gentes* proper, which deals with the relations between states. The second (related) difference is that Grotius does not conceive of international law as based on custom. Unlike Suárez, Grotius does not assume the moral unity of the human race as the source of international law. The *ius inter gentes* is directly based on natural law (and ultimately on human nature).[31]

The underlying purpose of this firm connection between international law and natural law is Grotius's political consideration to put an end to a state of affairs in which conflicts between states 'generally have Mars as their arbiter'.[32] A universal framework is required in order to regulate the conflicts between competing nations. These conflicts cannot be resolved by referring to customs as the expression of a brotherhood of mankind, because that is exactly what is lacking in international conflicts.

How can natural law provide for that framework? Partly by the same method as in municipal law, by mutual consent:

> [...] by mutual consent it has become possible that certain laws should originate as between all states, or a great many states; and it is apparent that the laws thus originating had in view the advantage, not of particular states, but of the great society of states.[33]

Here, the mutual consent of states is consistently dealt with by analogy with the consent that links the individual citizens together in society. Obviously, in the case of states, this consent is not the outcome of tacit and implied agreements, but is to be regarded as deliberate consent. The rationale behind this mutual consent is self-preservation. Just as individual citizens cannot hope to preserve themselves without society, states should enter into agreements in order to further their self-preservation.

---

[31] Van Eikema Hommes correctly criticises those authors (C. van Vollenhoven, W.J.M. van Eysinga and B. Fortuin) who maintain that Grotius's concept of international law is grounded in the universal brotherhood of mankind. In the JP it was indeed, but in the JBP it is directly grounded in natural law. See Van Eikema Hommes, 1983, p. 63.

[32] JBP Prol. 3.

[33] JBP Prol. 17.

In the JBP Grotius elaborates on this theme and explicitly criticises those who maintain that individuals and states cannot be compared, because nations contain all that is necessary for their preservation, whereas individuals cannot live outside society. According to Grotius, these people are in error, for

> [...] there is no state so powerful that it may not some time need the help of others outside itself, either for purposes of trade, or even to ward off the forces of many foreign nations united against it.[34]

States are not autonomous entities. Although to a lesser extent than individuals, states also have to rely upon mutual aid. Grotius's mentioning of 'trade' here is significant. No doubt, Dutch commercial activities had revealed the mutual dependence of states. Because states are not entirely self-sufficient, they should enter into mutual agreements.

6. *The right to wage war*

Grotius's emphasis on mutual consent is responsible for Grotius's fame as the founder of peace.[35] But there is another side, which is just as closely related to the need for self-preservation as the necessity of mutual agreement. For there is one important aspect in which states differ from individuals. Grotius asserts that it is not possible for states to forsake their 'life, liberty and limbs' in these international agreements. The contract *inter gentes* is entered into because it promises to ensure the self-preservation of states. This implies that it can be revoked as soon as the contract threatens to endanger that self-preservation. Whereas Grotius had denied to individuals any right to revoke the contract, he emphatically affirms the right of states to preserve themselves, even if that involves a breach of contract.

That is why Grotius, right at the beginning of the JBP, emphasises the right to war:

---

[34] JBP Prol. 22.

[35] Cf. James Brown Scott in his introduction to his edition of the JBP, who writes about Grotius that 'from The Hague he causes judgement to be passed on the nations through the Permanent Court of International Justice' (JBP p. xl).

In the first principles of nature there is nothing which is opposed to
war; rather, *all points are in its favour*. The end and aim of war being
the preservation of life and limb, and the keeping or acquiring of things
useful to life, war is in perfect accord with those first principles of
nature. If in order to achieve these ends it is necessary to use force, no
inconsistency with the first principles of nature is involved, since nature
has given to each animal strength sufficient for self-defence and self-
assistance [my emphasis].[36]

This is a surprising passage. We have seen that in dealing with
municipal law, the natural precept that exhorts us to keep promises
was the most important of all. On the basis of that precept, Grotius
even denies the citizen any 'vestige' of the right to govern after one
has consented to the alienation of this right. But when it comes to
states, the natural obligation to keep promises is apparently deemed to
be less important. And what is more, Grotius even asserts that 'all
points' (i.e. all four primary laws) are in favour of the right to wage
war.

We can only account for this apparent inconsistency by referring to
a conspicuous difference between individuals and states. Whereas
Grotius thought that individuals cannot live at all without society,
states can. Although states can hardly flourish in isolation, they can
nevertheless survive. That is why Grotius maintains that when states
are threatened by other states in their survival, liberty or property,
they are no longer obligated by agreements. Indeed, Grotius is merely
revealing the true character of the four primary principles of natural
law if he writes that 'all points' are in favour of war between states.

As I noted in section 3 of this chapter, the concept of human
nature that Grotius actually uses in his description of the role of
natural law is much more unified that it initially seemed to be.
Sociability and reason are in practice subordinated to self-preservation. That accounts for the fact thàt all four precepts are ultimately
informed by the need for self-preservation alone. Within the context
of municipal law, self-preservation of the individual can only be
furthered by following the precept on promises, thus ensuring sociability. That is why that precept gains an overriding importance. But
on the international level, all four precepts serve self-preservation of
states. As such, the precepts can be reformulated as rights, without

---

[36] JBP I, II, I, 4.

any loss of significance. This can be perceived, by comparing the function of the precepts on the level of individual citizens with the function it acquires on the level of states.

The natural law to abstain from another's property, for instance, does not inform the individual on how municipal law should be assessed. It assigns to the individual the right to property, but the implementation of that right is dependent on the way governments regulate property. In both Suárez's and Grotius's theories that natural precept is only operative within the context of civil society, but does not serve to criticise or justify human institutions as such. However, on the level of states, the precept plays a role which is more direct. It is not dependent on interpretations by public authority, but regains its full force as a natural precept. It can be reformulated as the (natural) right of states to defend their property against external enemies as well as to regulate it within their own borders. The same applies to the precept 'to inflict penalties upon men according to their deserts'. As I noted, the precept is of little use for the assessment of positive municipal law. But it does acquire significance if we read it as the right of a state to punish offenders both within and without its borders.

Once we see that the primary laws of nature are deduced from the need for self-preservation, they make sense. On the level of the individual citizen, only the precept concerning promises directly ensures that overriding aim. But on the level of states the right to punish, to exact compensation for losses, in short, to have true *dominium*, are all just as important in order to ensure self-preservation as the obligation to keep promises. In so far as international agreements further self-preservation, states should abide by them. But a state is absolved from that duty as soon as any of the other three rights are endangered by these agreements.

That is why the passages concerning the inalienability of rights only recur in the chapters of the JBP which are devoted to the *ius inter gentes*. I think this fact has been overlooked by Tuck, who concludes that the JBP 'is Janus-faced, and its two mouths speak the language of both absolutism and liberty'.[37] In fact, there is no Janus face at all here. Grotius's 'absolutist' mouth speaks of the alienability of *individual* rights; Grotius's 'liberal' mouth speaks of the inalienable rights of *states*. It is, however, understandable that confusion

---

[37] Tuck, 1993, p. 79.

might creep in, in view of Grotius's tendency to speak of states as if they are individuals. But both the liberal and the absolutist mouths speak the language of self-preservation alone. It is merely the difference between states and individuals which accounts for the fact that the rights of the individual can be alienated, whereas the rights of states are inalienable.

7. Perfect rights

The function of natural law had always been twofold: it provided for a justification of positive law that is congruent with natural law and for a derogation of laws which were thought to be conflicting with natural law. These two functions are taken over by the concept of inalienable rights that is developed by Grotius. Where rights are infringed, they serve as a justification of war. But since every state possesses those rights, including the enemy, they also serve as a limitation of war.

> It is not, then, contrary to the nature of society to look out for oneself and advance one's own interests, provided the rights of others are not infringed; and consequently the use of force which does not violate the rights of others is not unjust.[38]

And again:

> Right reason, moreover, and the nature of society [...] do not prohibit all use of force, but only that use of force which is in conflict with society, *that is which attempts to take away the rights of another* [my emphasis].[39]

It might seem as if Grotius is referring here to 'individuals' and to civil society. However, these passages figure in the chapter 'whether it is ever lawful to wage war', and as such refer to states and the society of states.

The term 'society' here does not point to an overall-plan. There is no integral conception of justice at the basis of the regulation of international relations. 'Society' merely refers to a context in which

---

[38] JBP I, II, I, 6.
[39] JBP I, II, I, 5.

rights are mutually respected. Natural law enjoins the states to protect their own rights and not to infringe the rights of others, but is not thought to provide for a comprehensive framework in which the nations can converge into a political or moral unity, or into true 'society' if we understand by that term more than 'abstaining from that which is another's'.

We might characterise Grotius's view of international relations as based on the model of what Aristotle called 'compensatory' or *restorative* justice. Restorative justice regulates some of the relations which can be established between two parties (if I owe something to somebody, I should 'restore' it to him). According to Grotius, restorative justice[40] is marked by the regulation of so-called perfect rights. A perfect right is something which a person *has*. Here, Grotius uses the traditional term *facultas*, which we already encountered in Suárez's work (IV.3). It is defined by Grotius as 'the right to one's own'.[41] This kind of perfect right is enforceable and legally binding.

The model of restorative justice which is at the basis of international relations is distinguished from '*distributive justice*'. Distributive justice[42] deals with the distribution of shares by an agent (e.g. public authority) among various persons. In itself, the distinction between these two types of justice is traditionally Aristotelian, but Grotius adds that distributive justice deals with so-called 'imperfect rights' or 'aptitudes'. An *aptitudo* is not legally binding, nor is it enforceable. It denotes merely 'that which is suitable, or fitting'. Connected with distributive justice, Grotius writes, are 'those virtues which have as their purpose to do good to other, as generosity, compassion, and foresight in matters of government'.[43] One cannot claim a (perfect) 'right' to be treated compassionately. One can only say that it would be suitable if a man is treated with compassion in a certain case.

Because distributive justice is regarded as only dealing with imperfect, not with perfect rights, Grotius takes the next step and cuts out distributive justice from the realm of law.[44]

---

[40] Grotius calls it 'expletive' justice.

[41] JBP I, I, V.

[42] Called by Grotius 'attributive justice'.

[43] JBP I, I, VIII, 1.

[44] Punishment is also regarded as a (special) form of expletive (restorative) justice. Cf. JBP II, XX, II, 1 and 3.

To this exercise of judgement belongs moreover the rational allotment to each man, or to each social group, of those things which are properly theirs, in such a way as to give the preference now to him who is more wise over the less wise, now to a kinsman rather than to a stranger, now to a poor man rather than to a man of means, as the conduct of each or the nature of the thing suggests. Long ago the view came to be held by many, that this discriminating allotment is a part of law, properly and strictly so called; nevertheless *law, properly defined, has a far different nature, because its essence lies in leaving to another that which belongs to him, or in fulfilling our obligations to him* [my emphasis].[45]

The focus on restorative justice as the regulation of perfect rights, which is expressed here, reflects the shift from natural law into natural rights. All four primary laws of nature can be regarded as formulations of duties on the part of party A, which correspond to the rights of party B. The duty of A to compensate for losses on the part of B is nothing else than the formulation of B's rights. As Finnis remarks:

[...] modern rights-talk is constructed primarily on the implicit model of a relationship between two individuals.[46]

If that assertion is right, we can see that Grotius paved the way for such a reduction to bi-polar relationships. His emphasis on perfect rights goes hand in hand with his emphasis on restorative justice as the paradigm-model for law. It cannot be otherwise: on the basis of a model of rights and correlative duties, we simply have to dispense with the required information about whether we should 'give preference' to the wise man, or the poor, or our kinsman. Reformulated as natural rights, natural law lacks the required substantial principles in order to carry out such deliberations. On the basis of Grotius's definition of natural law, there is no room for the Thomistic virtue of prudence, not because natural law is too inflexible (as it was in Suárez's work), but because it lacks the very principles which can be applied with prudence to everyday decisions. The only task that is left to natural law is the formulation of natural rights and the regulation

---

[45] JBP Prol. 10.
[46] NLNR p. 216.

of righteous claims between competing nations in a way comparable to that of the judge deciding civil law cases.[47]

The restriction of natural law as pertaining to perfect rights only is, I believe, to a large extent inspired by Grotius's wish to make law autonomous as a proper profession, as a discipline of its own, which should be separated from politics. This can be judged from Grotius's attack on Bodin:

> I have refrained from discussing topics which belong to another subject, such as those that teach what may be advantageous in practice. For such topics have their own special field, that of politics, which Aristotle rightly treats by itself, without introducing extraneous matter into it. Bodin, on the contrary, mixed up politics with the body of law with which we are concerned.[48]

If we read the JBP as an attempt to professionalise law, and to separate it from politics, it is clear why Grotius had to cut out 'distributive justice' from the sphere of law. Considerations pertaining to the distribution of shares inevitably involve political decisions; decisions that are made with an eye to external socially desirable goals.[49] In order to demarcate law from politics, law should be exclusively concerned with the regulation of perfect rights.

8. *The superfluity of a legislator*

We might agree with Finnis that the reduction of natural law to natural rights is to be deplored. The disappearance of the concept of a natural community as well as the limitation of law to restorative justice finally results in a conception of the state as a mere aggregate of abstract individuals. Furthermore, the reduction of law to the regulation of perfect rights only seems to curtail the scope of reason and to reduce it to instrumental reason alone, in which there is no

---

[47] Cf. Luig, 1996, p. 138: 'Da sich in Grotius' Völkerrechtssystem die einzelnen Subjekte des Völkerrechts wie Individuen einander gegenüberstehen, stellt sein Völkerrecht zugleich eine Rechstlehre eines natürlichen Privatrechts dar'.

[48] JBP Prol. 57.

[49] Weinrib, 1995, tries to carve out a niche for private law as an autonomous discipline by claiming that restorative justice is the proper basis for private law, whereas distributive considerations are 'contaminated' with politics.

room for moral deliberation about a comprehensive framework regulating the distribution of burdens and benefits.[50]

It should be noted, however, that the reformulation of primary laws of nature as perfect rights has two important advantages as well. It eliminates two awkward problems. The *first* problem we might call the problem of translation by the legislator. On the basis of a conception of natural law as a body of general natural precepts, the problem immediately presents itself that in order to be effective, these general precepts have to be translated into more specific precepts, appropriate to the regulation of human affairs in particular circumstances and societies. We have seen that Aquinas already acknowledged this problem and solved it by claiming that the general principles should be freely determined by the human legislator. Both Suárez and Grotius extended the room for manoeuvre on the part of the human legislator by means of their notion of human *dominium*. However, that implies that natural law as such can only play a modest role. Its precepts should first be interpreted, specified and translated by public authority before they can become operative. This reduces the scope of natural law as an instrument for critical assessment, as I have shown.

However, once these general precepts are reformulated as duties corresponding to natural rights, it is possible to circumvent the necessity of such a translation on the part of the legislator. In the form of natural rights, 'nature' can pass its verdict directly. The voice of nature is no longer only transmitted through the human lawgiver. Grotius has not yet drawn the full consequences of this position. On the level of municipal law he remains within the confines of the theory developed by Suárez, according to which public authority is the interpreter of natural law. Only on the level of international law does Grotius allow for the direct intervention of natural law in the form of natural rights, which are perfect and inalienable. Remarkably enough, on the level of states the right to property is *not* thought to be dependent on how 'property' is interpreted. It is Locke who extended this solution to the individual citizen as well, and it is in Locke's theory that the full critical potentiality of natural law is regained. There, rights are indeed more than privileges that have to

---

· [50] See NLNR p. 207; Van Eikema Hommes, 1972, p. 76. Both Max Weber and Jürgen Habermas stress the relation between what they call the 'process of autonomisation of subsystems' and the emergence of instrumental rationality. Cf. Habermas, 1981, I, II.4.

be *granted* by the legislator on the basis of his interpretation of natural law; they are directly derived from nature.

The *second* problem that is successfully avoided by the reformulation of natural law as natural rights is the problem of obligation. As we have seen in chapter III, this was Suárez's main problem in dealing with natural law. Nature and reason, taken by themselves, were regarded to be an insufficient basis for the obligation to follow the laws. That is why Suárez introduced an additional divine will. On the theoretical level, it is not easy to see how Grotius can avoid that notion. It is true that he thinks that our natural constitution is the product of God's will, but in itself, this move does not make the natural precepts obligatory. It is one thing to say that God has created us sociable, but another thing to derive from that wisdom the obligation to act accordingly.

However, his account of the application of natural law to international relations reveals that Grotius can indeed dispense with the decree of the divine will. We have seen that in practice sociability and reason are subordinated to self-preservation, which is viewed as a perfect right. This perfect right is immediately derived from God's will that creation preserves itself. But a right can also be *exercised*, not by God, but by the rights-holder. In Grotius's theory the perfect right of the one necessarily and by itself entails the perfect obligation of the other to respect that right. On the level of states, these rights are mutually enforceable. This implies that the problem of obligation is solved to a large extent. The disappearance of the notion of an overall legal framework that deals with the distribution of shares and the resolution of that framework into mutual relationships between rights-holders has the important advantage of there being no need for a will of God as an all-encompassing Sovereign.

The resolution of natural law into natural rights can therefore be regarded as solving problems by discarding them as irrelevant. On the level of municipal law there is no need for a human legislator who interprets and translates the primary precepts of natural law; on the level of natural law there is no need for a divine legislator who attaches sanctions to the precepts of natural law. Any attempt therefore to return to the notion of an overall system of natural law will inevitably hit upon the problem how to account for the legislator, whether human or divine. This is indeed the case in both Pufendorf's and Finnis's theories, as we shall see.

9. *Conclusion*

Grotius's theory presents a complex picture, which can best be evaluated according to the assumptions of my initial definition (see introduction). It is indeed true that Grotius thought that universal and eternally valid criteria and principles are grounded in nature (assumption b). But he unequivocally confines the meaning of nature to *human* nature, as we have seen in the preceding chapter. Human nature is conceived to be sociable, reasonable and inclining to self-preservation. However, if we look at the principles that are deduced from these fundamental traits (the four primary laws of nature), we see that they are all informed by the urge to self-preservation alone, to which reason and sociability are instrumental. This implies that natural law is based upon man's urge for self-preservation, and discoverable by man's rational perception of that inclination (assumption c).

These modified assumptions concerning the basis and promulgation of natural law are responsible for two—conflicting—tendencies in Grotius's work. On the level of municipal law, the tendency towards reduction of the role of natural law, already present in Suárez's theory, is reinforced. This is brought about by Grotius's identification of natural law with Suárez's natural law on *dominium*, and by his view of society as an artificial union to which people are bound by their (implied) consent. This consent cannot be guided by natural law, except in the general sense that living in society furthers our self-preservation. Natural law only tells us to obey those governments we have consented to. This implies that assumption a) that positive law can be justified/criticised by means of natural law is curtailed to the assumption that it can be justified on the basis of the notion of consent. This, furthermore, implies that we always have a moral obligation to comply with positive law. Assumption d) requiring a critical assessment of positive law in order to make it morally obligatory is no longer maintained, since Grotius takes 'consent' in a historical sense of that word.

On the level of international law, the precepts of natural law, reformulated as perfect rights, play a more direct and also a more important role. They are no longer translated and interpreted by public authority. States should abide by all four primary laws, which can be regarded as duties correlative to (perfect) rights of other states. These rights are mutually enforceable. This implies that international law is directly guided by natural law. Assumption a) that positive law should be justified/and criticised by means of these natural rights, as well as assumption d) concerning the moral obligation of states to abide by international regulations which are justified in terms of these rights are the basis of Grotius's entire theory of international law.

The difference between natural law and natural rights therefore seems to be crucial. Whereas natural law threatens to lose its critical potential, a theory of natural rights seems to allow for a scope of critical assessment which had been absent even in the writings of Aquinas.

CHAPTER VII

PUFENDORF'S DIVINE CONDUCTOR

It has been Pufendorf's fate to become known either as a predecessor or as a successor, who is seldom studied as a legal philosopher in his own right. Pufendorf himself already tried to refute the widespread view that he was mainly the follower of Grotius. In the preface to his main work, *De Jure Naturae et Gentium* (JNG),[1] he writes:

> [...] however much we cherish the fame of that man, so much so that we have been accorded the special designation of his 'Son', it must after all be acknowledged that he has entirely omitted not a few matters, some he has accorded but a passing touch, and introduced some other matters, which prove that after all even he was only a man.[2]

Nevertheless, his frequent mentioning of Grotius, John Selden and Thomas Hobbes, as well as his minute discussion and criticism of these authors must have contributed to the fact that Pufendorf was above all praised for his didactic qualities. The translations of his books were used as textbooks at universities in France, Scotland, and Holland, and they influenced generations of lawyers and philosophers to come. And that is one of the reasons why nowadays he is frequently studied as one of the major 'influences' on Kant, Locke, Rousseau, and Adam Smith, who devoted approving footmarks to Pufendorf.

Even in those studies that do treat Pufendorf as an independent natural lawyer, he is seldom presented as an original thinker. Krieger, for instance, characterises him as a 'mediator'.[3] But between what does Pufendorf mediate? Welzel regards Pufendorf's theory as a reconciliation between what he calls the 'existential' type of natural law that had been developed by Hobbes and the 'idealist' version of natural law designed by Grotius.[4] With the term 'idealist', Welzel means to designate the role of natural law as an 'ideal' standard

---

[1] Pufendorf, 1688.
[2] JNG pref., p. vi.
[3] Krieger, 1965, p. 3.
[4] Welzel, 1951, p. 130. See also Welzel, 1958.

against which positive law should be evaluated. With the term 'existential' he refers to the fact that for Hobbes natural law can only be implemented in the form of 'existing', positive law.[5]

On the basis of my analysis in the preceding chapter, this contrast is drawn too sharply. 'Idealism' can only be found if we confine ourselves to Grotius's *programme* as it has been developed in the Prolegomena of the JBP. There natural law is praised as an eternal and immutable standard against which positive law should be evaluated. But when it comes to the question how natural law in fact is *used*, we have seen that natural law is only effective on the international scene, which is conceived as a state of nature written large. On the level of municipal law, natural law hardly plays a role as a means to assess the moral qualities of the state or its laws. In Grotius's work we witnessed a gap between the programme and its implementation.

In fact, this implementation comes much closer to Hobbes's theory than to Grotius's own programme.[6] Hobbes also uses natural law mainly as an argument for the *necessity* of a sovereign state and not as a means to determine its *substance*,[7] but unlike Grotius he openly acknowledges this. He discards sociability from human nature, emphasises the natural right to self-preservation and only retains the precept that covenants should be performed;[8] a precept that can only be effective in the context of positive law. The natural laws that Hobbes mentions are 'rules of prudential morality',[9] technical rules people should observe in entering into a contract;[10] they are not meant as standards by means of which one can evaluate or criticise positive law. Finally, Hobbes does not understand 'distributive justice' in the Aristotelian sense of the word. Significantly, he understands it as the impartial treatment of an arbitrator.[11]

The main difference therefore between Hobbes and Grotius lies in their theoretical ambitions. Unlike Grotius, Hobbes openly and consistently deviates from the traditional programme of natural law theory and designs his own programme which emphasises not the nat-

---

[5] *Leviathan* (Hobbes, 1651) 26, 4.

[6] Also Tuck remarks that 'we constantly find echoes of Grotius in his [Hobbes's] works'. Cf. Tuck, 1989, p. 52.

[7] Cf. Welzel, 1951, p. 118.

[8] *Lev.* 15. Cf. also Raphael, 1988.

[9] Raphael, 1988, p. 161.

[10] Cf. e.g. Van Eikema Hommes, 1972, p. 86.

[11] Cf. *Lev.* 15; Raphael, 1988, p. 167.

ural qualities but the artificial, man-made character of society, justice and moral distinctions. We cannot properly speak of Hobbes as a natural lawyer because he no longer thought of natural law as an eternal standard for positive law.[12]

Thus, if we are to regard Pufendorf as a mediator, it is more appropriate to regard his theory as an attempt to reconcile Grotius's *programme* with that of Hobbes. Pufendorf tries to fit Hobbes's legacy into the traditional conceptual framework of natural law. As we shall see in this chapter Pufendorf thoroughly digested Hobbes's innovations. He discards 'sociability' from the description of human nature, he even extends Hobbes's theory of the artificial character of moral distinctions and endorses—albeit half-heartedly—Hobbes's concept of the state of nature as a means to abstract from cultural contingencies. Yet, this does not lead him to deny the existence of an immutable standard on the basis of which positive law can be evaluated. Instead, he takes natural law more seriously than Grotius, in the sense that he refuses it to be dissolved into a mere collection of natural rights. Once more he tries to provide for a unified concept of natural *law*.

It is this latter attempt which makes Pufendorf interesting for the purpose of this book. In the preceding chapter I concluded that a theory of natural *law* has to cope with two problems that are less acutely felt by a theory of natural rights: the problem of translation and of obligation. We shall see that both problems recur in Pufendorf's work. In this chapter, we shall see that the problem of obligation poses a serious difficulty for Pufendorf; a difficulty which is further enhanced by Pufendorf's particular conception of nature. On the basis of that conception, it is not only difficult to account for obligation, it is also impossible to conceive of nature as a normative order. In the following chapter, we see that the problem of translation is responsible for Pufendorf's difficulty in connecting the human normative order to the divine normative order. The upshot is that natural law theory finally succumbs to both problems.

My treatment of Pufendorf is structured along the same lines as that of his predecessors. In this chapter, the foundation and the status of natural law are examined; the next chapter will deal with Pufen-

---

[12] Haakonssen remarks that Hobbes's use of the 'antiquated language of natural law' mistakenly gave rise to interpretations of Hobbes as a 'genuine natural lawyer'. Cf. Haakonssen, 1996, p. 32.

dorf's views on how natural law can play a role in the assessment of positive law and human society.

1. *Weak and wicked*

Like Grotius, Pufendorf turns 'human nature' into the proximate source for natural law. It enables him, as it had enabled Grotius, to reconcile the fundamental freedom of God with the immutability of natural law. It is here that Pufendorf follows Grotius most closely. He asserts that God has been free in creating mankind as He saw fit, but once mankind had been created such as it is now,

> [...] it is no longer possible to believe that He will annul or change the law of nature so long as He makes no change in the nature of man [...].[13]

Natural law is therefore made 'coeval with the human race' as Locke put it.[14] And since human nature is the starting-point and foundation for natural law, Like Grotius, Pufendorf has to present human nature in an idealised form, as a 'rational and social animal'.[15] But whereas Grotius had treated this idealised concept as more or less corresponding to reality, Pufendorf is much more aware of the fact that it is a theoretical construct. Devoting a chapter to 'the certainty of moral sciences', Pufendorf writes:

> It is of little consequence here, whether or not the subject of a demonstrable proposition necessarily exists; but it is sufficient, if, when its existence is posited, certain affections are necessarily agreeable to it, and it can be shown by unquestionable principles that they are agreeable to it. Thus it is of little concern to mathematicians whether a triangle be something necessary or contingent, if only they can demonstrate that the sum of its angles equals two right angles.[16]

Whether triangles do exist in nature is beside the point. All that matters is that statements such as 'human nature is sociable' serve as

---

[13] JNG II, III, 5.
[14] Locke, 1661, Essay VII, p. 193.
[15] JNG II, III, 4.
[16] JNG I, II, 2.

'axioms', which 'need no further proof, but merit belief upon their own evidence [...]'.[17]

In chapter V, I argued that Grotius, by taking human nature as a proximate source, can short-circuit the discussion about the role of God. The so-called 'impious hypothesis' holds that the validity of natural law is independent from any belief in God. Pufendorf, however, is not prepared to draw this consequence. He calls Grotius's thesis 'an impious and idiotic theory'. Law, Pufendorf asserts, is only law if it has a superior.[18] Without a superior, law lacks obligatory force. According to Pufendorf, people are only obligated if they feel constrained to act in the prescribed manner. In other words, if there are sanctions attached to the precept.[19]

Pufendorf is evidently worried that people might not feel constrained enough by the perception of human characteristics alone. Grotius had argued that people are induced to sociability by a proper understanding of their long-term interests. Pufendorf thinks that such an understanding is insufficient:

> But if these dictates of reason are to have the force of law, there is need of a higher principle; for although their advantage is most manifest, still it alone could never lay so firm a restraint upon the spirits of men that they could not forsake such dictates if they should find satisfaction in disregarding this advantage, or believe that they could better consult their own advantage in some other way.[20]

Apparently, Pufendorf finds fault with Grotius's hypothesis not only because he is afraid of its alleged impiety, but also because he is more suspicious of human nature than Grotius professed to be. We have seen that for Grotius it was not even necessary to suppose that man is naturally sociable. Instrumental reasoning was so important in his description of human nature that he could confidently believe that man would be led to a social life on the basis of enlightened self-interest alone.

Pufendorf does not share this optimism. He was Lutheran enough to stress man's corrupted nature. Not only is man weaker than most animals, he is also more wicked than other animals, Pufendorf as-

---

[17] JNG I, II, 3.
[18] JNG II, III, 19.
[19] Cf. JNG I, VI, 14.
[20] JNG II, III, 20.

serts. One of the reasons for this greater wickedness is that man's desires are never satisfied. 'Man's desire [...] stirs him much more often than seems necessary for the preservation of his species', he complains.[21] The desires of man are manifold and unbounded.

> A craving for luxuries, ambition, honours, and the desire to surpass others, envy, jealousy, rivalries of wit, superstition, anxiety about the future, curiosity, all these continually trouble his mind, none of which touch the senses of the brutes.[22]

From this depraved condition of man Pufendorf concludes that man cannot live without a true law. And by 'law' he adopts Suárez's concept of 'law-as-precept': a decree issued by a superior, accompanied with sanctions. Without sanctions, the laws of nature would be no more compelling than the prescriptions of doctors, Pufendorf adds.[23] Reasonable people would surely take medical advice to heart, but the kind of beings Pufendorf had in mind cannot be entrusted to do so.

We see here that Pufendorf deviates from the idealised version of human nature that had been the starting-point for Grotius's programme of natural law. Instead of departing from the rational and social nature of man, Pufendorf engages in a description of human nature that is meant to be realistic, and which can be characterised as truly Hobbesian.[24] Yet, there are traces of the older conception. In his chapter on why mankind needs natural law, Pufendorf also mentions the traditional argument that man has been endowed by God with noble faculties, such as an immortal soul and dignity, by which mankind is elevated above the beasts. These noble faculties should be developed, since God gave them 'not for nothing'.[25] But immediately after having pointed out that man is elevated above the rest of the creation by these noble faculties, Pufendorf proceeds to point out that man needs a law, because he is more wicked and more passionate than the rest of the creation. And this remains the dominant theme of the book.

---

[21] JNG II, I, 6.

[22] JNG II, I, 6.

[23] JNG II, III, 19.

[24] Cf. Palladini, 1989.

[25] JNG II, I, 5. This passage has induced Behme to interpret Pufendorf as belonging firmly to the scholastic tradition. See Behme, 1996; Behme, 1995.

Pufendorf's sombre view of human nature explains why he had stressed the fact that the axiom of human nature is a theoretical construct, rather than a realistic description of reality. The problem is, of course, that the natural laws that are to be deduced from this theoretical construct should serve as standards for the behaviour of actual man, not for the virtual actions of a theoretical construct. And indeed, a serious attempt to actually carry out such a deduction is conspicuously lacking in the JNG.

2. *The orchestra of mankind*

Not only does Pufendorf depart from the traditional assumptions of natural law by emphasising man's fundamental wickedness, he also seems to share the scepticist view of mankind, according to which man is the product of local customs and cultures. Like Montaigne, Pufendorf emphasises the force of customs which 'when long established assume the specious appearance of natural law'[26] and he devotes many pages to the variety of customs that can be found all over the world. 'The Persians married their mothers, and the Egyptians their sisters', Pufendorf remarks dryly.[27]

But there is not only an extreme variety of cultures, individuals also differ from each other:

> [...] among men there are as many minds as there are heads, and to each one his own way seems best.[28]

In *De officio hominis et civis juxta legem naturalem* (DOH)[29] he elaborates on this theme:

> Men are not all moved by one simple uniform desire, but by a multiplicity of desires variously combined. [...] There is no less variety in men's occupations and habits and in their inclinations to exert their powers of mind, as may be observed nowadays in the almost unlimited kinds of life men choose.[30]

---

[26] JNG II, III, 9.

[27] JNG II, III, 8.

[28] JNG II, I, 7.

[29] Pufendorf, 1673.

[30] DOH I, 3, 6.

Whereas Grotius exerted himself in proving that 'beneath' or 'bey-ond' this multitude of customs and ways of life there is a universal hard core to be found in the essential nature of man, Pufendorf seems to abandon this search for uniformity. If there is something 'univer-sal' to be found, it is that human nature is universally passion-ridden, variable, diverse and multi-faceted. The theoretical construct Pufen-dorf has in mind should therefore not only abstract from the wicked character of man, but also from the fact that there is no such thing as universal human nature.

Yet, Pufendorf does attempt to derive natural laws from human nature, be it that he takes the 'realistic' version of human nature as his starting-point and not a theoretical construct. He argues for the need of natural law in a particularly revealing passage, where he claims that natural law, backed by the force of will of a superior, can elevate man to a level that is unattainable for the ordinary animal, although animals are naturally less wicked than men. The metaphor used here is that of the orchestra:

> Now the more voices there are, the more dreadful and unpleasant the sound in the ear, unless they unite in harmony. In the same way the greatest confusion would have prevailed among men, were not their dissimilarity of customs and appetites reduced to a seemly order through laws. And yet this variety in another way yields man a remark-able grace and reward, since out of it, if properly guided, *a marvellous orderliness and beauty may arise, which could not possibly have come from complete uniformity* [my emphasis].[31]

This is an interesting remark. True harmony is polyphony; it arises out of differences and contrasts, not uniformity.[32]

Clearly, Pufendorf did not regard harmony as the outcome of an organic development. It should be 'properly guided'. Harmony does not grow naturally and of itself; it should be brought about by an ordering principle. This ordering principle cannot be positive law, for positive law is nothing but codified custom. The conductor who ultimately achieves this harmony of voices is God.

---

[31] JNG II, I, 7.

[32] Kossmann points to the recurrence of this theme of harmony in conservative political thought, e.g. in Elie Luzac. Cf. Kossmann, 1987a.

One might say that to a certain extent Pufendorf remains loyal here to the programme of natural law. For indeed, it is on the basis of human nature (as weak, wicked and variable) that natural law is erected. But the relation between human nature and natural law is different. Aquinas had claimed that natural law served to *realise* the inclinations inherent in man's nature. The break-down of teleology induced Suárez and Grotius to assert that natural law should point out which actions *agree* with human nature. But Pufendorf claims that natural law serves as a corrective *counterweight*, so to speak. Human nature should be harmonised by natural law. Such a relation between human nature and natural law, however, is incompatible with the mathematical analogy. From a triangle it can only be deduced that the sum of its angles equal two right angles; not that they *should* equal three right angles in order to correct its properties.

So if we read Pufendorf's plea for sociability, he by no means refers to a trait inherent in human nature, but as a trait man *should* develop. Speaking about 'the basis of natural law', Pufendorf writes:

> It is quite clear that man is an animal extremely desirous of his own preservation, in himself exposed to want, unable to exist without the help of his fellow-creatures, fitted in a remarkable way to contribute to the common good, and yet at all times malicious, petulant, and easily irritated, as well as quick and powerful to do injury. For such an animal to live and enjoy the good things that in this world attend his condition, *it is necessary that he be sociable* [...] [my emphasis].[33]

When Pufendorf speaks about 'man's social nature'[34] he means nothing more than that human nature is such that it *needs* society.[35] By turning sociability into an imperative, Pufendorf puts an end to the uneasy and ambivalent position sociability had occupied in Grotius's theory.

---

[33] JNG II, III, 15.
[34] Ibid.
[35] I agree here with Palladini: 1989, p. 6, and 1990.

3. *Law versus rights*

Whereas Grotius thought that the imperatives were inherent in the characteristics of mankind (God willed these traits to exist in us and therefore he wills us to act conformingly), Pufendorf places these outside human nature. Human nature as such can only indicate that we need to be sociable; but it cannot oblige us to sociability.

We might attribute this view to Pufendorf's mixture of Lutheranism, scepticism and Hobbesianism, but it is worthwhile to keep in mind that the introduction of the additional will of God is a re-introduction of the concept. We have seen that also Suárez opts for this solution. Although Suárez did not share Hobbes' bleak vision of man, he introduced an additional obligation, coming directly from God. Apparently, we have to do here with a forced move, that can be explained by constraints within the theory itself. Both Pufendorf and Suárez felt that nature, taken in itself, could not be the sole foundation for natural law. Of course, we should take into account that the two men had a different concept of 'nature' in mind. Suárez thought of Vázquez's concept of 'rational nature' as an eternal order, regulating God's creation. Pufendorf refers to the Grotian notion of nature as 'human nature'. But these concepts of nature are criticised by both Pufendorf and Suárez *along the same lines*. Both men maintain that the rational perception of natural properties alone does not give rise to obligations.

I think that the similarity of Suárez's and Pufendorf's objections points to an underlying assumption they shared, an assumption which was not maintained by Grotius, who consequently did not perceive any difficulty here. This assumption has to do with the underlying conception of law. Grotius conceived of natural law as a set of duties correlative to natural and perfect rights. The laws that enjoin us to abstain from another's property, to punish transgressors of natural law, to compensate for losses inflicted by our faults, and even the law that we should fulfil promises, can all be deduced from our natural right to self-preservation. Here, the difference between law and right is that the law of nature *universalises* the perfect rights of the various partners. If I have a right to further my self-preservation, reason tells me that other people have the same rights. On the basis of this rational perception of other people's rights, a natural law can be formulated, which seeks to co-ordinate the right-claims of the various partners. That is why Grotius proposes to confine the term 'law' to the rules pertaining to the regulation of perfect rights only.

Both Suárez and Pufendorf, however, conceive of natural law as much more than a universal formulation of perfect rights. According to Pufendorf:

> [...] the term laws includes not only the things that pertain to justice properly speaking, as it regulates by a perfect obligation our attitudes towards others, but also the things which are concerned with other virtues and terminate in the agent himself.[36]

Not only does the natural law comprise both the duties 'towards others' and the duties we have 'towards ourselves',[37] also those duties 'towards others' entail a broader spectrum of virtues than in Grotius's version of natural law. In DOH, Pufendorf elaborates upon the latter by mentioning three types of such other-directed duties. Whereas the first two match the Grotian universalisation of natural rights (not to harm others, and to treat others as equals) the third clearly deviates from that familiar path. Pufendorf writes there:

> It is not enough not to have harmed, or not to have slighted, others. We must also give, or at least share, such things as will encourage mutual goodwill.[38]

This goodwill can be achieved by being useful to others, by benevolence, and by being grateful for that benevolence.

The inclusion of the latter type of obligations explains why Pufendorf was in need of an additional divine obligation to perform these duties. For of course the first two kinds of duties have to do with the mutual—perfect—rights of people. The duty to abstain from another's property and not to harm others can be enforced by the other partners, whose rights we violate if we do not perform these duties. But nobody has a perfect right to gratitude or benevolence. Such obligations cannot be enforced by equal others. They can only be enforced by a superior. In the case of natural duties (as opposed to the duties of a citizen), this superior can only be God.

We see therefore that a wider conception of law, including imperfect duties, requires the assumption of a superior. But such a wider conception also reverses the order of priority between law and rights.

---

[36] JNG I, VI, 4.
[37] JNG II, III, 24.
[38] DOH I, 8, 1.

As we have seen in the preceding chapter, Grotius's formulation of the four primary precepts of natural law is essentially based on his conception of perfect natural rights. These precepts reformulate these rights as duties. In practice, Grotius took the existence of rights as the starting-point for the formulation of law. Pufendorf, like Suárez, reverses that order. He maintains that rights can only be *derived* from a superior law. They cannot be conceived to exist prior to law. Pufendorf explicitly criticises Grotius for having presupposed 'the existence of something just and right before a law and norm'. This would entail the view that natural law merely points out 'a right already existing'.[39] This view is not acceptable to Pufendorf. Rights presuppose a law from which they are derived; not the other way round.[40] As we shall see in the next section, this view is further developed in Pufendorf's theory of moral entities.

Of course, a lot more can be said about the relationship between natural law and natural rights. But for my purpose it is sufficient to argue that it is apparently only in the form of universalised rights that natural law can live up to the traditional ideal that the rational perception of nature carries with it sufficient obligatory force. Of course it is an illusion: it is not natural law which enforces those rights, but the other partners, equally entitled with rights. Or more precisely, it is the risk that others might enforce their rights in a way that is unpleasant and unprofitable for us in the long run that induces us to respect those rights. In this sense one can indeed agree with Grotius that reasoning alone induces us to act according to natural law. He only needs to suppose that men are capable of instrumental reasoning. On the basis of calculation men will act according to natural law.

Such instrumental reasoning, however, is not sufficient for those who try to provide for a concept of natural law that comprises more substantial precepts than 'abstaining from that which is another's'. Such a broader concept of natural law requires a broader concept of rationality: men should be assumed to take into account other people's needs as well. Suárez already had his doubts about that capacity, but for Pufendorf it must have sounded like a fairy-tale. He therefore maintains that the rational perception of nature is not sufficient ground for obligation.

---

[39] JNG I, VI, 4.
[40] Cf. also Haakonssen, 1996, pp. 40-1.

4. *Moral entities*

Both Pufendorf and Suárez feel that the rational perception of nature, whether 'rational nature' or 'human nature', does not oblige people to follow the dictates of natural law. Both men maintain that the rational perception of nature alone does not produce any norms. Both think that the perception of natural facts does not produce ought-statements (cf. III.5-6).

But Pufendorf stretches his criticism even further. Suárez had maintained that although nature is not a sufficient foundation for natural law, it is nevertheless a necessary foundation. To him, nature provides the basis for natural law, God's reason its promulgation and God's will its obligatory force. But Pufendorf denies that nature can be considered as the basis of natural law. It is not even a necessary foundation of natural law; nature has nothing to do at all with natural law!

This is quite disturbing for a man who occupied a chair in natural law. But in fact, he states this view in the very beginning of the JNG, even before he writes about the necessary obligatory force of natural law. There, Pufendorf makes the important distinction between what he calls 'moral entities' (*entia moralia*), and physical entities. This distinction is taken from his teacher, the mathematician Erhard Weigel (1625-99),[41] and is developed by Pufendorf. The most important difference is that whereas physical entities are *created*, moral entities owe their existence to imposition (*impositio*):

> For they do not arise out of the intrinsic nature of the physical properties of things, but they are superadded, at the will of intelligent entities, to things already existent and physically complete [...], and indeed, come into existence only by the determination of their authors.[42]

This passage suggests that the choice for the word 'entia' is unfortunate. The idea is that there are physical substances, or *substrata*, to which a normative aspect is added. It would therefore be more appropriate to speak of moral properties rather than entities. This Pufendorf concedes: moral entities 'do not exist of themselves' and

---

[41] Cf. Röd, 1970, pp. 76-81.
[42] JNG I , I, 4.

'should not be classified as substances, but rather as modes', he writes.[43] But he justifies the terminology by pointing out that an analogy with physical substances has some heuristical value.[44]

These 'modes' are not generated by nature itself, they can only be added by intelligent beings, be it God or men, who have the intellectual power to *add* a normative aspect to nature. The necessity of *impositio* by an intelligent being in order to turn nature into a meaningful normative reality therefore not only applies to natural law, but to all kinds of norms and laws. The norms that regulate our daily lives are likewise the product of *impositio*; they are imposed by the free will of man. In the following chapter we shall examine this *impositio humana* more fully; here we focus solely on the consequences of this view for the concept of natural law.

To what extent is this distinction between nature and God's imposition, although phrased in unusual terms, really a new one? As we have seen in III.5 Suárez had also criticised Vázquez by maintaining that the divine judgement should intervene in order to turn nature into a normative and meaningful reality. To Suárez, too, God's reason is the *sine qua non* for law. Although Suárez is ambiguous about the precise role of God's reason, he seems to maintain the view that God should discern the agreement or lack of agreement of certain actions with nature. If that interpretation is correct, it is Suárez's view that reason expresses *what is already there*. God's judgement leads to statements about the nature He had created.

Pufendorf's claim is stronger: divine reason not only discovers or expresses moral entities, but invents them. God should *add* something to nature in order to turn it into a normative reality. That is why he speaks of divine imposition as indispensable for the existence of natural law. It is not only necessary in providing natural law with obligatory force; without imposition there is not even a norm, let alone an obligatory law.

This is an extraordinary view for a natural law theorist. The creation by itself is no longer the basis for natural law. God should *add* moral entities to his creation. How can we reconcile this idea with the notion that natural law is coeval with the human race? As I remarked in the first section of this chapter, Pufendorf repeats Grotius's view that by creating mankind God supplied for natural law.

---

[43] JNG I, I, 6.
[44] JNG I, I, 5.

That doctrine has clearly no need for an additional imposition. Instead, the creation of man *entails* the imposition of natural law.[45] The solution that Pufendorf offers is that God created man as 'an animal which could not be preserved alive unless he observed the natural law'.[46] God created man as an animal in need of law. He supplies for this need by His imposition. But this solution drastically limits the information nature can provide us about natural law. On the basis of man's natural disposition, we can only say that some sort of law is necessary. We cannot infer from nature what the substance of that law is.

There is a certain parallel here with Grotius and Hobbes, be it on a different level. For them, natural law had served as an argument for the necessity of a sovereign civil state, not as a means to determine its substance. Pufendorf extends this view to the level of natural law itself. Human nature only points to the necessity of natural law, but is silent on its substance. Where Hobbes had argued that it was for the sovereign ruler of a commonwealth to determine the substance of civil law, Pufendorf claims that it is to God alone to determine the substance of natural law.

So human nature is silent on the question what kind of natural laws we are to follow. God is assigned the important task of imposing natural law and determining its contents. The reason for that is not, I believe, because Pufendorf feared the impious consequences of intellectualism. Although he surely had his motives for turning natural law into a respectable science, he could have ensured this respectability in other ways as well. He could have stressed, more clearly than Grotius, God's will as manifest in nature. He could also have stressed, less equivocally than Suárez, the importance of God's reason in making sense of nature. Instead, he adopted the sharp distinction between natural and moral entities.

Why did he decide for that option? One of the reasons might be his Lutheranism. On the basis of the view that man corrupted and destroyed God's creation, an additional imperative is needed in order to restore that order. But there is another reason as well, which is Pufendorf's concept of nature.

---

[45] JNG II, III, 5.
[46] JNG II, III, 5.

5. *Unbridled nature*

In order to understand his view of nature, it is not sufficient to point to the development that was already noticeable in Suárez's work: the disappearance of teleological metaphysics. The decline of the belief in nature as constantly striving to a certain optimum state of affairs had led Suárez to deny the view that the rational perception of nature by itself can give rise to any norms. But it did not bring him to deny that reason and nature are necessary elements of the foundation of natural law.

Pufendorf's conception of nature is even further removed from traditional teleology. Not only does he deny the constant striving to ends, he discards the idea that any order can be found in nature. Animals, Pufendorf asserts, 'enjoy a liberty unrestrained by law'[47] and he understands by liberty 'negative liberty' in the sense coined by Isaiah Berlin, as absence of impediments.[48] Only man is bound to God's law; the rest of nature is unbridled. In dramatic terms Pufendorf depicts the life of animals as utterly cruel. In contrast to the passages in which he had asserted that man is even more wicked than animals, he warns the innocent spectator of nature not to be misled by appearances:

> Puppies play happily together, but throw a piece of meat among them, and at once you will see them fighting with one another.[49]

They even have no sense of ownership:

> Since they know no laws of ownership, on the gnawings of their hunger they often fight fiercely for what is common to all, and no sense of propriety prevents their seizing what others had stored up for their own use.[50]

Pufendorf also explains why animals have no law to guide them:

> For there seemed no need of great care in fostering and guarding the security of animals, which are not only produced by nature, in such

---

[47] JNG II, I, 4.
[48] Berlin, 1958.
[49] JNG II, I, 4.
[50] JNG II, I, 4.

great numbers, with high fecundity and little effort, but which also are
without an immortal soul, their life coming only from a minute disposition and motion of particles of matter. And the Creator is pleased to
manifest His power in producing and destroying them.[51]

Here nature is a scene of waste without any sense or order. The Car-
tesian flavour of this passage is coupled with the notion of nature as
capricious. It is impossible to find order or harmony within nature.
Nature is an aggregate of shrill voices, untempered by any ordering
principle. In the midst of this noise, man alone can understand the
instructions of the divine conductor.

In this sense we might say that this concept of nature is the reverse
of that of Suárez. Whereas in Suárez's philosophy the dynamic conception of nature is frozen into a perpetual 'state of affairs' that can
only be understood by theoretical reason, Pufendorf's view, like that
of Hobbes, is that of nature as perpetual motion. On the surface of it,
we might welcome this emphasis on motion as a return to the dynamic picture Aquinas had sketched. But of course Pufendorf's
motion is no longer understood as a movement towards a natural end:
it is only brought about by antecedent causes: the 'motion of particles
of matter'.[52]

It is in Pufendorf's work that we witness the consequences of the
shift from a teleological view towards a causal one. The replacement
of ends by causes turns nature into a meaningless whole. If we are to
discern any normative value in nature, it is only because intelligent
beings *put it in there*.

Of course, Pufendorf does not deny that as far as we are physical
beings, we participate in that world of perpetual motion of causes and
effects. But Pufendorf never tires to point out that this has nothing to
do with morality. Moral ideas are not innate. There is nothing in our
physical appearance that points to a natural disposition towards a
morally good life: the fact that our cheeks blush when we feel
ashamed does not prove a connection between nature and morals, he
writes, since we also blush when merely our reputation is at stake.[53]

---

[51] JNG II, I, 4.

[52] Denzer, 1972, pp. 60-6, gives a good overview of Pufendorf's conception of
nature. About the influence of the new mechanical concept of nature on natural law
theory in general cf. Tully, 1988a.

[53] JNG I, II, 7. Haakonssen, 1996, p. 41, remarks that it is this anti-essentialism
that explains 'Pufendorf's fear of considering rights as primary over law'.

6. *The sovereign legislator*

The denial of the possibility that nature might provide us with clues on the basis of which we might discern good and evil led Pufendorf to emphasise the importance of explicit legislation. It is only on the basis of an explicit law or generalised norm that we can arrive at moral distinctions. Unequivocally Pufendorf asserts:

> [...] that reason should be able to discover any morality in the actions of a man without reference to a law, is as impossible as for a man born blind to judge between colours.[54]

The actions of man would be indifferent, i.e. neither good nor evil, 'if every law both divine and human were removed'. Morality is not generated by nature, but only perceptible on the basis of norms that are imposed or added to nature, in Pufendorf's terminology.

Here again we see the influence of Hobbes and again his insights are translated to the realm of natural law. Hobbes had maintained that concepts like 'justice', 'equity' and 'moral virtue' could only acquire any sense on the basis of the—civil—laws issued by the sovereign. He held that indeed *civil* law is the *sine qua non* for moral distinctions.[55] Pufendorf transports Hobbes's views on civil law to the realm of natural law. We have already seen this happen in Pufendorf's argument for the necessity of natural law, rather than its substance (section 4). Now he claims that it is only within the framework of natural law that we are able to arrive at moral distinctions. And finally, as we have seen, he emphasises the need for coercive authority that attaches sanctions to law. One might conclude that Pufendorf's God performs the same function as Hobbes's sovereign.

This God, like Hobbes's temporal sovereign, is not bound to any 'higher law'. Since all law arises from the *impositio* of an intelligent being, and since we should not suppose that there is an intelligent being apart from ourselves and God, God is completely free. According to Pufendorf:

---

[54] JNG I, II, 6.
[55] *Lev.* 26, 4.

A liberty unfettered and free from every encumbrance and restriction belongs to the most Good and Great God alone [...].[56]

This view leads him to attenuate the claim that natural law is eternally valid:

[...] such eternity should not reach beyond the imposition of God, or the origin of the race of man.[57]

It is only by contrast with the changeable positive laws that we can speak of natural law as 'eternal'.[58]

Leibniz was incensed by this notion. In a fierce and also rather witty criticism of Pufendorf he wonders how, on the basis of such a theory, one can say that God is just. If 'just' derives its meaning from a law, and if we deny that God is bound by any higher law, the epitheta with which we adorn God are meaningless. We can only praise God as being just if we assess his conduct with reference to 'eternal truths'.[59] Whether or not we can praise God as just is not a mere theological trifle. In order to determine whether we should obey God's law, it is necessary that God is conceived as an authority and not merely as an arbitrary power. We are not bound by the laws of some God who is unjust.[60]

At first sight it seems as if we are back here at the familiar discussion between voluntarism and intellectualism. Once again all seems to revolve around the question whether God should be conceived as teacher or as legislator. But there is more to it than a mere repetition of moves on the eternal chess-board of natural law. The old-fashioned voluntarist had claimed that God has willed to create nature such as it is. It seems as if Pufendorf repeats that position when he tells us that by creating the human race, God created natural law. But his theory of moral entities tells us otherwise. God's intentions cannot be read in

---

[56] JNG II, I, 3.
[57] JNG I, II, 6.
[58] Ibid.
[59] Leibniz, 1706, p. 71.
[60] For a discussion of Leibniz's criticism and the reply by Barbeyrac, see Schneewind, 1996.

nature at all. God is supposed to have *added* a law to nature.[61] Pufendorf's voluntarism is much more radical than the older variety. The older voluntarist position could always be refuted by the claim, that whether God's will or reason was at the basis of nature, his intentions could always be *read* and understood by an investigation of nature. This path was chosen by Grotius. But it is now blocked.

In fact, Pufendorf's theory about law as *impositio* can be read as a criticism of the distinction between natural law and positive law as such. If law is not (im)posited, it is not law at all. That implies that all law is positive law. And indeed, Pufendorf implicitly criticises Grotius's distinction between natural and positive law when he writes:

> [...] we feel that we need not declare, with certain writers, that some things are noble or base of themselves without any imposition, and that these form the object of natural and perpetual law, while those, the good repute or baseness of which depends upon the will of a legislator, fall under the head of positive laws. For since good repute, or moral necessity, and turpitude, are affections of human actions *arising* from their conformity or non-conformity to some norm or law, and law is the bidding of a superior, *it does not appear that good repute or turpitude can be conceived to exist before law, and without the imposition of a superior* [my emphasis].[62]

This passage reveals the paradoxical outcome of Pufendorf's enterprise. His serious attempt to turn natural law into a genuine *law* which should serve as a framework for moral distinctions and which should be endowed with obligatory force in fact boils down to the dismissal of *natural* law.

The emphasis on God as the legislator of natural law also seriously undermines Pufendorf's own demarcation between natural law and divine positive law. In the preface to the DOH, Pufendorf claims that whereas natural law depends on 'right reason', the ultimate foundation of positive divine law is 'God's command'.[63] This statement, however, does not match with his theory of *impositio*, which main-

---

[61] This is insufficiently recognised by Haakonssen, 1996, p. 38, who writes that God 'created a moral world which has certain permanent features, namely those of basic human nature'. Such a view would have been in line with Grotius's theory. However, Pufendorf claims that God *superadded* a law to His creation.

[62] JNG I, II, 6.

[63] DOH p. 7.

tains that 'right reason' is unable to discern right and wrong independent of God's law, which is imposed and superadded to nature. The theory of imposition makes natural law dependent on God's command in just the same way as divine positive law.

The only difference therefore between positive divine law and natural law concerns their contents. Positive divine law has a wider scope: it reveals our duties towards God, seeks to ensure our future salvation, is not confined to worldly affairs, and focuses on inner thoughts as well.[64] Natural law is more limited in scope because it deals with worldly affairs and external actions only. But this distinction merely concerns the content of both bodies of law. Unlike Grotius, Pufendorf does not differentiate between natural and divine law on the ground of their different foundation. Both natural and divine law ultimately rest on God's imperatives. That is why it appears difficult to maintain that 'the doctrine of natural law [...] has nothing to do with theology'.[65] Although it is true that Pufendorf claims that natural law should be accessible to human reason, both disciplines are erected on the same logical foundation.[66]

7. The two faces of man

The sharp distinction between nature as a senseless and purposeless whole and morality as the product of the imposition by intelligent beings seems to exclude a serious theory of natural law. The investigation of nature leads to natural science, the investigation of human nature leads to what we nowadays might call social sciences, whereas an eternal standard for morality can only be provided by theology.

These conclusions are at odds with almost anything that Pufendorf asserts about his programme of natural law. Time and again he emphasises that the science of natural law is a genuine 'science', a 'discipline' which is independent from theology. He firmly criticises theologians in the preface to the JNG whom he accuses of meddling into affairs in which they have no authority at all[67] and he goes to all lengths in order to argue that certainty can be achieved in the

---

[64] DOH p. 7.
[65] D'Entrèves, 1951, p. 55.
[66] Cf. Laurent, 1982, p. 180.
[67] JNG p. vii.

science of morals, a science that is founded on the axioms provided by human nature.

Yet, we have seen that all that human nature reveals is the need for *a* law, not *what* law. How can his scientific ambitions be satisfied if he asserts that natural law is no law without God and that nature by itself is meaningless?

There might be an answer to these intriguing questions, but that answer is not explicitly given by Pufendorf. The only way out of this dilemma is to distinguish the different aspects of man. Man's physical aspects (like the blush on his cheeks; but also his passions and unbounded desires) should be sharply distinguished from man's 'nobler faculties'. It is only by the Kantian distinction of a phenomenal and a noumenal world that one can make any sense of the claim that natural law can be discovered by an investigation of man's nature. If we read 'human nature' consistently as 'man's noumenal aspects', and if we cut out man's physical aspects as *irrelevant* for the development of moral standards, it would be possible to rescue the programme of natural law. Such a law, however, would have little to do with nature and should more properly be called 'rational law'.

The problem is that this is Kant's solution and not Pufendorf's.[68] Pufendorf labels both man's rationality *and* his passions as 'human nature'. He persistently denies any innateness of moral ideas or an inborn moral sense. If he talks about man's social nature, he only intends saying that man needs society. If he refers to man's rationality, he does not point to an innate ability to participate in the noumenal order, but merely refers to the fact that man is able to understand God's law. Pufendorf, unlike Kant, does not abstract from that which links man to physical nature.

Pufendorf's distinction between physical and moral entities may indeed foreshadow Kant's distinction between a world of *Sein* and a world of *Sollen*,[69] but no more than that. Pufendorf keeps talking about human nature as a unified whole. A unified whole which stands alone in this world, because man is the only being who is required to follow the law of God and whose freedom is thereby restrained. Not human nature, but God is the axiom which is indispensable for 'the science of natural law'.

---

[68] Welzel's interpretation tends to turn Pufendorf into a proto-Kantian (although in a convincing manner). His interpretation is criticised by Denzer, 1972, I.4.

[69] Cf. the introduction by Tully to Pufendorf's DOH, 1673, p. 22.

This axiom seems to invalidate the whole enterprise, but in the next chapter we shall see how Pufendorf nevertheless finds room for 'a science of natural law' on the basis of these premisses.

8. *Conclusion*

It seems as if the relationship between Pufendorf and Grotius faithfully mirrors that between Suárez and Aquinas. Whereas Aquinas had conceived of natural law as based on a unified concept of eternal law, in which reason, will and nature could converge, Suárez supplanted it by a concept of law-as-precept, issued by a sovereign and accompanied by sanctions. This option is rejected by Grotius. Once more he tries to base natural law on *nature*, i.e. human nature, a concept in which he tries to reconcile the various competing elements. Pufendorf's dissatisfaction with Grotius's concept of human nature is similar to Suárez's objections to Aquinas's views. Like Suárez, he stresses the importance of a sovereign legislator who provides law with the necessary obligatory force. So we might say that whereas Aquinas and Grotius emphasise the 'natural' part of the concept of natural law; Suárez and Pufendorf draw attention to the 'law' part of natural law.

However, the discussion between 'naturalists' and 'legalists' is not a mere repetition of moves. Pufendorf radicalises the position of Suárez. Whereas Suárez still relies on nature as a partial foundation of natural law, Pufendorf thinks that natural law can only result from the *impositio* by intelligent beings, be it God or man. This theory of *impositio* is inspired by Hobbes's view that all moral distinctions are artificial in the sense that they can only be made by reference to law, as the product of an intelligent being.

In the process of rebuilding a theory of natural *law* as imposed by God, however, the tightrope that had still linked together reason, will and nature, snapped. In Pufendorf's theory these elements are no longer marked by an ever increasing tension; they definitely drift apart. On the basis of nature, it is no longer possible to arrive at rational judgements about good and evil. Moral distinctions are the product of a rational *impositio* that comes from *without* and that should be *added* to nature. But even if we have added reason to nature, the mixture cannot be regarded as law. It requires an additional obligation, provided by the will of God. It is in the hands of the first professor in natural law ever that the concept finally breaks down. In the following chapter, we shall investigate how a new and more interesting theory is erected upon its remains.

CHAPTER VIII

PUFENDORF'S RECONSTRUCTION OF RATIONALITY

At first sight, the demise of natural law as a *natural* law does not seem to affect Pufendorf's theories concerning the status of positive law. When one peruses his main oeuvre, the similarities with his forerunners catch the eye. Like Suárez and Grotius, he emphasises the importance of man-made institutions; like them, he stresses the fact that natural law mainly plays a role once these institutions are introduced by the free will of mankind, and he focuses on contracts, oaths and promises by means of which we are bound to obey positive law. It seems as if we are once again confronted with a gap between the programme of natural law and its implementation. Notwithstanding the fact that Pufendorf has turned natural law into a law posited by God, it does not seem to affect his theories about how natural law should be used in practice.

Yet, I shall argue in this chapter that this familiar vocabulary conceals some vital differences, which have to do with Pufendorf's dismissal of the notion that morals can be deduced from nature. As I noted in VII.7, the programme of natural law has in fact split into two parts, the 'natural' part and the 'law' part. In this chapter we shall see that the division of the unified programme of natural law into these two programmes is reflected in Pufendorf's writings on positive law. It leads on the one hand to an investigation of (human) nature that is meant to be realistic and empirical; on the other hand it tries to provide for moral standards, which are not deduced from 'nature' but from 'imposition'. Pufendorf's theory can indeed be characterised as a mixture of social science and moral theory.[1]

1. *The different roles of man*

In the preceding chapter we have seen that to Pufendorf it is by virtue of God's imposition of law that we can speak of natural law. Without

---

[1] For the interpretation of Pufendorf as a sociologist, cf. Wolf, 1927.

God's ordering activities, there is only 'nature'; an orderless scene of waste. But not only God imposes moral entities: *all* intelligent beings are able to add norms and values to what otherwise would have been a purposeless world. It is by virtue of these moral entities that the multiplicity of—natural—needs, desires and passions can be ordered and regulated.

As I remarked earlier, Pufendorf thought of these entities not as entities, but as modes 'superadded' to a physical *substratum*. The physical world acquires meaning, because *we* add value to it. It is by means of imposition that a mere piece of cloth is turned into a flag, and lumps of gold into money. But human beings impose values not only on things, but also on human beings. It is by means of human imposition that man is—literally—value-*laden*: human imposition turns 'man' into a 'person'.

Persona retains here its old meaning of 'mask' that enables an actor to play his role:

> So the same man can at the same time represent several persons, provided the various functions which attend such persons can be simultaneously met by the same person. For although by virtue of physical considerations the same person cannot be both husband and wife [...], or by virtue of moral considerations cannot be at once master and slave [...], yet nothing prevents the same person from being at one and the same time in his house the head of a family, in parliament a senator, in a court of justice a lawyer [...].[2]

Time and again Pufendorf stresses that in different situations men can assume different roles. Pufendorf hastens, however, to add that 'the imposition which produces real moral persons'[3] differs from the roles of actors in the theatre: whereas the latter serve no other purpose than to deceive the spectator, 'real' moral impositions should *order* man's lives. Like God's imposition of law, man's imposition serves to order the diversity of needs, desires and passions.

One might be tempted to ascribe to Pufendorf the rather modern view that it would be impossible to abstract from these imposed roles, and that these roles are constitutive of man. But such a view would ignore Pufendorf's view that human beings do not impose their values upon an empty world. Divine imposition is prior to human imposi-

---

[2] JNG I, I, 14.
[3] JNG I, I, 15.

tion. We are therefore not born as mere physical 'substrata' but as human beings. Human beings are not like pieces of cloth or lumps of gold, because they are already value-laden by God's imposition.

This view is at the basis of Pufendorf's remarks concerning abortion. As soon as the embryo in the mother's womb has acquired any 'human form', Pufendorf writes, it has the 'right of not suffering injury at the hands of others' and cannot legitimately be destroyed. Before that however, we cannot speak of that 'mass' as having sustained any injury.[4]

We should not identify his view with Grotius's view of man as endowed with natural rights. As I argued in VII.3, Pufendorf dismisses the view that there are any natural rights before the imposition of God's law. All rights are derived from God's law. They are the result of divine imposition and they cannot therefore be viewed as 'natural' but as 'moral' rights. The embryo should be conceived as something to which a moral right is added before it is born.

This has induced several interpreters to believe that Pufendorf can be regarded as a true forerunner of the modern conception of 'human' rights.[5] These interpreters maintain that the assumption of a moral right, which is *irreducible* to nature, is indispensable for any formulation of universal human rights, which emphasise human dignity, autonomy and liberty.[6]

However, despite the fact that there is indeed textual evidence for an embryonal conception of human rights,[7] I do not think that it was Pufendorf's main concern to develop a theory of individual rights in the modern sense of the word. He was much more concerned with what he called 'composite moral persons'. These arise when values are imposed on groups of individuals. These 'composite moral persons' arise

> [...] when several individual men so unite that whatever, by reason of that union, they want or do, is considered as one will, one act, and no more.[8]

---

[4] JNG I, I, 7.

[5] See Kobusch, 1996; and Welzel, 1958.

[6] If that interpretation is correct, we see at once the difficulty of a concept of human rights without the corresponding notion of a divine imposition. If it is not by nature, and not by God, how then is our physical *substratum* provided with any rights?

[7] E.g. JNG II, III, 17.

[8] JNG I, I, 13.

Pufendorf makes several distinctions in the description of these composite moral persons. They can be either public or private, sacred or civil, particular or general. Not only the state is such a moral person, but also corporations, synods, the church, the army, and even the family. This latter addition is surprising. We see here how far Pufendorf extends his view on the artificiality of collective bodies. To Grotius, only the state was an artificial, man-made institution. The family was a natural unit. To Pufendorf, *all* collective bodies are the product of moral imposition by intelligent human beings.

The elaborate description of these collective bodies reveals, however, the inadequacy of the antiquated language of 'substrata' and 'superadded entities'. Groups can hardly be viewed as such a substratum. Unlike the individual human being which is already value-laden as soon as it acquires a human form, there are no God-given groups. The association of different individuals in a group *constitutes* the moral entity. It is not an addition to an already existent substratum. Pufendorf was aware of that problem. In fact, Pufendorf himself complains about the 'paucity of vocabulary'.[9] We cannot avoid the impression that he struggles to express insights that were relatively new at the time he wrote.[10]

Despite the poor vocabulary, Pufendorf makes clear that we should conceive of these 'composite moral persons' as leading a life of their own. They are not to be viewed as a simple aggregate of individuals and their rights. Instead, these collective bodies may

> [...] obtain some special privileges and rights, which individuals as such in that body cannot claim or secure for themselves.[11]

As we shall see further on, this view of composite persons lies at the basis of his concept of the social contract. The power of the sovereign, instituted by the contract, should not be regarded as the *sum* of natural rights, as Grotius and also Locke maintain. It is not even regarded as the sum of individual *moral* rights, imposed by God. Pufendorf's theory of imposition leads him to the view that these

---

[9] JNG I, I, 11.

[10] Although Pufendorf's views seem to be inspired by Althusius, who also conceived of man as assuming different roles being a member of various communities and associations at the same time. Cf. Kossmann, 1987b, p. 108.

[11] JNG I, I, 13.

rights are created (or more precisely: 'imposed' by human imposition) as a *result* of that union.

2. *The state of nature*

According to Pufendorf, the whole social world in which we live can be regarded as the result of human imposition of moral entities. Man is conceived of as being able to play different roles in different situations and contexts, which are themselves the product of human imposition as well. In short, the whole social fabric is an artefact. In this sense Pufendorf is more radical than Hobbes, who only viewed the establishment of sovereign authority and the moral distinctions that are derived from its laws as a product of man's artifice.

This extension of man's artifice from politics to human culture as a whole can be said to be responsible for the curious concept of state of nature that Pufendorf uses. At first sight it seems as if he adopts the Hobbesian and abstract version of that concept, which serves as an analytical tool to justify public authority by pointing out its function in human society. Pufendorf is clearly attracted by the scientific ambitions of Hobbes's theory. In the very beginning of his essay *De Statu Hominum Naturali* (SHN),[12] he writes:

> Those who busily investigate the make-up of natural bodies do not consider it sufficient to inspect only the external appearances that immediately meet the eye at a first glance; rather, they also make extraordinary efforts to probe those bodies more deeply and to analyze them into their component parts.[13]

But *what* does Pufendorf want to investigate precisely? Not only the institution of the sovereign. He wants to unravel the rationality of all human artefacts. Pufendorf's state of nature therefore not only serves to abstract from civil authority, but from *all* human impositions, i.e. from culture as such. This, however, leads him to a version of the state of nature that is much closer to Grotius's account of primitive society than to Hobbes's fiction.

---

[12] Pufendorf, 1678.
[13] SHN 1.

Grotius had used the state of nature, not as an abstract analytical tool, but as a realistic concept, as primitive society, a state in which all conveniences and luxuries are lacking. His historical description of the state of nature served two goals. In the first place it had to explain the development towards a more refined mode of life. In the second place it served as a lesson: the state of nature served to gauge the immense advantages of civilised society as a state in which commerce can flourish and luxury becomes available.

In a curious blend of the two concepts, Pufendorf does all he can to depict the state of nature as realistically as possible. How did the first human beings come into existence? As children or as fully-grown men? And if the former, how could they have survived without arts or skills, if not 'some brute animal miraculously offered them its breasts'?[14] And if the latter, can it be that they invented all these arts and skills by themselves? How is it possible that man started to clothe himself, if we see that immediately after the Fall they only 'wove aprons for themselves out of fig-leaves'? Surely God must have taught them these things![15]

But even where he confines his account to the Hobbesian fiction of a state without any civil law, he cannot restrain himself from giving descriptions that are meant as historical explanations and not as a starting-point for a political analysis in the sense of Hobbes. Pufendorf immediately remarks that a state of nature where 'everyone is taken to be entirely his own master and free from any other's authority'[16] is a 'conceptual fiction'. Of course, Hobbes had designed it as such, but Pufendorf points out that man never had 'a right to everything' because he has always been bound by a Creator. Besides, men had always lived in families.[17] A 'real' state of nature therefore can emerge 'only when humans started multiplying into different families separated from one another'.[18]

Time and again we see that Pufendorf reverts to the idiom of a descriptive sociologist or historian, thereby hampering the scientific task he had set himself, in which the state of nature figures only as an analytical tool. The history he tells us is a history of ongoing

---

[14] SHN 4.

[15] SHN 5.

[16] SHN 7.

[17] Inconsistently, Pufendorf refers here to the family as a natural unit and not as an artificial 'composite moral person' as he had done in JNG I, I, 13.

[18] SHN 7.

civilisation; of increasing complexity, of a development towards luxury, commerce, and refined manners.[19] At the same time, however, he adds moralistic lessons to his accounts. Whether he abstracts from all human imposition or from civil society alone, he never fails to point out how much in fact we owe to God and how much we owe to each other. The historical descriptions exhort us to fulfil God's commands and to be sociable. The two aspects of Pufendorf's 'natural law' can readily be perceived in the mixture of sociology and moral theory that is provided by Pufendorf's history of civilisation.

3. *Reverse engineering*

However, Pufendorf's accounts of the state of nature cannot only be regarded as an uneasy reconciliation of Grotius and Hobbes. There is more to it than that. In order to appreciate the status of his rather naive histories of civilisation, we should realise once more the important differences between Grotius and Hobbes on the one hand and Pufendorf on the other.

Both Grotius and Hobbes had argued on the basis of the right to self-preservation, and they combined this right with the ability of men to calculate their proper interests. They were able to regard the contract as the logical outcome of the two features. Although we see that Grotius dwells on primitive society in order to congratulate ourselves in having escaped that unhappy state, these descriptions do not really form a vital element of his political theory as a justification of the state. He could have dispensed with them. The justification of the state can be sought in enlightened self-interest alone.

Pufendorf, however, faces an enormous problem when it comes to justifying human arrangements. His starting-point is not a natural right, but divine imposition. This implies that he cannot conceive of society as an organised regulation of right-claims. In order to be justified, human imposition should *match* with God's imposition.

The question that immediately arises at this stage is how we can be sure that these human arrangements are indeed in conformity with the divine imposition. The easiest way out would be to argue that our intelligence, imposed as it is by God, cannot fail to imitate God

---

[19] Cf. Hont, 1987. Hont points to the influence of Pufendorf's (and Grotius's) accounts on the theory of Adam Smith.

because there is a necessary harmony between God's imposition and ours. In fact, this is the solution offered by Aquinas, who maintained that we can reasonably expect that the human translations and *determinationes* of the general precepts of natural law somehow accord with God's intentions, since we can grasp the divine style by means of *synderesis*.

As we have seen in the preceding chapter, that option was not accessible to Pufendorf. In his blend of Lutheranism and scepticism, there is no room for the notion that man's rationality is capable of grasping the divine style. He cannot even maintain the more modest claim, put forward by Grotius, that man can discover his 'true' interest by means of instrumental rationality. Man's desires, passions and needs should be ordered from without. And indeed, we have seen that he thought of natural law as *taming* man's natural inclinations, not as realising or agreeing with them.

The dilemma he faces is that, on the one hand, he should maintain that human imposition can truly order our lives and passions in a way that is congruent with divine imposition and that for that reason we should comply with our self-imposed rules. On the other hand, he has no proper basis for the claim that human imposition can live up to that ideal. The argument from man's wicked and passionate nature would lead him to the claim that the social world we live in fails to comply with God's precepts to sociability.

So in some way or another he has to argue that although we are in a corrupted state and although we have no direct access to the will of God, there is after all *some* rationality in the way we order the world we live in and that we should therefore comply with its rules. Although he no longer shares the view that man can translate God's requirements, he has nevertheless to find a way by means of which human arrangements can be justified.

In this sense Pufendorf's task is similar to that faced by modern biologists, who no longer believe that nature is designed, but that it should be regarded as the outcome of a process of blind variation. Like Pufendorf's human agents, genes cannot be regarded as endowed with rationality. Like Pufendorf, post-Darwinian biologists can no longer believe that God put His rationality *within* nature (and unlike Pufendorf, they even have to dispense with the notion that nature can be ordered from without). And yet, serious biologists are confronted with problems like how did eyes evolve? Or, why did paradise-birds evolve these beautiful but clumsy tails? Biologists are supposed to make sense of natural evolution, in the same way as Pufendorf had to make sense of cultural evolution, without the prior assumption of rational agents.

Biologists usually proceed by the assumption of functionality, which underlies the method of so-called 'reverse engineering', so labelled by the contemporary philosopher of biology Daniel Dennett. In order to unravel the functionality of organisms, they are analysed as if they were artefacts. According to Dennett, the biologist proceeds in the same way as an engineer:

> When Raytheon wants to make an electronic widget to compete with General Electric's widget, they buy several of GE's widgets and proceed to analyze them: that's reverse engineering. They run them, benchmark them, X-ray them, take them apart, and subject every part of them to interpretive analysis: Why did GE make these wires so heavy? What are these extra ROM-registers for? Is this a double layer of insulation, and, if so, why did they bother with it? Notice that the reigning assumption is that all these 'why' questions have answers. Everything has a *raison d'être*. GE did nothing in vain.[20]

It should be noted that the assumption of the 'raison d'être' is *not* to assume that engineers are never stupid. But without the assumption that 'there is a good rationale for the features they observe, they cannot even begin their analysis'.[21] The same applies to natural evolution. Without the assumption of functionality we cannot make sense of evolution.

What applies to engineering and modern biology also applies to Pufendorf's attempt to make sense of human imposition. In order to understand the sociological make-up of society, we should assume that there is a good rationale for the features of society. This assumption does not rest on the concept of man as a rational being, but only on the idea that man's products can be *reconstructed* as having a raison d'être. The only difference between Pufendorf and modern biologists is that Pufendorf not only needs to show that there is *a* functional order in human society, but also that this order matches God's imposition, i.e. that this order is a rational and just order. He should not merely unravel the rationale of society, but also its rationality.

---

[20] Dennett, 1995, p. 212.
[21] Dennett, 1995, p. 213.

I think that Pufendorf's analysis of human society and its laws should be viewed in this light. It was his main object to *reconstruct* human arrangements as rational. This is clearly revealed by a passage in the JNG which immediately follows after his dismissal of the idea that moral ideas are innate. There he writes that although moral ideas are not innate but culturally acquired, this does not imply that man's activities cannot be reconstructed as moral and rational:

> It is no objection to our theory that most men do not know or under-
> stand the method whereby the commands of the law of nature are
> demonstrated, and that the majority of them usually learn this law and
> observe it as a matter of training or by following the general example
> of society; for we also daily see workmen do many things by imitation,
> or with tools whose method of use they cannot demonstrate, and yet
> such operations can nevertheless be called mathematical and based upon
> good reason.[22]

If we view Pufendorf's statements on the state of nature in this light, we can understand more fully why he was so concerned to give a realistic account of the beginning of society, rather than using it in the Hobbesian way as a thought-experiment. Like the engineer and the biologist, Pufendorf is concerned to form an adequate picture of the very make-up of the social fabric. How did man cope with a harsh climate? When and why was agriculture invented? When did people start to use iron? Why did people introduce ownership?

These questions can indeed only arise on the basis of the assump-tion that the *explanandum* is regarded as an artefact, as Dennett writes. This is nicely expressed by Pufendorf himself, where he criticises the notion that the development of states is a natural one:

> But to try to exclude the causes working throughout this natural devel-
> opment, and the pacts of men regarding the establishment of states, is
> as if one would say that a tree grows from a seed, from the tree are
> made planks and timbers, these properly brought together make a ship;
> therefore, a ship is made by natural development [...].[23]

But reverse engineering not only requires the assumption of artificiality; it also starts from the supposition that the artefacts outdo

---

[22] JNG II, III, 13.
[23] JNG VII, I, 5.

their artificers. The spider's web is much more ingenious than the spider itself. Pufendorf's sceptical view of mankind requires the assumption that man's products are more rational and more social than man's nature. Artefacts can transcend the inclinations of the artificers.

This assumption is, I think, responsible for Pufendorf's awareness of the importance of unintended consequences. It is in Hume that we encounter a fully developed theory of unintended consequences, but Pufendorf already hinted at the fact that society cannot be understood as only the result of man's deliberate intentions and motives. He has no difficulty in avowing that the first and foremost urge to live in society was not the urge for society, but the necessity of self-preservation. But, he goes on to argue,

> [...] after men had been brought into order by means of states, and so could be safe from injuries from each other, the natural consequence followed of a richer enjoyment of the benefits which tend to come to man from his fellows [...].[24]

He hints here at the fact that society, once instituted, acquires a dynamic quality of its own.[25] Society was originally established for selfish motives, but *once it was there*, it turned out that it generated other advantages as well. At that stage of human development, society is appreciated for its own sake. Although Pufendorf does not elaborate on the theme, we might even say that it is by means of a *List der Vernunft* (cunning of Reason), that human impositions contribute to a realisation of God's wishes, despite the fact that its artificers are weak, wicked and only endowed with limited rationality. The justification of human laws and rules is grounded in that—unintended—conformity with God's law.[26]

---

[24] DOH II, 5, 7.
[25] Cf. also JNG VII, I, 7.
[26] The claim that Hume's theory of justice as an unintended consequence is 'one of the boldest moves in the history of the philosophy of law' can therefore be attenuated. Pufendorf paved the way for this view. Cf. Haakonssen, 1981, pp. 19-21.

4. *Agreements*

The hope to find such a cunning of reason forms the most important difference between Pufendorf's enterprise and that of modern biologists. To him reverse engineering is not merely a scientific method, but the only possible method in order to *justify* human arrangements as rational and just.[27]

This underlying justificatory aim is responsible for the important role that Pufendorf assigns to agreements (*pacta*) as the basis for human institutions. Like Suárez and Grotius before him, Pufendorf thinks that most of the natural precepts are only applicable to a state of affairs introduced by men. He calls these precepts 'hypothetical', because they suppose a human framework in which they acquire their validity. As such they are distinguished from 'absolute' precepts, which are operative regardless of institutions.

This distinction echoes the well-known distinction drawn by Suárez between 'preceptive natural law' and 'natural law concerning *dominium*'. We saw in chapter V, that Grotius discarded the former from the realm of natural law and identified it with 'divine law', whereas he reserved the term natural law for natural law on *dominium* only. Here again, Pufendorf returns to Suárez's option. Once more the absolute precepts that can be found in the Decalogue, form part and parcel of natural law. This move is consistent, since we have seen that Pufendorf does not distinguish natural law from positive divine law. Both are erected on the basis of God's imposed law.

But the 'absolute' precepts of Pufendorf play a much more vital role than in Suárez's account. In fact, what we see is that preceptive law is combined with a theory of rights. Not as the natural rights that figured in Grotius's theory, but as moral rights, imposed on us by God. Absolute precepts and their corresponding duties arise on the basis of that inborn 'moral' right of human beings *as human beings*. They urge us to be sociable and to treat others as equals. Hypothetical duties, on the other hand, can be defined as the duties of men *in the various roles* society has assigned to them. The title of the DOH (On the Duty of Man *and* Citizen) refers to this combination of absolute and hypothetical duties. This implies that absolute duties, correspon-

---

[27] Interpreters who regard 17th century natural law theory as the starting-point for a science of human conduct generally overlook that ultimate aim. Cf. e.g. Tuck, 1993.

ding to the moral rights God endowed us with, can gain a critical importance that had been absent in Suárez's theory.

This enables us to understand why Pufendorf's account of consent is more critical than the account offered by Grotius. The function of agreements is, in terms of Pufendorf, that they serve as

> [...] a kind of bridge between the absolute and the hypothetical duties.[28]

Agreements are at the basis, not only of the state, but of all human institutions. The 'three most important human institutions upon which hypothetical precepts rest are speech, the possession of things, and human sovereignty'.[29]

In chapter VI, I argued that to Grotius these agreements formed the sole thread that links positive municipal law to natural law. On the basis of natural law it was not possible to decide which kind of government deserves our consent. Pufendorf does not agree with that view. He does not want to confine the scope of natural law to the injunction to fulfil promises only. In an extended criticism of Hobbes 'who appears to recognise but a single uniform justice which is nothing else but the keeping of faith and carrying out agreements', Pufendorf argues that agreements and pacts *themselves* should be subjected to a critical evaluation:

> [...] the statement that all justice can be resolved into performance of agreements, is so far from true, that, on the contrary, before it can be known whether an agreement should be carried out, one ought to make sure that the agreement was entered into at the command, or at least with the permission, of natural laws.[30]

Agreements are not binding because they are once entered into, as Grotius had held. Their mere existence is not sufficient ground for their validity. Agreements are only binding if they are entered into under conditions that turn them into valid agreements.

Consequently, in the DOH, Pufendorf devotes much attention to the conditions under which contracts or agreements are entered into. In order to make these agreements valid, the consenting party needs

---

[28] DOH I, 9, 1.
[29] DOH I, 9, 22.
[30] JNG I, VII, 13.

to understand 'whether the transaction in question suits him',[31] should have the required knowledge,[32] should not be subjected to fraud or wilful deceit,[33] should be capable of performing them,[34] and last but not least, the agreement should not be 'made on an immoral matter'.[35]

In chapter VI, I noted that Grotius had also provided criteria for the validity of contracts, but that these did not recur in his treatment of the social contract, which was conceived as an implied and tacit agreement. A similar and even greater difficulty can be found in Pufendorf, who also conceives of the origins of private property and even of speech as human institutions. He regards these as gradual developments, for which, of course, no explicit consent has been given. Here, like in Grotius's account, we see how a realistic description of the origins of these institutions is at odds with the justificatory ambitions of the notion of contract.

Nevertheless, unlike Grotius, Pufendorf links the above-mentioned stipulations concerning the validity of contracts to the kind of agreements that are at the basis of the major social institutions. He explicitly refers to these agreements as being only valid under the required conditions. How then does he reconcile these requirements with his realistic descriptions of the establishment of human institutions? The gradual development of culture seems to exclude the notion of an agreement between the rational, knowing, autonomous partners Pufendorf has in mind.

The answer should again be found in Pufendorf's main concern, which consists in justifying human institutions by arguing that they can be *reconstructed* as rational and legitimate phenomena. Although they can be regarded as the outcome of a contingent and gradual process, set in motion by agents which are not endowed with particular rationality or foresight, they can nevertheless be conceived of as valid contracts by means of rational reconstruction.

It is this emphasis on the *post hoc* reconstruction of rationality that enables Pufendorf to widen the scope of natural law. The influence of natural law (or more precisely: God's imposed law) is no longer limited to the precept that promises should be fulfilled. The terms of the

---

[31] DOH I, 9, 10.
[32] DOH I, 9, 12.
[33] DOH I, 9, 13.
[34] DOH I, 9, 17.
[35] DOH I, 9, 18.

contracts and agreements that lie at the basis of our institutions can be criticised by reference to the absolute duties, corresponding to the moral rights granted to us by God Himself. As soon as it transpires that these agreements require us to behave immorally or to inflict any harm on another, in short, if they require us to violate the rights God endowed us with, we are no longer bound by them.

5. *The social contract*

The implications of these views are shown by Pufendorf's conception of the contract that lies at the basis of the establishment of states. Here, Pufendorf unequivocally breaks with descriptive sociology and history. His analysis of the contract is not historical, but conceptual. His treatment of the social contract investigates the conditions that are required in order to turn such an agreement into a source for legitimate civil authority.

The starting-point for his analysis is the notion that collective bodies or 'composite moral entities' are the product of human imposition. Groups and nations are not merely aggregates of physical individuals. The association of individuals may be the result of an agreement which can be regarded as natural, but it creates a new entity which is not natural and transcends the intentions of the individuals. That is why Pufendorf introduces an analytical, three-staged model, which in fact comprises two contracts and a majority-decision.

The first stage consists of the association between individuals, who enter into agreement with *one another*. These individuals

> [...] are desirous of entering into a single and perpetual group, and of administrating the considerations of their safety and security by common council and leadership.[36]

This contract, which resembles Rousseau's notion of the social contract, turns a mere 'multitude' of men into a real unity. In an apparent effort to preserve some room for manoeuvre for the individual, Pufendorf allows for the possibility that one may enter such contract 'conditionally'. The allegiance of these conditional members depends on the kind of government that is chosen, whereas those who

---

[36] JNG VII, II, 7.

united 'unconditionally', are also unconditionally bound by that government.

The choice of a particular form of a government is the second stage of the contract. Pufendorf conceives of that choice as a decision by the majority of the union. This is remarkable in view of Pufendorf's idea that a single collective body should not be regarded as a sum-total of individuals. On these grounds one might have expected an early formulation of the concept of a 'general will' as being superior to individual preferences. However, both the possibility of a majority-decision and the fact that the conditional members are absolved from the duty of loyalty if the chosen type of government does not match their preferences indicate that in Pufendorf's theory society is less absorbing than in Rousseau's theory.

Finally, the third stage consists of the contract which

> will be necessary when the individual or body is constituted that receives the government of the group, by which pact the rulers bind themselves to the care of the common security and safety, and the rest to render them obedience [...].[37]

It seems that Pufendorf's complex account of the social contract ingeniously combines the contracts that were later to be designed by Rousseau and Locke: the first contract links individuals together; the second consists in a contract between the ruled and the ruler.

This complexity has contributed to the debate whether, and to what extent, Pufendorf allows for a right of resistance. There are many passages to be found where Pufendorf criticises any attempt to diminish, weaken or destroy civil sovereignty[38] and warns that these might lead to a return to the state of nature.[39] On the other hand, his three-staged model allows for some scope for dissent. Seidler argues that the first stage 'gives them a certain independence and leverage, both conceptual and real, which offsets the absolute authority of the sovereign'.[40] Pufendorf himself, however, clearly thought that his introduction not of the first, but of the third stage would allow for

---

[37] JNG VII, II, 8.

[38] E.g. JNG VII, VIII, 1.

[39] Cf. Wyduckel, 1996. Wyduckel interprets Pufendorf's theory as a moderate form of absolutism, partly on the basis of Pufendorf's use of the term 'decree' in the description of the second stage of the contract.

[40] Cf. Seidler, 1996, p. 91.

that 'independence'. Pufendorf explicitly introduces the contract between sovereign and subjects in order to avoid Hobbesian absolutism[41] and to guarantee that the king is also bound by the contract.

I tend to think that, although Pufendorf shared the concerns of Bodin and Hobbes and feared the consequences of a weak sovereignty, his version of the social contract can hardly be used as a defence of downright absolutism. Such an interpretation would be difficult to fit in with his claim that human imposition should be in conformity with divine imposition. Right in the beginning of his chapter on the creation of civil sovereignty, Pufendorf asserts that states and supreme sovereignty 'came from God as the author of natural law'.[42] This does not lead to a 'divine right of kings',[43] but it does put some important constraints upon the ruler:

> For a king cannot lawfully command anything more than agrees, or is supposed to agree, with the end of instituted civil society.[44]

King and subjects are bound by a mutual agreement that is only lawful when it can be reconstructed as conforming to the overall-plan of God's imposed law. If Pufendorf did not draw the consequences of this view himself,[45] the least we can say is that his *theory* allows for much more dissent than the rival theories of both Grotius and Hobbes.[46]

6. *The lack of a* ius gentium

So far I have analysed Pufendorf's theory concerning positive law as an attempt to reconstruct, along rational principles, the whole of the social fabric as the outcome of human imposition. In this sense we

---

[41] JNG VII, II, 9-10.

[42] JNG VII, III, 2.

[43] Cf. Seidler, 1996, pp. 88-9.

[44] JNG VII, II, 11.

[45] Presumably, he did. Seidler, 1996, points to Pufendorf's defence of the Glorious Revolution of 1688, in his essay *De rebus gestis Friderici Tertii, Electoris Brandenburgici, post Primi Borussiae Regis Commentariorum Libri Tres, complectentes annos 1688-1690*.

[46] It is significant that the Dutch editor and commentator of Grotius, Willem vander Muelen (1659-1739), combined his enthusiasm for Pufendorf's theory with a fervour for the Glorious Revolution. Cf. Kossmann, 1960, pp. 70-2.

might say that although Pufendorf has no place for a genuine natural law as 'natural', i.e. derived from nature, he nevertheless tries to reconstruct positive law as *rational*.

But there is one important area that is not treated in this way. In fact, it is hardly covered at all. And that is the field of international relations. This is surprising in view of the fact that Pufendorf occupied a chair in natural law *and* international law. Is it possible that he demolished the former and paid virtually no attention to the latter? Indeed, it is. According to Pufendorf, there is no body of law pertaining to the relations between states. There is no room for an independent *ius gentium*. International relations can either be regulated directly by natural law (i.e. God's imposed law), or they can be regulated according to customs, but since these are variable and contingent, they form a very insecure basis for international law.[47]

Why then did Pufendorf not develop a *ius gentium*? Where an independent body of law is lacking, there would seem to be all the more reason to try to justify or criticise wars or pacts on the basis of natural law. What else is the function of natural law? In fact, this is what Grotius did. Instead, we see that Pufendorf devotes very little attention to international affairs. Of the 1367 pages of the JNG, only 56 pages deal with the relations between states.

Tully explains this scarcity by pointing to the changes in the political situation. The peace of Westphalia had achieved a political stability that could not even be dreamt of by Grotius, who wrote during the Thirty Years War.[48] The result is that Pufendorf devotes much more attention to how individuals should live together as citizens than to international affairs.

Apart from these considerations, I think that his lack of enthusiasm for the development of international law testifies to a more fundamental difference with Grotius. I noted in VII.3 that Pufendorf, unlike Grotius, thought of law as an overall-framework. It is only on the *basis* of such a law that rights and duties can be derived, these are not conceived to exist prior to law. So whereas Grotius used these natural rights as a *starting-point* for the development of (international) law, Pufendorf conceives of rights and duties as the *result* of law. It is only within an overall system of law that it is possible to speak of rights and duties. At the root of this point of view is his theory that

---

[47] JNG II, III, 23.
[48] Tully, in his introduction to the DOH, pp. xix and xx.

moral distinctions are meaningless in the absence of law and only acquire any sense within an overall normative framework.

The idea that rights and duties can only arise on the basis of God's imposed law is quite troublesome for an international lawyer. For the problem with the rights and duties that are derived from God's imposition is that these rights are granted by God, and consequently, that the corresponding duties are equally regarded as primarily duties towards God, not towards other states. In line with his dismissal of 'natural rights', Pufendorf also attacks the idea, forwarded by both Grotius and Hobbes, that there is a natural right to punish. This right belongs exclusively to a superior. Since the only superior on the international scene is God, God alone has the right to punish.[49] Rights are not mutually enforceable by the rights-holder themselves. Obviously, this assumption makes it rather hard to make sense of any effective system of international law.

Pufendorf's omission to develop a *ius gentium* can therefore directly be traced to his conception of law as a legal framework consisting of a set of decrees issued by a sovereign and addressed to a collective body of citizens. It is only within that overall framework that people can assume their roles and their corresponding duties.[50]

Where there is no such sovereign (except for God) and where a collective body of subjects is absent, as is the case on the international level, Pufendorf does not see how he might develop such a legal framework. His dismissal of a concept of natural rights existing prior to law, leaves him empty-handed when it comes to a theory of international law. In terms of Pufendorf's own metaphor: he can only understand how a ship is built, (and see that it is right), but he is not able to build it all by himself.

In this sense we might say that Pufendorf's failure to be a professor of the law of nations is linked with his failure to develop a law of nature. A comparison with Aquinas is instructive here. As I argued in chapter II, Aquinas's principles of natural law have two functions. They serve as a justification or critical assessment of existing positive law, but they equally serve as a heuristical device in developing

---

[49] And that is why Pufendorf regards punishment as justified only in those cases where the punishable action can be regarded as a violation of the *law*. See Hartung, 1996.

[50] This, however, does not imply that Pufendorf could only conceive of rights as correlative to duties. For an elaborate account of Pufendorf's concept of rights, see Mautner, 1991.

positive law. The laws of the *ius gentium* were even regarded as the outcome of deduction from the general principles of natural law. Aquinas conceived the development of positive law as a more or less correct process of translation of the general precepts. But in Pufendorf's theory there *is* nothing to translate. The problem with a natural law that is imposed by God is that it is in fact inaccessible to human reason. And if the original text is inaccessible, it is not possible to translate. The option that logically follows from these assumptions is the one indeed chosen by Pufendorf: positive law results entirely from man's artifice. The scope of natural law as imposed by God is merely to justify these artefacts *post hoc*. Obviously, also this more modest task is hard to carry out if we lack the required knowledge of God's imposed law.

7. Conclusion

The conclusion seems to be justified that Pufendorf's theory marks the end of natural law theory, if we understand that theory as being supported by the four fundamental assumptions I outlined in the introduction to this book. As I argued in the preceding chapter, Pufendorf did not think that (assumption b) there are eternal moral criteria and principles grounded in nature. He emphatically discards the idea that nature, in whatever sense of the term, is or can give rise to a normative order. He equally denies the possibility for human beings to discover those principles by means of reason. All we can know is that man's nature needs to be governed by some sort of law. What that law is is promulgated by God, but is no subject for rational inquiry independent of that promulgation. Natural law and divine law are ontologically identical. This means that we can only judge or criticise positive law by means of that God-ordained law.

Surprisingly, this does not affect the critical potential of Pufendorf's theory. It is true that his principles are not derived from nature, but from God, but these principles are nevertheless important for our assessment of positive law. They derive that importance from the notion of rights. These rights pertain to mankind as a whole. 'Mankind' is not conceived as a natural species, but as a species which, as the only one in this universe, is endowed with a *moral* right. These moral rights flow from God's imposed law. The reason for the precept not to injure each other, Pufendorf writes, is not because it is to man's advantage, but 'because the other person also is a man'.[51] As we have seen, Pufendorf's evaluation of positive law, as well as the social contract that forms the basis of positive law is consistently informed by this notion of moral rights and the corresponding so-called 'absolute' duties. Here again, we see that the notion of rights (even if they are seen as *granted* by God) proves to be an important source for critical assessment. As a result, we might say that it has not only been Pufendorf's view that (assumption a) positive law should be justified/criticised in terms of moral rights, but also (assumption d) that we are only obliged to obey if positive law does not conflict with our moral rights.

In this sense, Pufendorf's natural law theory reveals a paradoxical outcome. Whereas the full-blown natural law theories of his predecessors are marked by a disappointing lack of critical potential, Pufendorf's dismissal of *natural* law allows him nevertheless to broaden the scope of eternal justificatory principles. However, we should keep in mind that he can only do so by stressing (moral) rights, not the body of divine law from which they are derived. Of course, this solution is vulnerable. God's law remains impenetrable to the human mind. The existence of human moral rights is made completely dependent upon the notion of God's law, into which we only have insight by means of His promulgated word.

However, we do not do justice to Pufendorf by measuring his merits according to the yardstick of natural law theory. Rather than assessing Pufendorf's relation to preceding natural lawyers, his significance should be estimated by focusing on the new theories that could be erected on the foundations he laid. In order to assess that contribution, I should refer to the conclusion I arrived at in the preceding chapter. There I concluded that Pufendorf's programme had disintegrated into a 'naturalist' part, analysing (human) nature in observational terms, and a 'moralist' part that tries to derive positive laws and norms from God's imposed law.

In this chapter we have seen how Pufendorf implements this two-fold programme. The emphasis on man's natural abilities and his powers to impose moral entities induced him to consider the steps in human civilisation in a way that is clearly meant to be as realistic as possible. Pufendorf's description of cultural developments reveals a genuine interest in social sciences, something which had been lacking

---

[51] JNG II, III, 18.

in Grotius, who had used these data mainly as an instrument in order to praise the conveniences of modern life.

On the other hand, Pufendorf does not write sociology for its own sake. He wants to discover some degree of rationality in order to justify the claim that we should comply with man-made rules. 'Natural law', in the sense of God's imposed law and God's granted moral rights, is used as a standard by means of which this rationality can be assessed.

Both these programmes are reconciled by the quite ingenious idea that cultural development can be understood as a set of unintended consequences with a dynamic of its own, which turns out to be more or less in harmony with God's law. It is this idea that induces Pufendorf to speak of 'natural law' as being completely different from 'divine positive law' and to his assertion that theology has nothing to do with natural jurisprudence. These statements do not refer to the different ontological status of both types of law. I argued in VII.6 that both rest on the same foundations. But the term 'natural law' in Pufendorf's work refers to the project of what I called reverse engineering: it refers to the attempt to reconstruct human artifice as being in conformity with God's law. And that task, indeed, has nothing to do with theology.

The reconciliation of the two tasks he had set himself indeed turns Pufendorf into a 'mediator'. But he does not merely reconcile Hobbes and Grotius, as it is commonly held.[52] He does not only mediate between his forerunners. On the contrary, he mediates between his successors!

The 'sociological' part, the attempt to establish a science of human conduct, was later to be developed more fully by Hume and Adam Smith. They focused, much more than Pufendorf had done, on the divergence between original motives leading to the establishment of society and the way society is sustained over time. Their main aim was to *explain* society and to understand why people actually *do* follow its rules, not whether they should do so.[53]

The 'rationalist' part of Pufendorf's enterprise, which seeks to develop criteria for a rational *justification* of human institutions, was to be the starting-point for Kant's deontological ethics with its emphasis on rational standards for legitimation and on the world of *Sollen* as

---

[52] See the references in my introduction to the preceding chapter.
[53] See Westerman, 1994.

a world of liberty, responsibility and moral autonomy of human beings.

I therefore prefer to regard Pufendorf's theory as the last attempt to provide for a theory in which an *explanation* of social phenomena and a *justification* of these phenomena in the light of universal principles are tied together within one comprehensive theoretical framework. After Pufendorf, two separate branches could develop which had nothing in common with natural law theory, but which shaped the intellectual world we now inhabit more thoroughly than any natural law theory that had preceded it.

PART III

CHAPTER IX

FINNIS'S NATURAL LAW WITHOUT NATURE[1]

The big leap from Pufendorf to the twentieth century does not imply that the intermediate centuries did not produce any natural law theory worth mentioning. On the contrary, seventeenth-century natural law theory was the starting-point for an enormous number of theoretical and political innovations.

The most important development, without which it is impossible to conceive of modern politics at all, is the development of theories of human rights. To say that the Grotian heritage of natural law as the sum-total of natural rights proved fertile is an understatement. Hobbesian and Lockean versions of this heritage were re-shaped and modified, implemented and exported to the world at large. Today, rights-talk has become the dominant way of discussing moral and political issues. In VI.8 on Grotius, I indicated a possible—theoretical—explanation of this success. If one conceives of rights as prior to law and if one regards law as a set of obligations corresponding to natural rights, it is easier to deal with what I called the problems of translation and of obligation.

Apart from political and social factors, these theoretical advantages may have contributed to the fact that in the 18th and 19th centuries natural law theory flourished in the form of rights theories. What is more: it was the only form in which natural law theory survived. This may sound as a very bold statement. Textbooks on natural law generally extend the meaning of the term 'natural law'. We are used to label Kant's moral and legal philosophy as a rationalist variety of natural law. D'Entrèves calls him 'the most forceful exponent of natural law in modern days'.[2] The thinkers belonging to the Scottish Enlightenment (notably David Hume and Adam Smith) are also said to have developed natural law theories.[3]

---

[1] See Weinreb, 1987, title of ch. IV.

[2] D'Entrèves, 1951, p. 110.

[3] Haakonssen, 1996; Forbes, 1975; Haakonssen, 1981; Buckle, 1991.

I think that these extensions of the number of natural lawyers rest on an inflatory use of the term 'natural law'. Either it is understood as an attempt to provide for eternal or universal principles, whether these are derived from nature or not, or it is conceived as an umbrella-term for all attempts to link morality with nature, no matter how the connection is established. For the sake of clarity, however, it seems to me advisable to reserve the title of natural law for those theories that set out to discover eternal criteria and principles, that are grounded in physical or human nature, discoverable by reason and that can serve as standards by means of which positive law can be justified and/or criticised (see my initial definition of natural law in the introduction).

On the basis of that definition we can see that although Kantian deontology as well as the Scottish philosophers can be regarded as branches of the tree of natural law theory, these are branches that decidedly grew their own way. The differences between these theoretical programmes reveal the deep chasm that already surfaced in Pufendorf's work. My thesis is that neither Kant nor Hume tried to provide for a unified and normative theory on the basis of (human) nature and therefore cannot be properly said to belong to the tradition of natural law.

As I argued elsewhere,[4] Hume did indeed take human nature as a starting-point, but not in order to justify man's conventions, but in order to explain them. He indeed acknowledges that man cherishes some universal principles beyond apparently conflicting moral views, but instead of using these principles as normative criteria for our moral judgements, he takes them as principles underlying these judgements. He does not tell us that sympathy with utility *ought* to guide our moral judgements, but that it always *is* at the bottom of our moral distinctions. And that is how he explains both the origins of our conventions as well as the motivation for people to follow rules. Despite the great similarities in vocabulary, Hume's enterprise is not that of a natural lawyer, if we restrict the meaning of the term of natural law theory to attempts to derive and justify moral principles from nature.

As for Kant, of course he does attempt to discover justifying principles. But at the same time he extended the gap between 'is' and 'ought', between *Sein* and *Sollen*, by claiming that they are not only

---

[4] Westerman, 1994.

logically, but also ontologically distinct. To Kant the empirical world is irrelevant to moral discourse. Unambiguously, Kant contrasts the empirical laws of nature with normative laws that can only be supplied by reason.[5] Inclinations and passions belong to the realm of nature.

According to Kant, these natural inclinations can only give rise to material and subjective aims, which can be achieved by following hypothetical imperatives. Hypothetical imperatives can inform us about how to proceed in order to achieve a subjective goal: if I want to become rich, or successful, or happy, I have to do x or y as the most efficient means to that goal. Hypothetical imperatives comprise prudential and technical rules. They inform us about means, not ends. Kant distinguishes these prudential and technical rules from moral laws such as the categorical imperative that informs us about how to achieve objective ends, which are universally reasonable and intrinsically good. These can only be discovered by pure reason.[6] Since we should regard other people as ends in themselves, not as mere instruments, our dealings with other people should not be guided by prudential considerations,[7] but on moral rules which are objective and universally valid and which can only be found out by reason. Nature plays no part at all in this realm. Kant emphasises that considerations, based on nature, are not only irrelevant, but even harmful to our pure reasoning on moral matters. I think therefore that if we want to take seriously the allusion to nature in the term 'natural law', we should abstain from calling Kant a natural lawyer.

This is not to deny that Kant and Hume can be regarded as successors of Pufendorf. Each developed and innovated one of the two programmes that we saw unfold in Pufendorf's theory (chapter VIII). Hume developed the tendency towards sociology which we detected in Pufendorf's attempts to give a realistic account of the origins of human conventions. He seriously attempted to analyse and explain social institutions as the product of human nature. Kant's theory, on the other hand, can be interpreted as an extension and further development of Pufendorf's theory of imposition. Kant indeed tried to provide for moral standards that can *justify* our institutions and not merely explain them, but unlike Hume he did not rely on man's nat-

---

[5] Kant, 1785, p. 49.
[6] Kant, 1785, p. 50.
[7] Kant, 1785, p. 51.

ural inclinations. 'Nature' is purely 'vernünftige Natur': reasonable
nature. The rational part of human nature is cut loose from the other
features we still saw figuring in Grotius's concept of human nature:
the urge to self-preservation and natural sociability. The works of
Hume and Kant show that the links between nature and reason had
snapped. Neither of them tried to develop one unified theory in which
nature and reason are reconciled and provided with the necessary
obligatory force.

So if we want to speak of natural law in the 18th and 19th centuries, we are forced to confine ourselves to theories of natural rights.
Only those theories tried to develop a political philosophy on the basis
of (human) nature. But here we should also be careful not to overestimate the role of nature. Many rights-theories have been shaped and
coloured by Kantian assumptions. Man's rights are conceived in the
Pufendorfian sense of the word, as rights of moral and rational beings, belonging to them by virtue of being moral and rational. The
fact that contemporary discourse does not refer to natural rights, but
to human rights, testifies to the dominance of Kantian assumptions.

1. *The ambitions of modern natural law theory*

There is, however, a good reason to omit rights-theories from this
book, even those which are devoid of Kantian overtones. They are
not instructive for the attempt of Finnis and Grisez to rehabilitate and
develop a theory of natural *law*, from which rights can be derived.
These modern natural lawyers do not take the existence of rights as a
starting-point for a theory of natural law. Instead, they try to reconstruct natural law as an overall moral framework which serves as a
foundation of rights. They do not regard law as merely a set of
obligations arising from these rights, but as the embodiment of the
common good. It is this ambition which inspires their attempt to
rehabilitate Aquinas's theory.

It is therefore fitting to turn directly to this attempt. In the preceding chapters we have tried to unravel the 'internal logic' that
prompted successive generations of natural law theorists to modify
Aquinas. I argued that the reformulations of natural law theory should
not be regarded as 'mistakes' or 'misinterpretations' but that Suárez,
Grotius and Pufendorf had good theoretical reasons for their particular theory of natural law. The question arises whether Grisez's and
Finnis's own theory of natural law is better suited to deal with these

internal problems. Is it able to circumvent the logical difficulties which confronted the preceding generations of natural lawyers? Or does it succumb to the same persistent problems?

I think we should gain a clear view of these matters, since the contemporary attempt to rebuild natural law theory is in itself an important one, even for those who are not attracted by the Roman Catholic overtones of the theory developed by Finnis and Grisez. This importance is primarily theoretical.

First of all, Finnis's attempt can shed light on the·frequently recurring demand for a foundation of human rights. His attempt to provide for a philosophical framework for our thinking on law and morals is meant to give us insight in the underlying values and principles on the basis of which competing right-claims can be resolved.[8] The success or failure of Finnis's attempt is therefore instructive for the debate whether a foundation of human rights is necessary and/or desirable.

Secondly, since it is Finnis's aim to unravel the underlying values and principles which inform our thinking on rights, his attempt can clarify the question whether, and if so to what extent, it is possible to argue and defend these values on the basis of philosophical argument alone. This has been one of Finnis's main concerns, and for that reason he relegates his discussion on religion and God to the final chapters of both the FE and the NLNR. He tries to articulate common values, independently from a particular religious orientation. His assumption that there are such values and that they have an objective (not only an intersubjective) basis, is at the root of his attempt to develop natural law theory.

Thirdly, related to his assumption concerning common values, is his view that modern society should be regarded as more than merely an aggregate of individuals. His view of human society as a community whose members 'share an aim'[9] is based on the assumption that co-operation should be regarded as more than merely the result of calculated self-interest. Finnis shares this criticism of liberal ideology with many contemporary 'communitarian' philosophers.[10] Most of these writers, however, phrase their criticism by means of the alleged

---

[8] NLNR p. 198.

[9] NLNR p. 152.

[10] For instance, MacIntyre, 1981; Williams, 1985.

contrast between virtue-theories and rights-theories.[11] Finnis's attempt is interesting in the sense that he tries to bridge that contrast and tries to accommodate for rights-theories as well. If this attempt is to succeed, the dead-lock between liberalism and communitarianism might be overcome.

In view of these three ambitions of the new theory of natural law, it is no wonder that it has been welcomed as an interesting innovation of legal and moral theory. The main attraction of Finnis's theory is that it aims at unification: it promises to furnish us with a unified theory of law and morals by means of which modern ethical and legal dilemmas can be reconciled. It remains to be seen now whether it succeeds in bridging the various gaps, or whether it is no more than an attempt to re-plaster underlying fissures.

In the following two chapters, I shall alternately refer to Finnis and Grisez. During Finnis's stay in Berkeley at 1965, he met Grisez, who at the time was engaged in developing a new theoretical framework for the Roman Catholic Church that would be more fit to cope with modern dilemma's than the traditional Thomist outlook. It is Finnis who developed these views and applied them to legal theory. Notwithstanding slight differences that have to do with these different backgrounds, their theoretical framework is the same throughout and can be regarded as a unified whole. The fruitful collaboration in which they engaged also includes Joseph Boyle, a former pupil of Grisez, and Robert P. George, who mainly contributes by explaining and disseminating the views of Finnis and Grisez. That is why we can regard this theory of natural law as a new—and influential—'research-programme'.

My treatment of this new programme will be organised roughly along the same lines as those on previous authors. In this chapter I shall focus on the foundation of contemporary natural law theory. The status and foundation of the basic principles will be explored and the role of nature is further examined. The second chapter will deal with Finnis's analysis of positive law.

---

[11] Cf. Hauerwas, 1981.

2. *A moral methodology*

Throughout the work of both Finnis and Grisez, the new theory of natural law is presented as a theory of practical reasonableness. The main aim of this theory is to provide principles (in the sense of *principia*: 'starting-points') that guide our reasoning on moral matters. Consistent with Grisez's and Finnis's interpretation of Aquinas, these principles should not be seen as general moral *precepts* from which more specific precepts can be derived. Rather, it is their view that we should restore Aquinas's concept of natural law as comprising general principles which serve as *guidelines* for practical deliberation. One of the main reasons for the modern natural lawyers to find fault with Suárez is that he underestimated the importance of these guidelines and reduced them to moral precepts. In my own terms: Finnis and Grisez want to restore the concept of natural law-as-style. This style of reasoning should enable us to deliberate on moral issues in both individual and collective affairs.

Finnis furnishes us with two ingredients for such a theory of natural law as practical reasonableness. The *first* ingredient consists of so-called 'basic goods' or basic forms of human flourishing'.[12] Finnis lists seven of such basic goods: life, knowledge, play, aesthetic experience, sociability or friendship, practical reasonableness and religion.[13] The idea is simply this: in reasoning about moral affairs, one has to orient oneself about the goods worth pursuing. In this sense, the basic goods can be compared to the quarters of the compass.[14] They are primary orientations, without which it is impossible to reason at all.

Although one can conceive of the seven basic goods as necessary conditions for any moral reasoning, they are not sufficient ones. Taken by themselves, they cannot guarantee that we arrive at sound conclusions about courses of action. This is because they do not serve as moral precepts. It would be a mistake to ascribe to Finnis the view that from the principle 'knowledge is a good to be pursued', specific precepts should be derived like 'reading books is morally right'. That would be a Suárezian account. Instead, Finnis allows for flexibility as

---

[12] NLNR p. 23.
[13] NLNR IV.2.
[14] This metaphor is not used by Finnis himself.

to *how* people weigh the various basic goods and how they set out to pursue these goods.

Finnis's assumption that the basic goods merely serve as starting-points for moral reasoning induces him to the assertion that basic goods are 'pre-moral'. Since these basic orientations are prior to any further deliberation, they do not yet contain an 'ought', but, in the hyphenated vocabulary of the natural lawyers, an 'is-to-be'.[15] This 'is-to-be' may give rise to an 'ought', but does not provide the 'ought' by itself without further reflection. Practical principles, such as 'knowledge is a good to be pursued',

> [...] are operative before moral issues arise. They are necessary conditions for the simple volition which gives rise to deliberation. So far forth, practical principles [= basic goods, P.W.] can be called 'pre-moral'.[16]

How then do we proceed from these pre-moral starting-points to moral judgements? By means of the *second* ingredient of Finnis's theory. This consists of methodological guidelines[17] that should direct our reasoning on the basis of these orientations. Finnis formulates nine such requirements: one should have a 'coherent plan of life'; there should be no arbitrary preferences amongst values, nor amongst persons; there should be enough detachment to one's projects in order to avoid fanaticism, but enough commitment to avoid apathy; the good should be pursued with a reasonable amount of efficiency; one should respect every basic value in every act; one should pursue the common good and, finally, one should follow one's conscience.[18] It is by following the methodological requirements that one can arrive at morally defensible judgements. The fanatical athlete who sacrifices his life, health, and friends by his single-minded devotion to the good of 'play' cannot be called practically reasonable.

Although the basic goods in themselves do not guarantee morally correct deliberation, it is clear that Finnis's and Grisez's theory of practical reasonableness stands or falls with the adequacy of the

---

[15] NLNR p. 90.

[16] Grisez, Boyle, and Finnis, 1987, p. 126.

[17] In the NLNR these guidelines are called 'requirements of practical reasonableness'; later they are labelled 'modes of responsibility', but their content remains the same. Cf. Grisez, Boyle, and Finnis, 1987.

[18] NLNR ch. V.

account of the 'basic goods'. If the (seven) quarters of the compass are inaccurate, we can never arrive at sound conclusions, even if we reason according to the methodological requirements. That is why most debates concerning Finnis's theory of natural law revolve around the status of these basic goods. This is not different from what we encountered in earlier debates on natural law theory. As we have seen, the debates on the status, the obligatory force, the certainty and the foundation of the main principles of natural law were extensive, despite the seeming triviality of those principles. The principle 'good is to be done and pursued, and evil avoided' is an example in point.

There are three claims attached to the assumption of the basic goods. The first is that there are no more nor less than seven of those goods. The second claim is that this selection is based on the fact that only these goods are self-evident. The third claim is that the basic goods are incommensurable. In order to assess the structure of the new natural law theory, we should examine these claims one by one.

3. *Selection of the basic goods*

Finnis and Grisez claim that there are only seven basic goods. 'Basic' means that they are not derived from some other good, and they are not instrumental to another good. The basic goods serve as irreducible and ultimate justifications for actions. All seven goods form independent principles for practical reasoning.

The most common objection to this view is the utilitarian one. How can the natural lawyers maintain that the basic goods cannot be reduced to the criterion of happiness? Is it not true that 'play' or 'aesthetic experience' are valuable by virtue of the fact that they contribute to someone's happiness? The natural lawyers, however, deny this emphatically. 'Happiness', they say, is a purpose. Purposes, however, cannot serve as ultimate justifications for actions.

We can clarify this view by taking the example of someone who goes to a lecture.[19] If, asked for his reasons, this person would reply that this contributes to his happiness, we generally do not take that as an ultimate or conclusive answer. We might be inclined to question him further: 'Why does attending a lecture make you happy?'; 'Why

---

[19] This is a modification of the example given by Finnis, FE p. 33. Another, but similar example has been adduced by George, 1991.

do you prefer a lecture-room to a park'? However, if he referred to one of the basic goods, saying that he wants to increase his knowledge, we generally find that a satisfactory answer. Why? Because we regard 'knowledge' as an intrinsic value. Only references to intrinsic values enable us to see 'the point' of a particular action, to use a favourite expression of Finnis and Grisez.

Why can only intrinsic values and not purposes serve as conclusive answers? The example of an artist might illustrate their point. If, when asked for his reasons to paint, the artist answers that he does it in order to become rich, or to provide himself with some cheap wall-decoration, we might be entitled to question the integrity of his enterprise. One does not engage in painting only in order to achieve some results. People who continually ask: 'And what do you *do* with all those canvasses?', are missing this vital point. Apparently, it is only the intrinsic worth of his painting that counts as justification. Painting, like reading, going to church, or sustaining a friendship are actions with an intrinsic value, or, in the vocabulary of the natural lawyers, 'the instantiations of a basic good'. Characteristic for intrinsic goods is that they do not require further justification in terms of an external purpose. On the contrary, reference to an external purpose *undermines* the justification of actions by which one 'participates' in these goods.[20]

So only those answers that are convincing as ultimate answers refer to the basic goods. But is it not true that there are many convincing answers? Is it not true that it depends on one's particular perspective whether one is convinced by an answer or not? We might, for instance, be satisfied with the answer of someone that he goes to a lecture in order to make a fool of the lecturer; certainly if we know that the lecturer is vain, pretentious, or has done our person some wrong. We cannot say that his reasons are not ultimate because they refer to a further purpose. Our revengeful man has no objective in view. It is enough for him to live out his revenge by simply being there and asking questions. He does not adduce any external purpose in order to justify his presence.

---

[20] MacIntyre's distinction between 'internal goods' and 'external goods' is inspired by similar considerations. However, MacIntyre extends this distinction, whereas Finnis does not. According to MacIntyre, external goods can only be enjoyed by the artist himself, whereas an internal good is a good for the society as a whole. Cf. MacIntyre, 1981, pp. 189-91. Finnis omits to include such a difference, which is partially responsible for his confusion about the common good, to be dealt with shortly in X.5.

However, in Finnis's view, revenge or dislike cannot count as intrinsic goods. Why not? Because they are not *goods*. Revenge is simply not one of the basic goods because it is not an 'aspect of well-being', or 'form of human flourishing', in the vocabulary of the natural lawyers. Only forms of flourishing are 'intelligible desirable for their own sakes'[21] and can count as reasons not requiring further reasons. In other words, the natural lawyers assert that good reasons *are* good reasons, irrespective of one's perspective. The basic goods are indeed the quarters of a compass; what is to be counted as 'north' and 'south' does not depend on one's perspective, but on reality itself. This is very clear in Finnis's denial of the possibility that revenge or hatred can ever count as ultimate reasons:

> The point [...] is that selfishness, cruelty, and the like, simply do not stand to something self-evidently good as the urge to self-preservation stands to the self-evident good of human life. Selfishness, cruelty, etc., stand in need of some explanation, in a way that curiosity, friendliness, etc., do not.[22]

The basic goods serve as ultimate reasons, because they are self-evidently good.

It is worthwhile to assess the precise scope of this argument so far. How do we select the basic goods? By asking whether they can serve as ultimate reasons. And how do we know which reasons are ultimate? Ultimate reasons are ultimate only if they have an intrinsic worth and are not conducive to an external purpose. How can we select non-instrumental arguments which refer to basic goods and distinguish them from non-instrumental arguments which do not? Only by answering the question whether the goods referred to are objectively desirable. How do we know which goods are objectively desirable and which are not? That is self-evident. This latter argument brings us to the second feature of the basic goods: their self-evidence.

---

[21] See George, 1992a, p. 34.

[22] NLNR p. 91. The term 'explanation' here is confusing and should, I think, be read as 'justification'. As I shall point out in the next chapter, Finnis tends to identify explanation and justification.

4. *The self-evidence of the basic goods*

Whereas basic goods are self-evidently good, non-basic goods are not. The question arises then how we can distinguish the former from the latter. A simple answer would be 'that which is found self-evident by all people all over the world'. Such an answer however will not do. Even though the natural lawyers think that there is more consensus on basic values than is commonly supposed by relativists, they do not maintain that there is unanimity on what should be counted as basic goods. Apart from that, they want to devise a compass for moral reasoning. It is no use then to ask people's opinions on what is to count as north or south.

The modern natural law thinkers therefore point out that self-evidence does not require that everybody assents to these goods. In this context, Finnis and Grisez repeatedly point out that Aquinas himself drew a distinction between that which is self-evident to everyone and that which is self-evident only to the wise.[23] Self-evidence does not require universal assent. A basic good such as knowledge simply *is* a self-evident good, irrespective of the fact that in large parts of the world knowledge is not considered so self-evidently a good at all.

How then does the wise man know that some goods are self-evident, while others are not? Is self-evidence no more than a philosophical disguise for strong but unargued personal convictions?[24] Finnis and Grisez have two answers to this criticism. The first is that indeed there *are* no arguments for the self-evidence of the basic goods, because self-evidence, by principle, need not be demonstrated or proven. Basic goods are basic, precisely because they rest on no further argument.[25] The most one can do, according to the natural lawyers, is to make plausible that a denial of the self-evidence of basic goods would violate the non-contradiction principle. They call such arguments 'dialectical arguments'.[26] In itself this solution is a curious one. The non-contradiction principle is—and in this they

---

[23] E.g. NLNR p. 32.

[24] Cf. Weinreb, 1987, p. 113. Cf. also Hittinger, 1987, p. 47: 'Turning to a good like religion, after the searching criticism of theorists like Hume, Feuerbach and Freud, is it philosophically advisable simply to posit religion as a basic good?'

[25] George, 1991, provides only one of the many instances that can be found of this familiar counter-argument.

[26] See Grisez, Boyle, and Finnis, 1987, p. 111.

agree with Aquinas—the first principle of theoretical reason. The view that the basic principles of practical reason can only be argued by means of the first principle of theoretical reason is, however, hard to reconcile with their recurrent plea for an autonomous sphere for practical reason as separate from theoretical reason.

There remains but one criterion for self-evidence. That is their ultimacy. Only those goods are self-evident that cannot be derived from any other principle.[27] One might point out that there is a circularity involved here, since the ultimacy of the basic goods is defended by the argument of self-evidence, whereas self-evidence is understood as ultimacy. But the natural lawyers would probably argue that such circles are unavoidable. One has to find a starting-point somewhere in order to avoid infinite regress.

Their second answer refers to Aquinas. Aquinas's first principle 'good is to be done and pursued, and evil avoided' is also a self-evident principle. The basic goods, being no more than an *extension* of that first principle, would rest on the same foundation.[28]

This answer is indeed consistent with their reading of Aquinas. But I think there is an important difference between Aquinas and the new natural lawyers. Whereas Finnis identifies the basic goods with principles for moral reasoning, Aquinas made a distinction between a principle as a proposition and that *about* which the principle is formulated. The first principle ('good is to be done ...') is indeed taken to be self-evident. This principle is accessible to us by means of our human capacity to understand God's eternal law by means of *synderesis*. But that does not imply that 'the good' is taken to be self-evident. On the contrary, what that good *consists* in, whether it is fame or happiness or wisdom, remains for us to reflect upon. The only thing which is self-evident is that there is a general tendency of things to strive upwards on the scales of being and goodness towards greater perfection. In the particular ends of other creatures, which are the expressions of God's style, we might find some information on the ends to be pursued, but it is for us to decide which is the more complete end (see I.5 and I.6). To Aquinas, the possibility of practical deliberation does not rest on the assumption of a *self-evident good*, but of a *self-evident principle*.

---

[27] Perry convincingly questions the view that non-derivability would entail self-evidence. Cf. Perry, 1988, p. 15.

[28] Finnis, 1987.

It is, however, easier to defend Aquinas's view than the view of the modern natural lawyers. Aquinas provided two arguments for the self-evidence of his first principle: the first consists of his notion of *synderesis*, the assumption that God's *exemplar* is accessible to human rationality. The second argument is that without a fixed principle that one should pursue the good (no matter how that good is defined), it is impossible to make sense of moral reasoning at all.

Neither of these two arguments can be adduced by Grisez and Finnis. The first cannot be adduced, since they do not want to base their account on a metaphysical assumption which is dependent on the assumption of God's existence. Nor is the second answer available. Grisez and Finnis do not merely refer to 'the good'. The first principles *define* what is to be understood by 'the good'. They are therefore more substantial than Aquinas's 'good'. The selection of 'knowledge', 'aesthetic experience' or 'religion' and the dismissal of 'respect', 'dignity' or 'happiness' as suitable candidates is, however, far from self-evident and requires, I think, some further argumentation.

5. *The incommensurability of the basic goods*

The third feature of the basic goods is their incommensurability. Finnis and Grisez maintain that the basic goods cannot be measured by means of one criterion, nor can they be compared to one another.

In I.5 we have seen that there is a tendency on the part of the contemporary natural lawyers to deny that Aquinas ordered the various ends (self-preservation, procreation, etc.) in a hierarchical way. According to Finnis and Grisez, all ends are 'basic forms of good and evil'. In a sense, they are right here. It certainly was not Aquinas's view that 'self-preservation' is subordinated to 'knowledge of God' in the sense that the former is *instrumental* to the latter. They have a value in themselves. That is why I also preferred to call these 'subends' rather than 'means'. However, this does not mean that Aquinas did not have an hierarchical ranking in mind. He conceived of self-preservation as a 'less complete' end. If Aquinas had drawn up a list of methodological requirements, he would have included 'try to find out which end is the more complete end'.

Grisez and Finnis emphasise, however, that not only Aquinas's theory of ends, but also their own theory of basic goods allow for a wide variety of basic goods, which are all equally important and cannot be reduced to one another. This view is informed by their concern to safeguard a fundamental freedom of choice. Finnis and Grisez repeatedly stress that this freedom of choice is dangerously curtailed by utilitarians, who subordinate all values to the ultimate goal of happiness alone. Finnis's and Grisez's analysis here is very much inspired by Kant. Kant, but also Neo-Kantians such as the sociologist Max Weber,[29] maintained that the choice between means is not a real choice; it is a matter of calculation; a technical affair in order to realise a given aim in the most efficient way.

In order to understand this view fully we should return to what I wrote on Kant in the introduction to this chapter. I noted there, that Kant sharply distinguished between a hypothetical and a categorical imperative. A hypothetical imperative does not inform us about the goals to be pursued, but merely points out what means are the most appropriate, *given* a certain end: 'If I want to get rich, I should not qualify as a philosopher, but as a manager'. The categorical imperative on the other hand, informs one about the *ends* to be pursued. These ends (*Zwecke*) are ultimate and not instrumental to another end.

The modern natural lawyers maintain this assumption. They strongly distinguish between technical and moral rules, between 'making' and 'doing'.[30] And on the basis of this assumption they criticise utilitarianism. They claim that utilitarians, by maintaining that happiness is the indisputable, ultimate and given end, reduce the scope for moral inquiry to an inquiry into the most efficient means to achieve that given end. In short, utilitarians are blamed for turning morality into a technical affair. This is all the more dangerous, according to the natural lawyers, because such a technical reduction does not allow for human freedom of choice. The question which means are most effective to a given end can be answered by calculations and is not open to debate.

In order to devise a theory of practical reasonableness, it is therefore of vital importance to assume that the various goods are equally important. And that is why the incommensurability-thesis is accompanied with the methodological requirements that we should not have arbitrary preferences, that we should respect every basic good and that we should avoid fanaticism.

---

[29] Weber, 1922.
[30] Grisez, Boyle, and Finnis, 1987, p. 100; Finnis, 1992, p. 134.

These claims sound perfectly reasonable, but cause some problems which are similar to the ones we encountered in Grotius's description of human nature. I noted at the end of chapter V, that the assumption of three features of human nature entailed the problem of priority. Are we to choose in favour of sociability or in favour of self-preservation? In practice, we saw that Grotius subordinated all features of human nature to self-preservation alone, but theoretically the dilemma was there.

The same applies to Finnis's and Grisez's plurality of principles. What am I to do if I am forced to choose between basic goods? This dilemma recurs both in trivial situations (am I to help my friend or read a book), as well as in more dramatic dilemmas (am I to sacrifice my life for the good of religion). In short, on the basis of which considerations am I to *select from* the list of the seven basic goods? Which is more important, 'friendship', 'play', 'knowledge' or 'religion'? Finnis's methodological requirements do not bring me any further, since they only admonish me to take all basic goods into equal consideration. Yet, since time is short, I inevitably sin against that prescription.

We might wonder, therefore, whether the assumption of ultimate and incommensurable values really can provide for freedom of choice, if we mean by 'choice' something more than a blind guess. Is there any scope for moral reasoning left? Weber thought that indeed there are no such criteria for regulating these choices. He thought that the assumption that ultimate values are incommensurable implies that the choice for one or the other is an arbitrary affair, for which no moral methodology can be designed. Although one can rationally decide on means, there is no rational way of choosing between ends.

Finnis, although sharing Weber's assumption on the ultimacy of values, does not draw this conclusion. In fact, he blames Weber for having exaggerated the arbitrariness of moral choice. In a discussion of Sartre's well-known moral dilemma of the soldier who is confronted with the option either to serve his country against the invading forces, or to stay home in order to take care of his sick mother, Finnis confidently announces that both courses of actions are laudable. What is important, he adds, is that the irresponsible courses of action (shoot the mother, join the occupying forces) are not taken into account. It is the job of practical reason to dismiss these immoral actions.[31]

These are obviously trivial remarks. It seems as if Finnis's practical reason is indeed, to quote Clifford Geertz, like a 'sprinkler-system that turns off when the fire gets too hot'.[32] That 'ignorance' is better than 'knowledge', that 'art [...] is better than trash',[33] who will deny it? The problem, apart from the obvious difficulty that we differ on what we should count as 'knowledge' or 'art', is how we can choose between them.

Finnis and Grisez could have tried to answer this problem by developing a theory concerning *prudentia*, the virtue of reasoning well. By describing the qualities required for sound practical reasoning they probably could have avoided the arbitrariness which inevitably accompanies a Weberian theory of ultimate and incommensurable values. It should be noted, however, that in that case, they could not have contented themselves by simply taking over Aquinas's theory of *prudentia*. As we saw in chapter II, Aquinas's concept of *prudentia* only refers to reasoning about means, not ends, since he thought that the latter were directly accessible to us by means of *synderesis*. However, Finnis and Grisez neither maintain the possibility of *synderesis*, nor do they adopt an—extended—theory of *prudentia*. The result is that they cannot escape from arbitrariness when ultimate values conflict.

6. *The irrelevance of nature*

We might be inclined to think that theorists who set out to develop a theory of natural law try to answer these questions by referring to nature, or to human nature. One would expect natural lawyers to infer the basic goods from (human) nature, or at least to provide an argument, derived from some conception of nature, which might shed light on how we can select from the various basic goods that present themselves. But they do not. They assert that nature is irrelevant to our reasoning on moral matters. What is more, they also deny that nature ever played an important part in natural law theory. That is

---

[31] NLNR p. 176.

[32] Geertz, 1983, p. 217, used this metaphor in a description of law.

[33] NLNR p. 220.

why Finnis thinks that 'natural law' is an 'unhappy term'.[34] He includes the term in the title of his book merely to pay tribute to Aquinas.

Finnis explicitly denies that Aquinas or any other natural lawyer ever tried to derive norms from facts. To the question: 'Have the natural lawyers shown that they can derive ethical norms from facts?', Finnis replies:

> [...] the answer can be brisk: They have not, nor do they need to, nor did the classical exponents of the theory dream of attempting any such derivation.[35]

According to Finnis and Grisez, even Aquinas is not guilty of having committed the naturalistic fallacy. Instead, they argue that this criticism rests on a misinterpretation. We can remain faithful to the ground-structure of Aquinas's programme without falling into naturalistic traps.

Finnis and Grisez argue this point by referring to Aquinas's distinction between theoretical reason and practical reason. Practical reason is about moral affairs; theoretical reason inquires into nature. There is no conflation between 'is' and 'ought'.[36] Although nature indeed plays some role in Aquinas's teachings, we should regard it as a subordinate one. Nature is a mere 'speculative appendage',[37] something that is *added later* to the immediate grasp of self-evident goods and the purposiveness of human life, but which is irrelevant to our knowledge of good and evil. We have come across this interpretation in I.4.

In fact, according to Grisez's and Finnis's interpretation, Aquinas does not reason *from* nature *to* morality, but the other way round:

> [...] the teleological conception of nature was made plausible, indeed conceivable, by analogy with the *intro*spectively luminous, self-evident structure of human well-being, practical reasoning, and human purposive action [...].[38]

---

[34] NLNR p. 374.
[35] NLNR p. 33.
[36] NLNR p. 20.
[37] NLNR p. 36.
[38] NLNR p. 52.

According to Finnis, the teleological view of nature is merely an *extrapolation* of the experienced purposiveness of human actions. That is why we can do very well without a teleological concept of nature; we can indeed do without any conception of nature at all. Nature is a mere afterthought, with which the theory of natural law is decorated; it does not form its foundation.

This view has met with fierce criticism on the part of some Neo-Thomists, who see Aquinas's heritage squandered.[39] In the words of Veatch:

> [...] rather than being embarrassed or apologetic over his failure to demonstrate that natural law is indeed natural, he [i.e. Finnis, P.W.] would appear rather to want to make a virtue out of his very necessity. [...] Yes, and as if to puzzle and perplex his readers even more, Finnis apparently wants to claim no less a one than St. Thomas Aquinas as being on his side in this regard.[40]

In chapter I, I already dealt with the conflicting interpretations of Aquinas and opted for a middle-course (I.3). Finnis and Grisez are right in stressing that it is certainly not Aquinas's view that we can infer directly norms from the observation of nature. The ability to reason does not boil down to our ability to copy God's artefacts. But that does not imply that nature does not play a role at all. According to the interpretation I suggested, it is Aquinas's view that we have access to God's style directly by means of *synderesis*, as well as indirectly by means of the examples that can be found of God's style as it is expressed in nature.

If my interpretation of Aquinas's theory is correct, this would imply that nature plays a less important role than is commonly assumed by Neo-Thomists, but a more important one than Finnis allowed for. The intelligibility of God's normative order (i.e. natural law) depends in fact on two assumptions. The first is the assumption of our immediate grasp of the divine style (*synderesis*); the second is the assumption that our reasoning is further informed by the examples God provided. Finnis emphasises the former at the expense of the latter.

---

[39] Bourke, 1981; Veatch, 1981a; Veatch, 1981b.
[40] Veatch, 1981a, p. 256.

However, even if Finnis's and Grisez's interpretation of Aquinas is one-sided, this is not an argument against the kind of natural law theory they want to develop for themselves. Their claim is that it is the purposiveness of *human action* which is an important assumption for a theory of practical reasonableness, and that this purposiveness is not dependent on any concept of nature. If they are right, that is an important argument. Bourke may criticise Finnis and Grisez on the grounds that they are 'bypassing the complete metaphysics of finality',[41] but if that implies that they can *also* by-pass all the problems that have been the result of this kind of metaphysics, that would be a tremendous advantage.

In part II of this book, we have seen the enormous problems pertaining to the role of nature. Nature was found to be 'inert', not giving rise to obligations (Suárez), or could not form the foundation of natural law (Pufendorf) and where it indeed played a vital role, its role was reduced to the emphasis on self-preservation (Grotius). If the natural lawyers succeeded in grounding moral theory in the purposiveness of human action, without reference to nature, many problems would indeed be discarded. It is therefore worthwhile to examine the quality of the argument.

7. *Practical reason curtailed*

At first sight it is indeed plausible that the teleological view of nature was developed by analogy with human action. In this sense, we might agree that it is an extrapolation of human experience. But can we say that this extrapolation is irrelevant to natural law theory?

In order to answer that question, we should keep in mind that the old conception of teleological nature did not merely assert that there is *a* purpose to be found in nature, in the sense that we might say that all human action serves *a* purpose, no matter what it is. For a plant, the end of self-preservation is a *suitable* and a *good* end, since God had designed it in that way. And for a human being, sociability is a good and valuable end, since God had meant him to live in society. It is true that we human beings can select from these various ends and decide which end is the most complete in the given circumstances, but all these ends derive their intrinsic value (as sub-ends) from the fact

---

[41] Bourke, 1981, p. 245.

that God had intended these to be fulfilled by the various creatures. In this sense is it possible to infer from natural inclinations the various possible values that present themselves.

But this solution is not acceptable to Finnis. Although he does believe in God, he does not want to turn this belief into an underlying foundation for his theory. And without the assumption that God intends us to have natural desires and inclinations, we cannot guarantee that these natural desires are morally good. Whereas Aquinas could render depraved inclinations (greed, hatred, egoism) intelligible by maintaining that these inclinations nevertheless tend to a good, but to a good which is incorrectly understood, Finnis and Grisez cannot maintain that assumption. The fact that man's natural inclinations can be morally indefensible turns them into unsuitable starting-points for moral reasoning.

In this respect, they find themselves in the same position as Grotius, who likewise had to account for man's evil natural inclinations. But whereas Grotius opts for an idealised account of human nature, Finnis and Grisez discard human nature as a reliable standard. This may be clear from the passage in which desires as such are discarded as starting-points for moral reasoning:

> [...] we should say not that practical reasoning begins with *wants* (or desires) and seeks satisfactory ways of *satisfying* them; but that practical reasoning begins by identifying *something wanted* (or desired), i.e. something considered (*practically* considered) desirable.[42]

Practical reasoning is informed, not by natural inclinations, but by basic orientations, the things that are worthwhile pursuing. These basic orientations cannot be back traced to natural inclinations at all. Only the basic goods can form reliable starting-points. This is indeed the only consistent answer in view of the assumptions of the natural lawyers. 'Nature' as such is unreliable, if we do not maintain the a priori assumption that it is God's creation.

It should be noted, however, that this position is a reversal of Aquinas's. Whereas Aquinas starts with natural inclinations and desires which can only be turned into desirable goods by means of practical reasoning, Finnis starts with what is desir*able*. Practical reasoning does not *result* in a formulation of the desirable good, but

---

[42] FE p. 35.

finds its *starting-point* there. The orientations with which we set out to reflect on our moral conduct are already supposed to be objectively good, intelligible and self-evidently desirable.

However, this move narrows down the scope for practical reasoning. In the theory of Finnis and Grisez, practical reasoning might enable us to strike a balance between the various incommensurable goods. We might follow the requirements that we should not directly harm one of these goods, or that we should have no arbitrary preferences. By following these requirements we translate or implement the desirable goods into desirable courses of actions. But these are small tasks, compared to the role Aquinas assigned to practical reasoning: to discern what is really desirable. In fact, in Finnis's theory this important task is already carried out before practical reasoning comes in. Practical reason cannot determine which goods are desirable and which are not. That is the reason why Finnis and Grisez recur to the notion that they are self-evident. They are presupposed. This status of the basic goods seems hard to reconcile with the view that they are 'pre-moral': an is-to-be rather than an 'ought'. As expressions of the 'desirable' these basic goods are completely moral. The only way to understand that claim is to identify the term 'pre-moral' with 'pre-rational'. They come in before practical reflection is carried out.

It should be noted that not only compared to Aquinas the scope of practical reason is curtailed. We see the same if we compare Finnis's position to that of Kant. This can be judged from Finnis's criticism of Kant. According to Finnis, Kant unnecessarily limited 'human flourishing' to the basic good of practical reasonableness alone and did not take seriously enough the other basic goods. Kant considers 'play' or 'friendship' as 'mere' objects of natural inclinations, Finnis asserts, not as *intelligibly* desirable:

> There is impoverishment to the extent that Kant's understanding of understanding (reason) overlooks the *intelligible* goodness of the specific, substantive aspects of human flourishing, and seeks to make do with reason's 'a priori' power of universalizing.[43]

At first sight, this criticism seems reasonable. The rigid distinction between reason and nature is indeed problematic. But if we compare Kant's theory with that of Finnis, Kant's solution is much more

---

[43] FE p. 74.

plausible than Finnis's. Kant did not opt for the unaccountable normativity of basic goods as *starting-points* for practical reasoning. He consistently argued that without practical reasoning one cannot speak of something 'desirable' at all, but only of 'desires'. Without human practical judgements there are no practical 'goods' or 'truths' at all; there are merely natural inclinations and their objects. Since Kant correctly refused to rely on the problematic notion of 'self-evidence', practical reasoning is the *sine qua non* for all moral distinctions. Its role is much more important in Kant's moral philosophy than in the theory of practical reasonableness, developed by Grisez and Finnis.

There is a remarkable paradox involved here. The attempt to reconstruct natural law as a theory of practical reasonableness necessitates the argument that nature is irrelevant to human reasoning. However, that argument in turn undermines practical reasonableness as well. The new theory of natural law throws out the baby with the bathwater.

8. *The hidden role of nature*

The sole reason for rejecting the view that natural inclinations are morally relevant is the reluctance to ground natural law in a '*pious* hypothesis'. The existence of God should not serve as an indispensable foundation for natural law. But Grisez was much less hampered by that consideration than Finnis. Consequently, we see that in Grisez's articles, but also in joint articles, there is less reluctance to allow nature some role. In an attempt to justify the multiplicity of the basic goods, the thesis is maintained that:

> The diversity of the basic goods is neither a mere contingent fact about human psychology nor an accident of history. Rather, being aspects of the fulfillment of persons, these goods correspond to the inherent complexities of human nature [...].[44]

Even the very wording of this view reminds one of Aquinas's thesis: 'The order of the precepts of the natural law *corresponds* to the order of our natural inclinations'.[45] And indeed, like Aquinas, the authors

---

[44] Grisez, Boyle, and Finnis, 1987, p. 107.
[45] ST I, II, 94, 2, concl.

proceed to distinguish different aspects of human beings. Human persons can be regarded 'as animate', 'as rational', and 'as simultaneously rational and animate'.[46] As 'animate', people cherish life itself; as 'rational', people cherish 'knowledge and aesthetic experience' and as both they cherish 'work and play'.[47] The assignment of basic goods to different aspects of human nature is relevant because the basic goods are regarded as being 'perfective' of those aspects. Finnis asserts that the basic goods 'would not perfect that nature, were it other than it is'.[48]

Despite protestations to the contrary, a conception of nature does come in here; a thoroughly teleological conception. And it not only serves as an argument for the plurality of the basic goods; it equally answers the question why we should select exactly these goods as basic. They are basic, *not* because they are ultimate and self-evident, but because they correspond to and are perfective of—different aspects of—man's nature.

So it seems that nature does play a role after all. How do the natural lawyers reconcile this role with their view that nature is irrelevant to natural law? They maintain that there is no inconsistency here and that their teleological conception of nature does not give rise to moral 'ought'-statements. This is argued by means of a rigorous distinction between epistemology and ontology. The natural lawyers assert that, *epistemologically* speaking, it is impossible to infer the existence of basic goods from human nature. But *ontologically* speaking, the basic goods are grounded in nature.[49] Since it has been Hume's criticism that we should not *infer* norms from facts, Finnis and Grisez think that they can avoid that charge by making a distinction between epistemology and ontology. Although norms are grounded in nature, they do not infer norms from nature.

I am afraid that this argument does not rescue their position from the charge of naturalistic fallacy. The selection of the basic goods is clearly informed by their belief that these seven basic goods are truly 'perfective' of man's nature. Because they are perfective of man's nature, they are regarded as intrinsic values. It is no good pretending

---

[46] Grisez, Boyle, and Finnis, 1987, p. 107.

[47] Grisez's list of the basic goods is slightly different from that of Finnis in the NLNR; an indication that their self-evidence is inaccessible, even to 'the wise'.

[48] Cf. Finnis, 1987, pp. 46-7.

[49] Cf. Finnis, 1987, p. 46, and George, 1992a, p. 35.

that the basic goods are first selected on the basis of their 'self-evidence', and only afterwards 'happen' to be perfective of human nature.

Apart from that, the argument is not necessary. There is no reason to shun the naturalistic fallacy, if one adheres to a teleological ontology. Inferences from nature to norms would not be fallacious at all. We have seen in the chapter on Suárez's foundation of natural law (chapter III) that problems only arise when one no longer believes in the theological assumption that God has performed His role as Legislator, *in* and *by* creating the world. Suárez conceived of God's activity in three successive stages: he thought that God first created, then added a judgement, and after that added obligatory force. That is why he thought that 'nature' taken by itself formed an insufficient foundation and had to be coupled with explicit decrees and obligatory force.

But Finnis and Grisez are much more loyal to Aquinas than Suárez. They apparently believe that God created man in such a way (as animate, rational etc.) that some values are perfective of nature. On the basis of this view, God's rational judgement is *implied* in His creation. So if one maintains that human beings tend to perfect themselves, and that there is a God who created us to that end, there is no reason why one should shrink from the conclusion that we should indeed perfect ourselves. Both the assumption of teleology and the assumption of God's existence are clearly present in the work of the modern natural lawyers. Within that framework, inferences from facts to norms are no fallacies at all, and can be drawn without any logical mistake whatsoever.[50]

There are indeed indications that these inferences are drawn in the application of the theory to practical matters. In a recent article, Finnis argues that homosexuality is 'intrinsically unreasonable and unnatural' on the grounds that the 'reproductive organs of homosexuals cannot make them a biological (and therefore personal) unit'.[51] Yet, even here Finnis denies committing the naturalistic fallacy. He professes merely to 'apply the relevant practical reasons [...] and moral principles [...] to the realities of our constitution, intentions and

---

[50] It should be noted that Finnis and Grisez take the is-ought distinction much more seriously than most contemporary philosophers of science, who generally assume that the perception of facts is value-laden.

[51] Finnis, 1996, pp. 14-15.

circumstances'.[52] However, this 'application' is clearly informed by supposedly biological arguments; not by practical reasons.

The conclusion seems to be justified that the modern formulation of natural law rests on a hidden assumption of teleology, coupled with the belief in God.

9. *Conclusion*

We have seen that the new theory of natural law decidedly presents itself as a theory of practical reasonableness, rather than as a theory of natural law. The first principles such as 'knowledge should be pursued' or 'play should be pursued' are not to be taken as precepts but as general and basic orientations on the basis of which we should reason about moral matters. These basic goods, although they are grounded in nature, are not inferred from human nature. They are taken to be self-evident. That means that, strictly speaking, the new theory of natural law neither has anything to do with law nor with nature.

It is, however, not certain whether the reformulation of natural law theory as a theory of practical reasonableness is better suited to cope with the various traditional dilemmas of natural law theory. It is true that we need not worry about the naturalistic fallacy but instead, the natural lawyers face the far more serious problem of a lacking foundation. The foundation in nature might not have been adequate (Suárez's and Pufendorf's qualms testify to this fundamental inadequacy), but the alternative candidate which is proposed, self-evidence, is even less convincing as a foundation. In order to turn 'self-evidence' into more than a debate-stopper or a disguise for this lack of foundation, a theory would be required in which it is argued that man has immediate access to those self-evident forms of human flourishing. If we are not supposed to rely on nature, a (modern) equivalent of *synderesis* should be developed. Such a theory is absent.

Apart from the problem of foundation, there is still the familiar problem of obligation. Even if we recognise the seven basic goods as real basic goods, why should we be obliged to take these goods as a starting-point for our moral reasoning? What compelling reasons are there to abstain from, for instance, the utilitarian criterion? Suárez's

---

[52] Finnis, 1996, p. 16.

problem is far from solved, even if we do not conceive of the first principles as precepts, but as general orientations. The point is: why should we be guided by Finnis's compass rather than by our own sense of direction?

It seems then that the modern theory of natural law has to deal with both the problem of foundation and of obligation. Yet, Finnis and Grisez argue that their theory is a theory of practical reasonableness; not of natural law. There are, however, reasons to suppose that their theory fails to achieve the aim of broadening the scope for moral inquiry as well.

In the first place, since all basic goods are regarded as ultimate, irreducible to each other or to any other—external—purpose, and inherently incommensurable, it is difficult if not impossible to decide on the basis of these first principles which basic good should be given priority in case of conflict. The extension of one first principle to seven first principles may appear to widen the scope for practical reasoning but in fact turns reasoning into a somewhat arbitrary affair. Since all goods are deemed equally important, the methodological requirements of practical reasoning only inform us that we should not directly act against one of these seven goods. In the second place, the scope of practical reasoning is curtailed by that fact that it no longer plays a role in deciding which goods are really desirable. The seven selected desirable goods form the starting-point for our enquiry. Their self-evidence excludes critical reflection on the value of these basic goods.

These shortcomings as a theory of practical reasonableness can only be amended, I think, by explicit references to the teleological view of human nature, which is at the basis of Finnis's and Grisez's selection of the basic goods. If their anxiety of committing the naturalistic fallacy had not prevented them from openly acknowledging these underlying assumptions, we could have gained a more informative account, be it that by doing so, they would have been confronted with the familiar problem of nature as an inadequate foundation as well as the problem posed by the assumption that God created us in order to perfect ourselves.

In the introduction, I noted that Finnis's attempt is theoretically interesting in three aspects, one of which is the attempt to unravel underlying and objective values on the basis of philosophical argument alone, without assuming the existence of God. On the basis of this chapter, we might conclude that this task can only be carried out by assigning an important place to the notion of self-evidence. This self-evidence, however, is not embedded within a wider conceptual framework which might elucidate the kind of rationality required to 'see' this self-evidence and therefore remains unargued. As for the other two ambitions of modern natural law theory (to provide a foundation of rights and to criticise liberalism on the basis of natural law), we should turn to the next chapter.

CHAPTER X

FINNIS'S DECISIONISM

In the preceding chapters we have seen that a recurrent problem in natural law theory was the question how we can translate and specify the general principles of natural law. Suárez's notion of *dominium* and the attending permission for human beings to change the *materia* of natural law which has to do with *dominium* have been the starting-point for a development in which more and more room was assigned to human legislators to determine positive law in view of the contingent and variable requirements of human societies. ·

We might expect Finnis to run into similar difficulties. At first sight it is not easy to see how Finnis's principles of natural law, consisting of the seven basic goods coupled with a set of methodological requirements for practical reasoning, can be applied to the analysis and justification of positive law. How can a basic good such as 'play' or 'aesthetic experience' be sensibly linked to our understanding of positive law? How can he hope to provide a foundation for rights on the basis of these goods?

These are the questions to be dealt with in this chapter. After a description of Finnis's methodological point of view (section 1), attention will be paid to Finnis's double-sided picture of law (section 2). His views on how positive law can be linked to natural law will be the subject of section 3, after which his concept of the common good will be analysed in sections 4-6. The practical implication of his analysis will be further examined in section 7.

1. *Ideals and ideal-types*

In part II of this book, we have seen that in the natural law theories of Suárez, Grotius and Pufendorf, natural law was partly used to provide a justification of positive law, partly by the attempt to explain the origins of human institutions in terms of historical or (proto) sociological descriptions. We have seen that both aims are at times hard to reconcile, which is, for instance, shown by the double function of consent in Grotius's and Pufendorf's theories. Pufendorf's attempt to reconstruct and to unravel the rationality of human institutions was, I noted, the last ingenious attempt to combine both sociology and moral theory within one theory.

It is therefore all the more surprising to encounter in Finnis's theory the same blend of justification and explanation.[1] This may be judged from the passage in which he states his intention to

> [...] develop a concept [of law, P.W.] which would explain the various phenomena referred to (in an unfocused way) by 'ordinary' talk about law—and explain them by showing how they answer [...] to the standing requirements of practical reasonableness [...].[2]

Obviously, an explanation of terms by showing 'how they answer to the requirements of practical reasonableness' is nothing else than to *justify* them in terms of the basic goods along with the methodological requirements. And this is indeed what Finnis has in mind when he writes:

> As always, the explanation of social institutions [...] is primarily a matter of grasping their rationale.[3]

It seems then that Finnis tries to spawn here the gap between the two programmes we saw emerging within Pufendorf's theory, and to reconcile 'sociology' and 'moral theory' once more within one theory.

This is not to say that Finnis was aware of that attempt. He more or less seems to take for granted that explanation and justification are one and the same thing. This is apparent from his view that his method can be compared to that of Max Weber. Finnis claims that in order to make sense of legal institutions, we should take over Weber's concept of 'Idealtypen': ideal-types. In order to analyse 'law', 'community', or 'obligation', we should, according to Finnis, start by defining the *'focal meaning'* of these terms. The state of affairs that is described by this focal meaning of terms is called the *'central case'*.[4] Focal meanings are distinguished from secondary meanings. The rules

---

[1] In the preceding chapter (IX.2), we came across the same identification where he ventured his opinion that only reasons referring to intrinsic values do not require any further explanation. Cf. NLNR p. 91.

[2] NLNR p. 279.

[3] NLNR p. 170.

[4] NLNR pp. 9-10. Finnis borrows the term from Raz, 1978, p. 133.

of a mafia-gang may be called 'law' but only in a secondary, not in a focal meaning of the term. Consequently, central cases are to be distinguished from 'borderline' cases. The friendship between business-associates, who have a calculated interest in mutual co-operation is a borderline-case of 'friendship', not a central case.

By focusing on these focal meanings, Finnis asserts, it is possible to

> differentiate the mature from the undeveloped in human affairs, the sophisticated from the primitive, the flourishing from the corrupt, the fine specimen from the deviant case [...].[5]

It should be noted that this normative use of ideal-types is not what Weber had in mind. Weber constructed ideal-types for ordering empirical phenomena in intelligible categories, thus making sense of them within a particular and explicated point of view ('Wertbeziehung'). He explicitly warns us not to confuse ideal-types with ideals, and remarks dryly that 'there are ideal-types of brothels as well as of religions [...]'.[6]

However, for Finnis, to understand a cultural phenomenon such as law, normative judgements on the quality of that system of law are required. Understanding is impossible without evaluation.[7] That is why Finnis adopts the perspective of the reasonable man. According to Finnis, positive law should be analysed from:

> [...] the viewpoint of those who not only appeal to practical reasonableness but also *are* practically reasonable, that is to say: consistent; attentive to all aspects of human opportunity and flourishing, and aware of their limited commensurability [...].[8]

---

[5] NLNR pp. 10-11.

[6] Weber, 1904, p. 200.

[7] This led Ted Honderich to the remark: 'It is no good practice to run together the idea that one has to "understand" the values, which is, to be sympathetic to them [...] and the idea that one has to "understand" them in the sense of knowing about them'. See Honderich, 1980.

[8] NLNR p. 15.

Positive law should be analysed from the viewpoint of the just man.[9] Apparently, it is Finnis's—implicit—view that if something is understood by this just and reasonable spectator, it is justified as well.

2. *The moral and technical aspects of law*

How is the reasonable man to understand (i.e. assess) the system of law? He has to understand it in the 'focal meaning' of the term. That is, as the 'law and legal system of a complete community'.[10] A complete community, Finnis informs us, is 'self-sufficient':

> [...] there is no aspect of human affairs that as such is outside the range of such a complete community.[11]

This is not to say that 'complete' communities do exist in reality.[12] But the modern territorial state, Finnis writes, *claims* to be such a complete community. And it is from this claim that law derives its meaning. As a legal system of a complete community, law regulates all forms of human behaviour. It gives legal force to other normative associations and it regulates the conditions under which the members of the community can participate in other normative associations. As such it is the supreme authority.[13]

Since law can be understood on the basis of the claim of states to be complete communities, we should examine this latter concept before we proceed to the analysis of law. The most conspicuous trait then of Finnis's concept of community is his view that it is a unified whole. Finnis does not differentiate between 'society' and 'community'; between *Gesellschaft* and *Gemeinschaft*.[14] There is no room in his analysis for the notion that a state might consist of an aggregate of individuals who have little in common with one another. The members of a community share an aim. What unites people into a com-

---

[9] A curious reversal of the viewpoint proposed by Holmes: that of the bad man. Cf. Holmes, 1920.

[10] NLNR p. 148.

[11] NLNR p. 148.

[12] NLNR pp. 149-50.

[13] NLNR p. 148.

[14] NLNR p. 135.

munity is not their frequency of interaction;[15] we should not conceive of communities as a rush-hour crowd.[16] Communities have

> [...] some more or less shared objective or, more precisely, some shared conception of the point of continuing co-operation. This point we may call the common good.[17]

What then is the common good? In relation to communities, the common good is defined as:

> [...] a set of conditions which enables the members of a community to attain for themselves reasonable objectives, or to realize reasonably for themselves the value(s), for the sake of which they have reason to collaborate with each other [...] in a community.[18]

In short, the common good consists of the conditions which are required in order to participate in the basic goods. This implies that law is only indirectly—by means of the common good—linked to the basic goods. The rationale of law is to further the common good. And the common good in turn enables the members of society to pursue the basic goods. It seems then that a lot depends on how the intermediate link, the common good, is perceived.

These 'central cases' of 'law', 'community' and the 'common good' serve as a sketch of the *moral rationale*, the *raison d'être* of a legal system. Any legal system should 'instantiate' the common good by co-ordinating the actions of members of a complete community. If the reasonable spectator is to understand institutional arrangements as (true) law, it is on the basis of these 'ideal-types'.

However, the recurrence of idealised notions as 'complete community' and 'common good' does not imply that Finnis is blind to the formal aspects of law. On the contrary, next to his sketch of the moral *raison d'être* of legal systems, Finnis devotes much attention to these formal aspects. These formal features should be understood, according to Finnis, as signs that law is not merely a moral system, but also a technical one, in the Kantian sense of comprising a set of tools or means in order to bring about a given end.

---

[15] Here Finnis criticises Homans: NLNR p. 151.
[16] NLNR p. 150.
[17] NLNR p. 153.
[18] NLNR p. 155.

> Lawyers' tools of trade [...] are means in the service of a purpose
> sufficiently definite to constitute a technique, a mode of technical
> reasoning. The purpose [...] is the unequivocal resolution of every
> dispute [...] which can be in some way foreseen and provided for.[19]

The given ends for which law supplies the means are certainty,
predictability and stability.

Finnis distinguishes five formal features of law which can be
understood on the basis of this quest for certainty:[20]

> a) law is a self-generating system, which regulates its own
> creation;
> b) law brings predictability into human interaction by the mech-
> anism that rules or institutions, once validly created, remain
> valid until they are repealed according to its own terms;
> c) law regulates the conditions under which a private individual
> can modify the application of the rules (as e.g. in marriages or
> contracts);
> d) this predictability is enhanced by the special mechanism that
> past acts are seen as an—exclusionary—reason for 'acting in a
> way *then* provided for';
> e) law presents itself as a seamless web.

Law, according to Finnis, can be distinguished from other sets of
rules (convention, etiquette) because it is a coercive order which
regulates its own creation.

This technical aspect of law as a set of tools in order to bring
about a given end implies that its vocabulary should not be seen as a
mere translation of moral discourse. Law is not simply a set of moral
precepts plus the force of sanctions.[21] Since law's overall aim is
predictability and certainty, its vocabulary acquires a different form:

> Legal reasoning [...] is (at least in large part) technical reasoning—not
> moral reasoning. Like all technical reasoning, it is concerned to achieve
> a particular purpose, a definite state of affairs attainable by efficient

---

[19] Finnis, 1992, p. 142.
[20] NLNR pp. 268-9.
[21] NLNR p. 281.

dispositions of means to end. The particular end here is the resolution of disputes [...].[22]

Finnis points out that moral precepts such as 'Thou shalt not kill' are absent in legal formulations. These rather take the form of propositions such as: 'It is an offence to kill'.[23] The fact that normative discourse is rephrased in the 'indicative propositional form',[24] Finnis adds, is due to the fact that a lawyer

> sees the desired future social order from a professionally structured viewpoint, as a stylized and manageable drama. In this drama, many characters, situations, and actions known to common sense, sociology, and ethics are missing, while many other characters, relationships, and transactions known only [...] to the lawyer are introduced.[25]

And he adds that there are not only reasonable or unreasonable acts to be found on that scene, but things like 'crime', 'offence', or 'tort'. He concludes that:

> [...] it is the business of the draftsman to specify, precisely, into which of these costumes and relationships an act of killing-under-such-and-such-circumstances fits.[26]

3. *Determination and deduction*

Finnis therefore presents us with a double-sided picture of positive law. On the one hand, law is thought to strive for an open-ended and inexhaustible 'common good' as the condition which enables people to pursue the basic goods; on the other hand law is seen as a tool, a means to the definite end of predictability and certainty. Finnis claims that in order to understand law correctly, we should take into account *both* aspects, and see that the technical aspect is subordinated to its moral aspect:

---

[22] Finnis, 1992, p. 142.

[23] NLNR p. 282.

· [24] This seems to be an oversimplified view, disregarding the fact that performative speech plays an important role in law.

[25] NLNR pp. 282-3.

[26] NLNR p. 283.

> [...] this quest for certainty, for a complete set of uniquely correct answers, is itself in the service of a wider good which, like all basic human goods, is not reducible to a definite goal but is rather an open-ended good [...].[27]

The question arises how law's immediate goals (certainty, predictability) are related to that wider common good. Can we obtain a unified concept of law in which the technical aspects of law as a set of tools aiming at certainty and predictability can sensibly be linked to the 'wider' common good as the set of conditions in which men can pursue the basic goods?

In order to answer that question Finnis makes use of Aquinas's notion that positive law can either be the result of *determinatio* or of a *deductio*, carried out by one of more syllogisms (cf. II.6). By the concept of *determinatio*, Aquinas allowed for a scope of freedom and choice on the part of the legislator to *shape* these general principles into particular rules. Aquinas compared the task of the legislator to that of the architect who has to determine not only that *a* house has to be built, but what kind of house and in which style.[28] By contrast, laws that are the result of *deductio*, such as the *ius gentium*, are more firmly connected to these principles (although error might creep in even there).

Finnis adopts this insight and conceives of legislation as a combination of both methods. To a large extent, legislation is brought about by *determinatio*. The example he mentions is a familiar one: the regulation of property.

> If material goods are to be used efficiently for human well-being, there must normally be a regime of private property. [...]. But precisely what rules should be laid down in order to constitute such a regime is not settled ('determined') by this general requirement of justice. Reasonable choice of such rules is to some extent guided by the circumstances of a particular society, and to some extent 'arbitrary'.[29]

The creation of the 'stylised drama' of law is to some extent the result of arbitrary decisions in view of the contingency of human affairs.

---

[27] Finnis, 1992, p. 142.
[28] ST I, II, 95, 2.
[29] NLNR pp. 285-6.

However, we should not overestimate the degree of arbitrariness involved. The legislator is not entirely free to draft the legal system as he sees fit. He has to take into account several principles which, according to Finnis, are deduced from the first principles of natural law (i.e. the basic goods).[30]

Which are the principles Finnis has in mind? Not only the kind of principles Aquinas allowed for, the principles prohibiting murder, or theft, which can be regarded as deductions from the various ends for mankind. Finnis deviates from that view and presents us with a rather complex variety of such deduced principles.

First of all, the legislator should be guided by the desiderata of the Rule of Law. The Rule of Law, as it is described by Finnis, seems to comprise no more than the eight requirements, devised by Lon Fuller,[31] that a legal system should meet in order to count as law. According to Fuller, laws should be publicised, understandable, not changed overnight, not retroactive, not be impossible to comply with, internally coherent, applied by rules that are stable, clear and coherent, and administered by persons who can be held accountable and who are consistent.[32]

In the second place, the 'reasonable legislator' is guided by

> [...] a multitude of other substantive principles related, some very closely, others more remotely, some invariably and others contingently, to the basic principles and methodological requirements of practical reason.[33]

These principles are a mixed bag, as can be judged from Finnis's enumeration. Fundamental principles such as 'no criminal liability without *mens rea*' or '*pacta sunt servanda*' go hand in hand with procedural rules of evidence, such as estoppel, which precludes someone from denying the truth of a statement he has previously asserted.[34]

---

[30] Finnis distinguishes first-order from second-order principles. The former guide legislation, the latter regulate the application of the rule. He remarks that often a second-order principle is a mere translation of the first-order principles and vice versa, since their shared rationale is predictability and stability: NLNR pp. 286-7.

[31] Fuller, 1969, ch. II.

[32] NLNR pp. 270-1.

[33] NLNR p. 286.

[34] NLNR p. 288.

The relation between *determinatio* and *deductio* is a complex one. For instance, the legislator who wants to integrate the law of property (the product of *determinatio*) in the entire system of law, has to take into account principles, such as the requirements of the Rule of Law, which result from *deductio*. At the same time, this attempt to integration requires 'countless elaborations'.[35] These in turn cannot be carried out without *determinatio*. That is why Finnis points out that the two methods are not 'two streams flowing in separate channels.'[36]

However, complex as the relation might be, it is Finnis's view that a particular *determinatio* should not be conflicting with the principles which are the result of *deductio*: the eight desiderata of the Rule of Law as well as the mixed bag of principles that are 'closely or remotely' deduced from the basic goods together with the methodological requirements.

4. *The Rule of Law and the common good*

Finnis's complex conception of the principles that are the result of a *deductio* induces us to consider the question to what extent this mixture of procedural and substantial principles can indeed be regarded as deductions of the basic goods, as Finnis claims. This may seem a technical question, but it is important if we want to assess the scope of natural law for these deduced principles check the arbitrariness of *determinatio*. If Finnis can argue that the Rule of Law together with the other principles are deductions from the seven basic goods, the theory of the basic goods might indeed be regarded as a successful attempt to unify modern substantial as well as procedural requirements within one theory of natural law.

However, an explicit argument is lacking. As for the variety of substantial principles Finnis adduces (such as *pacta sunt servanda* or 'no one should be allowed to judge his own cause'), we might see these as deductions from the basic goods and the methodological requirements, although Finnis does not actually carry out these deductions. But it is more difficult to see how the Rule of Law can be regarded as 'deductions' from the basic goods. How can the prohib-

---

[35] NLNR p. 288.
[36] NLNR p. 289.

ition of retroactive legislation enable us to pursue the good of 'play'? Or how does the promulgation of law help us pursue the basic good of 'religion'? These questions seem to suggest that the Rule of Law is very 'remotely' linked to the basic goods indeed.

We have to keep in mind, however, that the common good serves as an intermediate link between the basic goods and law. And according to Finnis, the common good of communities should be regarded as a set of conditions which enable the members of society to pursue the basic goods as they see fit. As such, the common good provides for the necessary co-ordination without which the basic goods cannot be pursued. The common good is a boundary condition.

If we regard the common good in this light, it is indeed possible to see how the Rule of Law can be directly linked to the common good (and therefore—indirectly—to the basic goods). Finnis remarks:

> The fundamental point of the desiderata [i.e. the Rule of Law, P.W.] is to secure to the subjects of authority the dignity of self-direction and freedom from certain forms of manipulation.[37]

It is only by a stable, effective and predictable system of law that citizens have the possibility to pursue the basic goods.

Finnis could have rested at that. However, he is evidently not satisfied with that analysis. After having outlined that the Rule of Law is of great importance in order to ensure certainty and predictability, he keeps stressing that the common good should not be identified with these aims. The common good is 'a wider good', to which the aim of certainty is subordinate. He keeps stressing the distinction between the technical aspect of law (as a tool aiming at certainty, etc.) and the moral aspect of law as furthering the common good. Therefore Finnis attenuates the importance of the Rule of Law. It

> does not guarantee every aspect of the common good, and sometimes it does not secure even the substance of the common good.[38]

That is why we should not always give priority to the Rule of Law. After having outlined that the Rule of Law falls short of the common good, Finnis argues that it is sometimes necessary to depart from the

---

[37] NLNR p. 273.
[38] NLNR p. 274.

Rule of Law, 'temporarily but sometimes drastically'. According to Finnis, the written constitution is not a 'suicide-pact'. In extreme conditions, true 'statesmanship' is required.[39] Since stability and certainty are in the service of a 'wider good', it is sometimes necessary that these virtues should be sacrificed in order to instantiate that wider good.

These are puzzling remarks. As a way of enabling people to pursue the various basic goods, the Rule of Law is of vital importance in creating the desired climate. The Rule of Law may be merely a part of the common good, but an important part. How then can Finnis write that the common good can require a departure from the Rule of Law? How can he say that it does not secure even the 'substance of the common good'? The Rule of Law *is* the substance of the common good![40]

Moreover, if the Rule of Law only serves to realise aims that are thought to be *subordinated* to the common good, how can we make sense of Finnis's statement that the Rule of Law is to be regarded as deductions of the principles of natural law (capable of checking particular determinations)? If the Rule of Law is not seen as a—vital—ingredient of the common good, but merely as subordinated, to be brushed aside in case of conflict with the common good, how then can these subordinate principles serve as standards by means of which the determinations can be justified and/or criticised?

I think that this confusion is due to an ambiguity of the concept of the common good itself. This ambiguity can be illustrated by a recent article in which Finnis distinguishes two concepts of the common good.[41] The common good can be instrumental or non-instrumental, he writes.[42] The instrumental common good is the common good we have come across so far. It is a set of conditions, necessary for the participation in a basic good. The common good of a political community is instrumental in the sense that it provides for the required co-ordination without which basic goods cannot be enjoyed.

But there is a non-instrumental common good as well. That kind of common good can be *identified* with (one) of the basic goods. This is,

---

[39] NLNR p. 275.

[40] This is Fuller's own view of the Rule of Law. According to Fuller, it is misleading to regard law as a (technical) instrument in order to bring about certain ultimate values or ends. Law *is* a form of order itself. Fuller, 1958, p. 60.

[41] Finnis, 1996.

[42] Finnis, 1996, p. 5.

for instance, the case in a community of religious believers. Their shared aim *consists* in the participation in one of the basic goods: religion. The same applies to friends: their shared aim *is* friendship, to be enjoyed for its own sake, and not with an eye to some external aim. If there were such an external purpose, friendship is not understood in the focal meaning of the term.[43]

It seems to me that it is Finnis's view that although the Rule of Law forms an important ingredient of the instrumental common good, it falls short of the kind of common good in the non-instrumental sense of the word. Whereas he has an instrumental common good in mind if he praises the advantages of the Rule of Law in securing a climate in which the members of society are free from manipulation, he has a 'higher' non-instrumental common good in mind in those passages where he concedes that the Rule of Law cannot 'secure the substance' of the common good.

5. *Rights and the common good*

The notion of the common good seems to be elusive. Despite the notion that the common good of a political community is instrumental for citizens to pursue the basic goods, Finnis evidently uses a more extensive conception of the common good as well.

This ambiguity is even more apparent in Finnis's analysis of rights. On the basis of an instrumental common good, it is not easy to see why the common good should be seen as more than a list of rights. Rights can also be regarded as a set of conditions which should be met in order to enable members of society to participate in the basic goods. Partly, this is conceded by Finnis. Speaking about the various declarations of rights, he concludes:

> When we survey this list [of rights, P.W.] we realize what the modern 'manifesto' conception of human rights amounts to. It is simply a way of sketching the *outlines of the common good*, the various aspects of

---

[43] Finnis also includes the common good of married couples in the list of non-instrumental common goods, but in fact, there is no basic good that can account for this inclusion. On the other hand, Finnis *excludes* the community of scientists from his list, although we might say that their 'shared aim' consists of 'knowledge' and as such the common good of these communities should be understood in the non-instrumental sense.

individual well-being in community. What the reference to rights contributes in this sketch is simply a pointed expression of what is implicit in the term *'common* good', namely that *each* and everyone's well-being, in each of its basic aspects, must be considered and favoured at *all* times by those responsible for co-ordinating the common life.[44]

And he points to an advantage of rights-talk as well. It is much more specified than general references to the common good.[45]

Despite this advantage of rights-talk, Finnis nevertheless keeps referring to an unspecified common good. Why? Because he thinks that rights can only *flourish* within the common good. Finnis remarks that

> [...] human rights can only be securely enjoyed in certain sorts of milieu—a context or framework of mutual respect and trust and common understanding [...].[46]

It is this 'milieu' that counts, not the individual rights as such. If the rights of a minority are infringed, Finnis adds, it is not only the minority which suffers, but it is a public affair, concerning us all.

He concludes that human rights are important *components* of the common good, and as such they are 'subject to or limited by other aspects of the common good'.[47] These other aspects can be described by expressions such as 'public morality', 'public health', 'public order'.[48] As components of that public order, rights should not be ascribed prematurely 'a conclusory or absolute status',[49] but should fit in an overall 'pattern', a 'conception of the human good.'[50]

However, it is not easy to understand these allusions to 'public order' or 'overall pattern' on the basis of an instrumental common good. If the common good is a set of conditions which enables the members of society to pursue the basic goods, it is difficult to see

---

[44] NLNR p. 214.
[45] NLNR p. 221.
[46] NLNR p. 216.
[47] NLNR p. 218.
[48] NLNR p. 218.
[49] NLNR pp. 220-1.
[50] NLNR p. 219.

how human rights can ever be subject to or limited by that common good, or how we can speak of the common good as the milieu in which rights flourish. Rather, this milieu *consists*, among other things, in the recognition of these rights.

Here again, we come across the same difficulty as we encountered in Finnis's conception of the Rule of Law. Both human rights and the Rule of Law are alleged to be embedded within and, in case of conflict, *subordinated* to the common good. But this claim cannot be understood on the basis of the instrumental notion of the common good.

I think therefore that Finnis's tendency to subordinate both rights and the Rule of Law to the common good can indeed only be understood if we interpret his notion of the common good in the noninstrumental meaning of the term. It is instructive to examine his views on that kind of common good, which is exemplified in his analysis of friendship. In the NLNR, this analysis immediately precedes that of 'community'. In friendship there is not only a shared objective, external to the relation, Finnis asserts. One does not form a friendship merely to further one's own interest. Each of the parties involved acts for the sake of the other. The unity between friends, thus constituted, forms in itself a point of view which is not reducible to the perspective of one or the other, but is a

> unique perspective from which one's own good and one's friend's good are equally 'in view' [...].[51]

It is from this vantage-point that the common good can be discerned.

Translated to the common good of a political community, it seems to be Finnis's view that right-claims should be judged in the light of such a vantage-point. The 'unique perspective', in which the good of the society as a whole is in view, can indeed be regarded as more than the sum-total of rights.

In fact, it is perfectly possible to regard the common good of a political community as the direct participation of one of the seven basic goods. One of the goods is termed, somewhat ambiguously, 'sociability (friendship)'. 'In its weakest form' it is 'realized by a minimum of peace and harmony amongst men', in its strongest form

---

[51] NLNR p. 143.

it results in the true union of friends described above.[52] If living in society is in itself the participation in the basic good of 'sociability', there is no reason to conceive it as an instrumental common good. The common good of members of society is itself the participation of one of the basic goods: 'sociability', just as the common good of a group of religious believers is itself a basic good: 'religion'.

However, Finnis does not draw this consequence. I think that his reluctance is partly due to his conception of the basic goods. In the preceding chapter, we have seen that Finnis emphasises that these are all equally and intrinsically valuable. They cannot be reduced to each other, and they are even alleged to be incommensurable. He clings to this thesis because he thinks that the assumption of one overriding aim (happiness, or even sociability) would hamper man's fundamental freedom of choice. He keeps stressing the (Neo-)Kantian view that the assumption of one ultimate aim would reduce the moral debate on ends into a technical calculation of means. That is, I think, why he is reluctant to conceive of the common good in the non-instrumental sense of the term. It would exalt the virtue of 'sociability' above the other basic goods.

So we see that Finnis faces a dilemma. On the one hand, he wants to conceive of the common good as more than the sum-total of human rights. Parallel to that view is his concept of society as more than an aggregate of individuals. Consequently, 'public interest' is more than the sum-total of individual interests. But in order to provide human rights with such an overall foundation, a more substantial concept of the common good is required than the instrumental one he offers. However, such a substantial, non-instrumental concept is at odds with the plurality of principles of natural law (basic goods) and cannot be developed or even openly acknowledged.

6. Decisionism

In the preceding chapter (IX.5), I remarked that the assumption of the incommensurability of basic goods, although intended to widen the scope for practical reasoning, in fact reduced that scope. Finnis's theory of natural law provides no information that can guide our selection among the basic goods in case they conflict. The methodo-

---

[52] NLNR p. 88.

logical requirements do not help us further. The choice for a basic good is ultimately an arbitrary one.

It seems as if this problem does not only affect our daily choices between 'going to church' or 'helping friends', but is equally responsible for his analysis of positive law. On the one hand, Finnis unequivocally stresses the importance of the common good. His analysis of the Rule of Law and of human rights indicates that it is Finnis's view that procedural constraints, important as they may be as instruments to the wider good, are nevertheless 'instruments' and as such subordinated to that common good. As we saw in section 4, he even allows for departures from the Rule of Law in order to safeguard the common good.

But what *is* this wider good? It is not to be understood in the non-instrumental sense as merely the participation in the basic good of sociability: that would narrow down the scope for moral debate. Nor is it to be regarded as an instrumental common good. According to Finnis, the common good is 'more' than the conditions created by the Rule of Law and is 'more' than human rights to freedom and equality.

Is the common good then the sum-total of basic goods? We might think that Finnis conceives of the ideal society as furthering the participation of all basic goods alike (funding sports, culture, religion). However, any society, even an affluent one, has to confront, sooner or later, the choice between the incommensurable basic values. On the basis of Finnis's view that the incommensurability of the basic goods is the *sine qua non* for moral debate, this debate is apparently about the desirability of the various basic goods. We might think that the issues to be decided upon refer to a *particular conception* of the common good. A fundamentalist may regard 'religion' as one of the pillars of the common good. It is true that Finnis adds that we should not directly harm one of the basic goods, but nevertheless there is room for a society to decide whether 'knowledge', or 'play', or 'religion' should have top-priority or not.

But how can we deliberate on these topics if the basic goods are incommensurable? Does not that imply that the choice for a *particular conception* of the common good is an arbitrary affair, just as the choice of an individual between the competing basic goods is ultimately an arbitrary one? This indeed seems to be Finnis's view, explicated in his article of 1992. There, he draws the full consequences of his incommensurability-thesis which he defends against Dworkin as well as the adherents of the so-called 'Economic Analysis of Law', who are criticised for maintaining that the goals for human society can be rationally decided upon and that the means towards their achievement are a matter of—technical—calculation. In this article, Finnis claims that all moral norms—both on the individual and the collective level—ultimately rest on *a pre-moral choice*.[53]

Even the Golden Rule ('Do to others as you would have them do to you; do not impose on others what you would not want to be obliged by them to accept') is not exempt from this arbitrariness. Finnis argues that here a commensuration is required of what would *count* as burdens and benefits. But this cannot be carried out in a rational way. They are incommensurable. The only option available is to rely on one's *'feelings* towards various goods and bads'.[54] The same applies to collective decision-making:

> Analogously, in the life of a community, the preliminary commensuration of rationally incommensurable factors is accomplished not by rationally determined judgements, but by *decisions* (choices).[55]

The examples he furnishes are to some extent trivial. He speaks about 'the decision to permit road traffic to proceed faster than 10 m.p.h.', or 'to define trusts as English law does'.[56] These are relatively innocent examples. In fact, we might view these decisions as *determinationes*. But as determinations, they should, according to Finnis's own theory expounded in the NLNR, be judged in the light of deduced principles. Here, however, he does not allow for that possibility. He asserts that we do not have a 'rational critique' of that society's decision.

It seems to me that in this article he draws the full consequence of his view that the Rule of Law is subordinate to the common good. In quiet times and stable societies the Rule of Law is a suitable instrument to bring about that common good. But the Rule of Law is not a suitable standard by means of which a particular conception of the common good can be evaluated. Despite his claim that a *determinatio* should be judged along the principles that are the outcome of deduction, the principles of the Rule of Law simply do not qualify as such

---

[53] Finnis, 1992, p. 148.
[54] Finnis, 1992, p. 149.
[55] Ibid.
[56] Finnis, 1992, p. 150.

standards. In section 4, I already wondered how we can conceive of the Rule of Law as deductions; here we see again that they cannot exercise their critical task.

This is, I think, a potentially dangerous view. If one comes to think of it, only those conceptions of the 'common good' in which a basic good is systematically violated are excluded by Finnis. The particular conception of a religious fundamentalist regime, for instance, can be justified by Finnis's theory. It can justify its choice by referring to the importance of the basic good of religion. It can emphasise (if fact it *does*) that the particular conception of the common good it has opted for does more justice to the basic good of 'sociability' since it knits its members together in 'more than an aggregate of individuals'. It might emphasise that it includes the basic good of 'knowledge' as well, be it that it is understood as 'true' (divinely inspired) knowledge. It might concede that it does not allow much room for 'play', but nevertheless it does not directly violate that basic good either. In fact, since freedom is not included in the list of basic goods, there is no basic good that is directly harmed by such a regime.

This is not to say that Finnis is a religious fundamentalist. But there is nothing in his theory of natural law that excludes a 'choice' for a fundamentalist conception of the common good. Finnis's theory only seems to regard actions *within* a given normative and/or legal framework, but it does not raise the question whether that framework and the common good it is said to 'instantiate' are justified in themselves. Not only does it omit to raise that question; Finnis concedes that it is impossible to justify or criticise the ultimate choices that shaped these systems. The establishment of a legal system and the particular conception of the common good that underlies that system are matters of—arbitrary—choice.

In this sense, Finnis's theory can certainly be regarded as a worthy successor of natural law tradition, which is marked, as we have witnessed in the preceding chapters, by an ongoing tendency to confine the critical potentiality of natural law. The beginnings can be found in Aquinas's concept of the free *determinatio* by the legislator in framing the principles into particular rules. Yet, Aquinas still thought that the latter should be justified in terms of the former principles. Suárez widened the scope for human intervention by claiming that the affairs over which man has *dominium* can be regulated as the legislator sees fit. Grotius enhanced the discretionary powers of man even further. The main institutions of society cannot be criticised by means of natural law. Natural law prescribes only that we should obey these institutions once we have consented to them. And finally, in Pufendorf's theory, we only have criteria for a *post hoc* reconstruction of the rationality of human institutions. It is only where 'rights' are formulated (such as Grotius's perfect rights of states, and Pufendorf's 'moral' rights) that natural law can become effective as social criticism.

Finnis's argument can be regarded as a continuation of this development. Although he professes to agree with Aquinas that the *determinatio* should be justified in the light of principles deduced from the main principles of natural law, he in fact creates a gap between the common good on the one hand and on the other hand the 'deduced' principles (such as the Rule of Law) which are not deduced from the basic goods nor from any conception of the common good at all. It is ultimately the common good that gains priority. But this common good is not itself a subject for critical reflection. It is 'rationally underdetermined' to use Finnis's expression.[57] It is the result of choice and decision.

That is why even Pufendorf's modest criteria are no longer available to Finnis. The rational criteria Pufendorf had in mind and that were developed further by Kant are said to have no bearing on the matter how to assess the weight of the various competing values. These criteria come in only *after* we made an arbitrary decision on what is to be counted as good or bad.

7. *Civil obedience*

Despite the fact that the ultimate choice of the common good is premoral, rationally underdetermined and not subject to the criticism of the Rule of Law, since the latter is subordinated to the former, Finnis emphasises that we not only have a legal but also a moral obligation to obey the law.

His argument is inspired by Raz's concept of 'exclusionary reasons'.[58] An exclusionary reason is a reason one can have for disregarding other reasons. Raz mentions the example of a woman who is

---

[57] Finnis, 1992, p. 150.
[58] Finnis explicitly refers to Raz: NLNR p. 243. For Raz's exposition: cf. Raz, 1978; and Raz, 1975.

asked to make up her mind—quickly—about a particular, complicated investment-scheme. She is tired, and conscious of not being able to weigh the different reasons for or against the investment. Therefore, she decides to disregard all the various reasons for or against this investment. Such a decision is an exclusionary reason which is located at a different level than the other reasons in favour or against the investment. The decision counts as a (second-order) reason not to regard (first-order) reasons which pertain to the matter at hand.

Authority can also function as such an exclusionary reason. The rules laid down by an authoritative source can function as exclusionary reasons for disregarding other reasons. It is on the basis of the viewpoint of the just and reasonable man that Finnis defines the 'central case' of authority:

> A person treats something [...] as authoritative if and only if he treats it as giving him sufficient reason for believing or acting in accordance with it *notwithstanding* that he himself cannot otherwise see good reason for so believing or acting [...].[59]

In this sense, legal systems can have authority, but also books and doctors. However, the reasons on the basis of which the reasonable and just man decides to consider a *political or legal system* as authoritative (i.e. as exclusionary reason for action), differ from those which induce one to treat doctors as authoritative. The reason for treating rulers as authoritative is, according to Finnis, that they can 'settle co-ordination problems for the community'.[60]

Since the 'common good requires that co-ordination problems be solved',[61] the effectiveness of a (legal or political) system in settling these co-ordination problems is of overriding importance. Finnis claims that:

> for an understanding of the authoritativeness of rulers, as a concern of practical reasonableness, it is the sheer fact of effectiveness that is presumptively (not indefeasibly) decisive.[62]

---

[59] NLNR p. 233.

[60] NLNR p. 246.

[61] NLNR p. 244.

[62] NLNR p. 247. Note that 'understanding' here is understanding by the reasonable spectator, i.e. justification.

This emphasis on effectiveness induces Finnis to emphasise the importance of the Rule of Law:

> In short, it is the values of the Rule of Law that give the legal system its distinctive entitlement to be treated as the source of authoritative solutions.[63]

By 'values' Finnis refers to the stability and predictability of the legal system. As we have seen earlier, Finnis attaches much importance to these values (be it that they are subordinated to the common good) because they ensure that the five formal features of law (enumerated in section 2) are 'instantiated'. The self-generating quality of a legal coercive order is enhanced by following Fuller's requirements.

What does this analysis imply for our moral obligation to obey the law? The mere fact that it counts as an exclusionary reason does not in itself point to such an obligation. Raz points out that although exclusionary reasons cannot be countervailed by first-order reasons (for that is the definition of an exclusionary reason), they *can* be countervailed by other exclusionary reasons. If, for instance, I have decided not to serve my country as a soldier as long as that army occupies a neighbouring country, that decision counts to me as an exclusionary reason, which collides with the exclusionary reason furnished by legal authority.

But although Raz wants to make room for such deliberation between exclusionary reasons,[64] Finnis does not want to allow for such a scope of moral reasoning. Referring to the formal feature of law that it presents itself 'as a seamless web', he asserts:

> Its subjects are not permitted to pick and choose among the law's prescriptions and regulations.[65]

Why not? Finnis adduces two arguments, which might be referred to as a Socratic and a Kantian argument.[66] The Socratic argument points to the benefits one has acquired thanks to law's proper functioning. The Kantian argument points out that the legal system as a whole can only be effective if it is universally followed.

---

[63] Finnis, 1991a, II, p. 280.
[64] See Raz, 1994, p. 348.
[65] Finnis, 1991a, II, p. 264.
[66] Ibid. Cf. also NLNR p. 361.

According to Raz, both arguments fail to convince. Since one has no choice but to accept the benefits, which most of the time are not even requested, the Socratic argument is unsatisfactory. The Kantian argument leads to circularity. Raz points out that nor law's claim to be a seamless web, neither the need for co-ordination, are in themselves sufficient justifications for a general obligation to obey the law. It is only on the assumption that one has to obey the law that one can argue from the seamless web to a general obligation.[67]

This criticism seems to be justified. We have seen that Finnis differentiates between the moral rationale of law and its technical aspects. We saw that Finnis thinks that the Rule of Law proves to be insufficient as a bridge to link both aspects. But since the Rule of Law falls short of the common good, he can hardly argue now that the common good is achieved (or instantiated) by following the Rule of Law alone. Indeed, Raz is right to criticise Finnis's position that the technical quality of law is a sufficient foundation for a moral obligation to obey the law.

Yet, this is precisely Finnis's claim. According to Finnis, only if law is effective, can the common good be instantiated. Even in cases where a particular law seems to clash with the requirements of practical reasonableness disobedience is not justified. It would impede law to exercise its co-ordinative functions which instantiate the common good in a far more important way than it would be served by departure from the law in particular instances.

Here at last, we see that the Rule of Law and the effectiveness of the formal features of law are linked with the common good. And not only linked, but identified. If one reads Finnis's accounts on civil disobedience, his statement is clearly that the common good can only be instantiated by an effective and smooth functioning of the law. Notwithstanding his reservations concerning the ability of the Rule of Law to guarantee the common good, his position here is that the Rule of Law is nevertheless a surer path to the common good than the individual's own practical deliberation can afford. Civil disobedience is therefore out of the question for Finnis and it is in vain that Raz warns him for the (moral) risks of 'uncritical acceptance of authority'.[68] One has a moral obligation to obey positive law, no matter

---

[67] Raz, 1994, pp. 350-2.
[68] Raz, 1994, p. 351.

how it is 'determined', because it is the only means to secure the common good.

We see here a curious reversal of the position outlined in section 4. There, he concedes that the procedural safeguards, presented by the Rule of Law, still are subordinated to the common good, since the values of the Rule of Law (certainty, predictability) are merely tools for a wider aim. But when it comes to establishing the authority of legal systems and our moral duty to comply with them, he identifies the common good with certainty and predictability, since it is the only way to co-ordinate the actions of citizens. And co-ordination is fundamental to the common good.

This contradiction can only be solved if we understand Finnis's Rule of Law as a two-sided concept. As a set of procedural safeguards for individual citizens, the Rule of Law should be subordinated to the common good; as mechanisms by means of which rulers can co-ordinate, the Rule of Law is identified with the common good. The Rule of Law cannot serve as a standard by means of which positive law can be criticised, but it is an all-important tool for the justification of positive law.

8. *Conclusion*

If we regard Finnis's theory in the light of the four assumptions which served me to evaluate the contributions of the other natural law theorists who are discussed in this book, a remarkable picture can be sketched.

It is indeed Finnis's view (assumption a) that there are eternal principles which serve as standards for the evaluation of positive law. These standards, however, can justify almost any legal system, including systems which limit or violate human rights of liberty and equality, if the common good requires such violations. The particular conception of the common good itself can only be criticised if it systematically violates one or more of the basic goods.

Assumption b (these eternal principles are grounded in human nature) is indeed maintained by Finnis, but he does not infer from that view that we can discover these principles by an examination of human nature. We have access to these principles by reason (assumption c), but by 'reason' the modern natural lawyers do not refer to rational perception of nature, but only to the immediate grasp of self-evidence which remains unargued (see chapter IX).

Finally, Finnis does not maintain assumption d) that our moral duty to obedience is dependent on the justification of positive law in the light of eternal principles. It is Finnis's view that we have a general duty to obedience. In the first place, this view is a direct implication of the limited critical potential of the list of basic goods (see assumption a). But even those legal systems that violate one of the basic goods (and are *not* justified in the light of Finnis's natural law) should nevertheless be obeyed, since they can carry out their co-ordinative task only by such civil obedience. There remains but one criterion which exempts us from that duty, and that is ineffectiveness. However, that criterion does not figure on the list of the basic goods and is properly speaking not a principle of natural law.

These are disappointing conclusions for anyone who has been taught that natural law theory can avoid the dangers and pitfalls of legal positivism by allowing for moral and critical evaluation of positive law. In fact, Finnis's theory of natural law exhorts us to be more uncritically law-abiding than any legal positivist has ever dared to suggest. I think that this disappointing result is due to the fact that Finnis's theory is a mixture of two traditions: Neo-Kantianism and natural law theory.

The (Neo-)Kantian conceptual framework of Finnis's theory is, I think, responsible for the decisionist account of the common good. This chapter has shown that the criteria Finnis develops (the need for co-ordination, predictability) come in *after* a decision on the kind of common good to be pursued, a decision which has to be based on feelings rather than reasons, since the competing values are incommensurable.

The incommensurability-thesis is inspired by the persistent dichotomy between means and ends and consequently, between the technical and the moral aspects of law. Already in Kant's work this division is responsible for a dividing line between law and morals. Yet, Kant believed that it is possible to decide between ends in a rational way. Neo-Kantians stressed that such a rational decision is not possible. According to people like Hans Kelsen and Max Weber, the ultimate values cannot be reconciled. This view has widened the gap between law and morals (or for that matter, between science and morals) even further. It is no coincidence that Neo-Kantians such as Kelsen could, without much difficulty, develop their programme of legal positivism.

But this further development into (the German type of) legal positivism does not lead to the kind of unconditional surrender to the status quo that is proposed by Finnis. Weber as well as Kelsen thought of politics as the domain where values could be chosen—arbitrarily—, but of science as the domain where means can be calculated. Distorted as this separation might be, it leaves some room for scientists to create their own *niche*, where the mind can be free, as Kelsen once expressed it.

The problem with Finnis is that he does not want to rest at that. And it is here where the second element of his theory comes in: natural law tradition. As a result, Finnis keeps stressing that law is *not* a mere technique and ends up identifying the technical and the moral aspects of law, by reducing the latter to the former. Consequently, there is no niche to be found in Finnis for autonomous scientists and professional lawyers, in Weber's sense. That implies that there is no room left for a moral evaluation, *separate* from a formal analysis of law as a technical enterprise. This is due to the particular viewpoint Finnis decides upon which is equally inspired by natural law theory: that of the just and reasonable man. His view that a phenomenon such as law can only be understood if we understand its moral rationale, precludes the possibility of a moral critique apart from a formal analysis.

In this sense, I should modify my opinion, expressed in section 1 of this chapter, where I asserted that Finnis's methodology is similar to Pufendorf's, since both authors combine explanation and justification. This chapter reveals that Finnis's method is exactly the *reverse* of that of Pufendorf. Pufendorf tried to unravel the moral rationale of human institutions by explaining them. Finnis, however, sets out to explain human institutions by treating them as having a moral rationale. Since Pufendorf seriously sets out to unravel the various factors that contributed to the establishment of human institutions, he has the possibility to decide, after he has carried out his analysis, whether these institutions match the divine imposition or not. That is why we saw that Pufendorf in fact allowed for a considerable scope of criticism. But Finnis presupposes the moral 'point' of these institutions. Without a moral rationale, they are unintelligible to him. That is why we see that once Finnis 'understands' these institutions, they are justified as well and there is no room left for a critical evaluation.

In the introduction to the preceding chapter, I sketched three ambitions of contemporary natural law theory: a) to provide for a foundation of rights; b) to unravel common values on the basis of philosophical argument alone; and c) to criticise liberalism by means of natural law rather than by a theory based on the concept of 'virtues'. In the preceding chapter I already remarked that aim b) is not convincingly carried out. As for aim a), to provide for a foundation of human rights, we see indeed that Finnis tries to accommodate for rights-talk on the basis of a conception of the common good as the 'milieu' in which rights can flourish. However, the concept of 'common good' is unsatisfactorily developed. It seems to waver between an instrumental and a non-instrumental meaning, neither of which are fully explicated. This problem is enhanced by the fact that the particular conception of the common good is not rationally informed, but a product of pre-moral choice. It seems to me that human rights are more secure without a foundation than with this arbitrary foundation, especially when the foundation of these rights can be used in order to abrogate these rights, a possibility Finnis's theory allows for.

The arbitrariness and insufficiency of the notion of the common good might be traced to Finnis's neglect of virtues. The third aim I distinguished is Finnis's intention to criticise liberalism without recourse to a virtues-idiom. I am not in a position to judge whether Finnis fares much better than the theorists who start from the concept of virtues as developed by Aristotle and Aquinas. However, if one compares Finnis's analysis of the common good with MacIntyres's, one cannot escape the impression that the ambiguities between an instrumental and a non-instrumental common good can, to a large extent, be clarified and maybe even resolved by an analysis in terms of practices and virtues.[69] The fundamental ambiguity of Finnis's concept of the common good does not contribute to the attractiveness of his theory as an alternative to 'rights-talk'.

---

[69] Hittinger, 1992, criticises Finnis for having unnecessarily curtailed virtues in his account of natural law.

EPILOGUE

I

If there is any continuity to be found in the successive natural law theories analysed in this book, it is the increasing difficulty to provide natural law theory with an adequate foundation. Aquinas had erected the whole edifice on the assumption that God created the world according to an ordering principle, a style, which He expressed in nature. Human beings have access to that normative order by means of *synderesis*, the angel's eye which perceives at a glance the divine plan and its expression in nature.

Suárez's theory reveals that as soon as one questions this particular conception of creation, Aquinas's foundation is no longer available. Suárez understands creatures as representations, as finished products which do not reveal by themselves a normative order. Nature can only gain normative significance by means of God's rational judgement and explicit will. In order to rescue natural law from falling apart, Aquinas's foundation had to be fortified with two additional foundations: God's judgement and God's will.

The increasing tension between the three pillars of natural law induced Grotius to introduce an intermediate link. Natural law may be ultimately grounded in God, but proximately in human nature. Since we can only be certain about that latter foundation, this should be the starting-point for the deduction of natural law. However, the tensions between reason, will and nature that mark Suárez's foundation return on the level of human nature in its three features: self-preservation, sociability and rationality. The latter two features tend to be reduced to the all-important urge to self-preservation.

Pufendorf's return to Suárez's concept of law as a set of obligatory precepts, induced him to criticise Grotius's concept of human nature in the same way as Suárez had criticised Aquinas. Pufendorf discards the entire notion that (human) nature can give rise to norms. It is not even a partial foundation of natural law. Norms can only be imposed by either God or human beings. Imposition and creation are sharply distinguished. The edifice of natural law breaks down along precisely those fissures that had surfaced in Suárez's theory. After Pufendorf, natural law theory is divided into two programmes, neither of which can be regarded as justificatory attempts to connect law with nature. The first is a 'naturalistic' programme, in which human society is explained by reference to human nature; the second is the 'rationalist' programme, in which universal justificatory principles are formulated on the basis of reason alone.

Finnis's theory of natural law can be regarded as a continuation of this latter programme. The—professed—anxiety to commit the naturalistic fallacy as well as his foundation in ultimate and incommensurable values testify to the dominance of (Neo-)Kantian assumptions. The ultimate values he discerns (the seven basic goods) lack a foundation, although there are indications that nature is—secretly—allowed to play its traditional role. The blend of Neo-Kantianism and natural law result in a theory in which morality is identified with the effectiveness of law and exhorts us to a moral obligation to obedience even to those regimes that have opted for a conception of the common good which cannot be defended by Finnis's theory.

One might say that the failure of Finnis's Neo-Kantian formulation of natural law does not imply that natural law as such is a dead-end. Would it not be possible to start working at the other side of the post-Pufendorfian divide and to develop a natural law theory which emphasises nature rather than reason? Is it not possible, for instance, to start from the assumption that there are certain natural ends to be pursued (e.g. evolutionary success, cultural diversification) and to develop a theory of natural law that is informed by modern biological theories?

On the basis of my analysis of Finnis alone we cannot decide that question. It can be expected, however, that such a theory would not be able to solve the dilemmas inherent in any form of natural law which is not supported by a concept of God as the creator of a meaningful and normative order, i.e. a concept of eternal law in Aquinas's sense of the term. In the first place, such a theory needs to argue that it is reasonable to act according to nature. It is of no use to point out that there is a limited rationality perceptible in nature (in the economic cost-benefit sense of the term rationality), for why should that be the kind of rationality we should strive for? In the second place, even if there would be agreement upon the concept of rationality, the problem of obligation would have to be dealt with. Nature may indicate desirable courses of actions, but can never oblige. Suárez's addition of the divine will (already an uneasy addition in his own theory) is not accessible to us.

In the third place, we have to take into account the enormous problem of translation. Even if it can be conceded that there is 'something' in nature which is reasonable and even obligatory, one cannot hope to translate that 'something' into guidelines for the regulation of human affairs. All the principles and guidelines that the discussed authors have come up with, suffer from an incurable generality. They could only be applied to practice by means of a *determinatio* which is often so arbitrary that we can as well do without these general principles. So even if it is assumed that there is some foundation of morals in nature, in the sense that human beings have naturally evolved and that their ethics can hardly be said to have been developed out of thin air,[1] this does not help determine the moral merits of basic human institutions or the way we should reason about personal affairs.

Off-hand, we might conclude that there is no reason to believe that a naturalistic programme would fare so much better than Finnis's development of natural law theory on the basis of a Kantian programme in which reason is given priority to nature. The theoretical reconstruction of successive natural law theories reveals that it is only by combining and reconciling will, reason and nature within one unified concept that we can hope to establish some form of natural law theory. I do not see how such a reconciliation can be brought about other than by Thomistic assumptions. Exactly those assumptions have been undermined. We might deplore that loss. We might regret to have forsaken our 'angel's eye' by questioning the possibility of *synderesis*. In that case, however, it is advisable to convert to Thomism rather than to develop a new theory of natural law.

II

There is another reason not to try to develop a new variety of natural law doctrine. This reason is not immediately revealed by any particular natural law theory, but by the story of decline of which the theories discussed are the successive episodes.

It is important to note that the gradual undermining of the foundations of Aquinas's edifice is not due to bad maintenance or neglect. On the contrary, the history of natural law is marked by constant

---

[1] Cf. Dennett, 1995, p. 467.

attempts at renovation. These attempts seem to be inspired by the belief that natural law theory can serve as a bulwark, a fixed point in the contingencies of human affairs. As such it had to be fortified.

Suárez rehabilitated and developed natural law theory in order to avert the undermining influence of Lutheranism and voluntarism. Grotius renewed the foundations of natural law in order to rescue it from the crumbling forces of scepticism. Pufendorf used it in order to avoid the arbitrariness inherent in a purely theological account of politics and law. Finnis tries to restore natural law theory in order to rescue legal theory from proceduralism and technicality.

Paradoxically, these renovations achieved exactly the opposite effect of the intended one. The reformulations of natural law theory largely consist in the effort to disarm the enemy forces by incorporating them. This strategy turns out to be a dangerous one: once the enemy is encapsulated, it undermines natural law theory from within.

Suárez's attempt to stem Lutheranism and voluntarism resulted in a concept of natural law which incorporated the divine will. This incorporation led to increasing tensions within the theory itself which could not be reconciled. Grotius's enterprise of securing natural law against scepticism induced him to emphasise self-preservation and to situate it on the level of universal human nature. His attempt resulted in a natural law theory which can be regarded as a universal foundation of 'expediency'. Pufendorf's aim to demarcate natural law from theology resulted in a foundation of natural law which was identical to that of divine law. And finally, Finnis's attempt to criticise purely technical analyses of law resulted in a theory in which morality threatens to be identified with technicality.

We might be tempted to explain this paradox by pursuing the metaphor of fortification further. We might regard these renovations as coming 'too late'. It is unwise to lay bare the foundations of a building in bad weather. No wonder, the rain creeps in at that stage. I think, however, that we should abandon the metaphor altogether and assume that it is the *metaphor itself* which is to blame for the failures of all these ingenious and intelligent renovators. It is the dominant view of natural law as a bulwark, cherished by each of the authors discussed, that can be held responsible for the demise of natural law theory. The failure of natural law theory should be ascribed to its foundational aspirations.

A comparison between Finnis and Grotius might clarify this point. As I noted in chapter V, Grotius's account of natural law is marked by the tendency to short-circuit the discussion on foundations. This does not imply that he abstains from searching for such a foundation, but he situates the foundation of natural law at a more 'superficial' level. He refrains from discussing whether it is God's will, or His judgement or His lessons which are at the basis of natural law. He resolves not to uncover these foundations, but to stop short at human nature. This decision enables him to formulate some natural rights, corresponding to human nature. Theoretically, this move might be unsatisfactory, but it is sufficient for the aim he has in mind. There is no need within his theory to ask further and to inquire into the foundations of these rights by investigating the foundations of human nature. His decision to abstain from a search for 'deeper' foundations has to a large extent been successful. Rights-language seemed (and still seems) to be appropriate for discussing moral and legal topics in everyday life.

We have seen that Finnis is not satisfied to rest at that level. He wants to inquire into the common values which are at the root of this rights-talk. But what does this digging for 'underlying' foundations amount to? A formulation of so-called 'basic goods'. In so far as these goods are proper foundations, in the sense that there is not a level to be found which is 'deeper', they are to a large extent trivial ('art' is better than 'trash'). In so far as they are not trivial, they are being contested (why 'religion' instead of 'dignity') and therefore apparently not fit to serve as foundations. His search for foundations has merely transferred the problem to another level. In Finnis's theory there may be a foundation of rights, but there is no foundation for the basic goods. Consequently, the concept of the common good can only be defended on decisionist grounds.

Finnis's theory testifies to the risk that this search for deeper levels of justification can overshoot the mark. In fact, his deeper foundation results in a discussion on a level which is much *too* deep for the topics for which the theory was designed. That is why it is in vain that one looks in Finnis's theory for a discussion of topics such as the problems pertaining to the aftermath of dictatorial regimes and the justification of retrospective legislation. He is honest enough to admit this omission, but adds that natural law theory cannot clarify these issues. Significantly, he writes:

> Much can be said on such questions, but little that is not highly contingent upon social, political and cultural variables.[2]

It is indeed. But natural law theory was designed to pass a verdict on contingent matters from a fixed and universal point of view. The discussion concerning the principles of practical reasoning is meaningful in so far as it can contribute to our understanding of the moral dilemmas which arise in a contingent world. If a theory of natural law relegates the discussion of such topics to the realm of the 'contingent', it has lost any practical significance.

I think therefore, that little can be gained by the constant search for justifications and explanations on a 'deeper level'. The persistence of a terminology in which reference is made to 'fundamental' reasons and 'underlying assumptions' testifies to the dominance of the metaphor which treats theories as buildings.[3] But theories are not buildings. They are more aptly compared to tools, as the pragmatist says. And the appropriateness of tools can only be decided by their effectiveness in dealing with certain problems, not by an examination of the firmness of their 'foundations'.

III

Despite the dominance of the foundational idiom, the natural lawyers discussed in this book, Finnis excepted, never quite forgot this instrumental value of natural law theory. In fact, we have seen in each second chapter on a particular author, how the natural law theorists tried to turn natural law theory into such a tool for coping with the dilemmas and practices posed by political and legal reality. Whereas the first chapters described the effort to fortify the building of natural law, the second chapters analysed the attempt to turn these buildings into tools, capable of analysing and justifying existing practices.

It is no wonder then, that there are dramatic discrepancies between the first and second chapters. Most of the buildings designed are simply not appropriate for the problems at hand. They are too general and too abstract in order to make legal and political institutions

---

[2] NLNR p. 362.
[3] Cf. also Lakoff and Johnson, 1980, ch. 17 and 18.

intelligible. In fact, the more these theories are fortified, the less versatile they are in dealing with practical problems. The solution for which the natural lawyers opted was to smuggle in another—more appropriate—tool under the disguise of natural law theory, which was better able to cope with reality than natural law proper. Aquinas relied on the virtue of *prudentia*, Suárez introduced the notion of 'custom', Grotius introduced and developed the concepts of 'consent' and 'rights', whereas Pufendorf focused on the way human beings 'impose' normative values and social roles. These tools were successful, but were only loosely connected to their programme of natural law.

This state of affairs is not a particular feature of natural law theory only. The same applies to mathematics. It achieved it greatest successes in its applications to physics, biology, electrical engineering, and computer science. This is in shrill contrast to its attempts to provide for a foundation. In the words of the historian of mathematics, Kline:

> The attempts to erect mathematics on an unshakable foundation have ended in failure. The successive attempts to provide a solid foundation, from Euclid through Weierstrass to the modern foundational schools, do not give any indication of an evolutionary advance which promises eventual success.[4]

This similarity between mathematics and natural law theory is not coincidental. Grotius may have been the first but not the last to have maintained that the science of natural law should adopt the mathematical method. For a long time, the main ambition of natural law theory was to link morality by means of a chain of inferences to first and firm principles *more geometrico*.

It seems then, that the history of mathematics indeed contains some valuable lessons for natural lawyers. If we are to take seriously the successes of mathematics, we should indeed proceed *more geometrico*, i.e. we should start theorising not about fundamentals but about applications.

---

[4] Kline, 1980, p. 320.

IV

In fact, such an approach has been proposed by Jonsen and Toulmin in their plea for a rehabilitation of casuistry.[5] They interestingly relate their experience as members of the National Commission for the Protection of Human Subjects of Biomedical and Behavioral Research and note that despite the widely varying backgrounds of the participants, agreement was much more easily reached about particular cases than about general principles. General principles led to the adoption of irreconcilable standpoints, whereas one tended to agree surprisingly easily about particular cases.[6] Jonsen and Toulmin therefore propose to abandon the search for universal principles and to develop and refine a casuistry better suited to cope with this kind of moral dilemmas.

Although I see no reason to enthuse over 16th century Spanish casuistry, we might regard their argument as a plea for the development of more specific concepts. In fact, these concepts should be specified to such an extent that they are effective in coping with a *particular* kind of problem. This might sound strange. Most philosophers see it as their main task to discover *universal* concepts and principles, not specific ones. But as soon as we abandon architectural metaphors and revert to the idiom of the engineer, in which concepts are compared to tools, it is easy to see why specific concepts are more successful than universal ones. The painter does not take a 'universal' brush, no matter the size of the painting or the material he intends to use.

In fact, we have seen (X.5) that Finnis himself praises the advantages of more specified concepts. 'Reference to rights' he remarks, 'is simply a *pointed* expression of what is implicit in the term "common good"' [my emphasis].[7] Indeed it is, and that is why the concept of 'rights' is more effective than the notion of the 'common good'. Not for all purposes, it should be noted. The notion of 'rights' can be a very blunt or improper tool as well, as is for instance revealed by the confused discussion of animal-rights. So we are left to determine which degree of conceptual specificity is needed for the issue at hand. That question can only be decided by the criterion of effectiveness.

---

[5] Jonsen and Toulmin, 1988.
[6] Jonsen and Toulmin, 1988, pp. 16-20.
[7] NLNR p. 214.

If we compare concepts with tools, it seems that the history of technology is no less instructive for our purpose than the history of mathematics. Apart from its lesson concerning the appropriateness of specific tools, it also teaches us that concepts should not be unnecessarily complex. We all know the famous stories of multi-purpose apparatuses which promise to make coffee, to cut onions as well as to squeeze oranges. These machines are never successful. Recently, the combination of a TV-set and a VCR in one apparatus met with a similar fate. These devices fail, because every consumer knows that if one element breaks down, the whole apparatus loses most of its use.

The successive attempts to reformulate natural law can be regarded as precisely the attempt to develop such a multi-purpose tool. It is used in order to deal with the nature of obligation, with promises, with the establishment of human society, with the gradual introduction of property, it should justify penal law and it should even inform us in our deliberation about personal affairs. But in order to do all these things, the concept had to be furnished with all sorts of additional devices. Not only the double function of 'consent' testifies to that tendency; Grotius's account of human nature as well as Suárez's three-fold foundation are conspicuous examples. And indeed, as soon as one element breaks down ('the divine will'), the whole edifice is useless.

V

Some readers might object that to regard concepts as tools is merely metaphorical language. Philosophy should not be compared with technology. Not only Finnis, but most philosophers cherish the notion that it is dangerous to reduce philosophy to a technique. These readers are right, but in a different sense than they think they are.

Usually they start from the (Kantian) assumption that there is a clear distinction between on the one hand 'means' and on the other hand 'ends'. Whereas ultimate values are the proper subjects for 'debate', the selection of tools is merely a matter of 'calculation'. In the discussion of Finnis's views we repeatedly came across this assumption.

Fuller convincingly argues that such a division is not tenable. He eloquently points out that the argument displays an enormous lack of understanding of what technique is about and underestimates the amount of deliberation required in order to devise these 'means'.[8] On the other hand, the Kantian argument mistakenly supposes the existence of desirable end-states as independent variables. In Fuller's words:

> [...] human aims and impulses do not arrange themselves in a neat row of desired 'end-states'. Instead they move in circles of interaction. We eat to live and we live to eat.[9]

Ends are not independent from how they are brought about. The end 'consists' of means. Referring to an 'ultimate end' such as 'equality', Fuller remarks:

> Until we find some means by which equal treatment can be defined and administered, we do not know the meaning of equality itself.[10]

This insight enables us to clarify the futility of Finnis's attempt to conceive of an 'ultimate' common good, to which 'rights' should be subordinated, or to which the Rule of Law is a mere means. As I noted (X.4 and X.5), the common good *consists in*, among other things, the mutual recognition of rights, the Rule of Law, and some procedural and ethical rules of thumb. What are these rules and principles? Tools or ends? That is apparently a wrong question.

The fact that this question cannot be asked, let alone answered, reveals, however, that in speaking about concepts as tools, the value of engineering metaphors is limited. We should not think of 'end' as a definite one, such as a chair or a CD-ROM. It is therefore not appropriate to speak of conceptual tools as 'mere' instruments. We might rather think of Aquinas's artist, who not merely aims at 'making a picture', but wants to create a work of art according to a certain style. The 'tools' needed for such an enterprise do not only comprise pencils and brushes. He needs this equipment, but he needs also experience, some stylistic guidelines and, indeed, exemplars. I think that our concepts can more aptly be compared to the latter kind of equipment than to instruments in the narrow sense of that word.

---

[8] Fuller, 1958, p. 56.
[9] Fuller, 1958, p. 54.
[10] Fuller, 1958, p. 62.

Rights, procedural principles, substantial guidelines are all elements which together make up a picture, that can only *post hoc* be evaluated as the realisation of an ultimate value, such as 'democracy'. But such *post hoc* reflection does not turn these concepts into mere means. As such, the kind of concepts we use can more properly be compared to Aquinas's 'sub-ends'. They are not 'complete ends' in the sense that we should regard them as ultimate values, to be cherished and pursued for their own sakes. But nor are they 'mere' means. Parliaments, policies and principles are more than mere instruments to bring about democracy. They form its component parts, have a value in themselves and move in 'circles of interaction'.

I think that these 'circles of interaction' are overlooked by the natural lawyers discussed in this book. That is why they keep looking for ends and 'first principles', whereas the concepts they needed were already there. They could have contented themselves with the notions which are described in my second chapters on each author, without bothering about the first principles at all. The search for ultimate foundations and last ends is as elusive as the search for a foundation of mathematics or the end of the world. There is no 'ultimate' horizon. In order to do justice to that wisdom, we should modify Aquinas and maintain that our 'most complete end' consists in taking seriously all those sub-ends.

REFERENCES

This bibliography lists only those works directly referred to or quoted in the text. The date after the name of the author refers to the original date. If a later edition is used, this is indicated in the reference after the full title. Footnotes in the main text refer to the original date; pages refer to the edition actually used.

Adler, Mortimer J. (1981), *Six Great Ideas*, New York.

An-Na'im, A.A. (1992), *Toward an Islamic Reformation*, Cairo.

Aquinas, Thomas (1266-73a), *Summa Theologiae*, Blackfriars edition, Cambridge, 1966. (abbrev. ST)

— (1266-73b), 'Summa Theologiae', in: *Basic Writings of Saint Thomas Aquinas*, ed. A.C. Pegis, New York, 1944.

— (1256-9), *De Veritate*, ed. Leonina, Rome, 1970. (abbrev. *De Ver.*)

Behme, Thomas (1995), *Samuel von Pufendorf: Naturrecht und Staat*, Göttingen.

— (1996), 'Gegensätzliche Einflüsse in Pufendorfs Naturrecht', in: Palladini and Hartung, 1996, pp. 74-82.

Berlin, Isaiah (1958), *Two Concepts of Liberty* (inaugural lecture), Oxford.

Besselink, Leonard (1988), 'The Impious Hypothesis Revisited', *Grotiana*, 9, pp. 3-63.

— (1992), Review of Eyffinger and Vermeulen, 'Hugo de Groot, Denken over Oorlog en Vrede', *Recht en Kritiek*, 18, 4, pp. 384-90.

Bourke, Vernon (1981), Review of Finnis's NLNR, *American Journal of Jurisprudence*, 26, pp. 243-7.

Boyle, Joseph (1992), 'Natural Law and the Ethics of Traditions', in: George, 1992, pp. 3-30.

Buckle, Stephen (1991), *Natural law and the theory of property: Grotius and Hume*, Oxford.

Chiappelli, F. (ed.) (1976), *First Images of America: the Impact of the New World on the Old*, Berkeley.

Chroust, Anton-Hermann (1943), 'Hugo Grotius and the Scholastic Natural Law Tradition', *The New Scholasticism*, XVII, pp. 101-33.

— (1981), 'A Summary of the Main Achievements of the Spanish Jurist-Theologians in the History of Jurisprudence', *The American Journal of Jurisprudence*, 26, pp. 112-24.

Crowe, M.B. (1976), 'The impious hypothesis: a paradox in Hugo Grotius?', *Tijdschrift voor Filosofie*, 38, pp. 397-410.

D'Arcy, Eric (1961), *Conscience and its Right to Freedom*, London.

Dennett, Daniel D. (1995), *Darwin's Dangerous Idea: Evolution and the Meanings of Life*, London.

D'Entrèves, A.P. (1951), *Natural Law: An Introduction to Legal Philosophy*, 2nd ed., London, 1971.

Denzer, Horst (1972), *Moralphilosophie und Naturrecht bei Samuel Pufendorf: Eine geistes- und wissenschaftsgeschichtliche Untersuchung zur Geburt des Naturrechts aus der praktischen Philosophie*, München.

Dufour, A. (1984), 'Grotius et le droit naturel du dix-septième siècle', in: *The World of Hugo Grotius (1583-1645)*, Amsterdam & Maarssen, pp. 15-41.

Duska, Ronald (1974), 'Aquinas's definition of good: ethical-theoretical notes on "De Veritate", Q. 21', *The Monist*, 58, pp. 151-62.

Eco, Umberto (1988), *The Aesthetics of Thomas Aquinas*, trans. Hugh Bredin, Cambridge, Mass.

Farrell, Walter, O.P. (1930), *The Natural Moral Law according to St Thomas and Suárez*, Ditchling.

Fernández-Santamaria, J.A. (1977), *The State, War and Peace: Spanish Political Thought in the Renaissance 1516-59*, Cambridge.

Finnis, John (1980), *Natural Law and Natural Rights*, Clarendon Law Series, Oxford. (abbrev. NLNR)

— (1983), *Fundamentals of Ethics*, Oxford. (abbrev. FE)

— (1987), 'Natural Inclinations and Natural Rights: Deriving "Ought" from "Is" According to Aquinas', in: L.J. Elders, and K. Hedwig (eds.), *Lex et Libertas: Freedom and Law according to St. Thomas Aquinas*, Studi Tomistici, 30, Città del Vaticano, pp. 43-55.

— (ed.) (1991), *Natural Law*, 2 vols., Aldershot.

— (1991a), 'The Authority of Law in the Predicament of Contemporary Social Theory', in: Finnis, 1991, II, pp. 259-81.

— (1992), 'Natural Law and Legal Reasoning', in: George, 1992, pp. 134-57.

— (1996), 'Is Natural Law Theory Compatible with Limited Government?', in: George, 1996, pp. 1-26.

Fiore, Robert L. (1975), *Drama and Ethos: Natural-Law Ethics in Spanish Golden Age Theater*, Kentucky.

Fleck, Ludwik (1935), *Entstehung und Entwicklung einer wissenschaftlichen Tatsache: Einführung in die Lehre vom Denkstil und Denkkollektiv*, Frankfurt a. M., 1980.

Forbes, Duncan (1975), *Hume's philosophical politics*, Cambridge.

Fruin, Robert (1868), 'Een onuitgegeven werk van Hugo de Groot', in: P.J. Blok et al. (eds.), *Robert Fruins Verspreide Geschriften*, III, The Hague, 1901, pp. 367-445.

Fuller, Lon Luvois (ca. 1958), 'Means and Ends', in: Kenneth I. Winston (ed.), *Principles of Social Order*, Durham, 1981, pp. 47-64.

— (1964), *The Morality of Law*, rev. ed., London, 1969.

Geertz, Clifford (1983), *Local Knowledge*, New York.

George, Robert P. (1991), 'Recent Criticism of Natural Law Theory', in: Finnis, 1991, I, pp. 353-411.

— (ed.) (1992), *Natural Law Theory: Contemporary Essays*, Oxford.

— (1992a), 'Natural Law and Human Nature', in: George, 1992, pp. 31-41.

— (ed.) (1996), *Natural Law, Liberalism, and Morality*, Oxford.

Gombrich, E.H. (1950), *The Story of Art*, London, 1972.

Greenawalt, Kent (1982), Review of Finnis's NLNR, *Political Theory*, 10, pp. 133-6.

Grisez, Germain G. (1965), 'The first principle of practical reason: a commentary on the Summa Theologiae I, II, qu. 94 art. 2', in: Anthony Kenny, *Aquinas: a Collection of Critical Essays*, Notre Dame, Indiana, 1976, pp. 340-82.

— and Finnis, J. (1981), 'The basic principles of natural law: a reply to Ralph McInerny', *American Journal of Jurisprudence*, 26, pp. 21-31.

— Boyle, J., and Finnis, J. (1987), 'Practical Principles, Moral Truth, and Ultimate Ends', *American Journal of Jurisprudence*, 32, pp. 99-151.

Grotius, Hugo (1604), *De Jure Praedae Commentarius*, ed. James Brown Scott, trans. G.L. Williams, in: The Classics of International Law, Oxford, 1950. (abbrev. JP)

— (1625), *De Jure Belli ac Pacis Libri Tres*, ed. James Brown Scott, trans. F.W. Kelsey, in: The Classics of International Law, Oxford, 1925. (abbrev. JBP)

Haakonssen, Knud (1981), *The Science of a Legislator: The Natural Jurisprudence of David Hume and Adam Smith*, Cambridge.

— (1996), *Natural Law and Moral Philosophy: From Grotius to the Scottish Enlightenment*, Cambridge.

Habermas, Jürgen (1981), *Theorie des kommunikativen Handelns*, Frankfurt a.M.

Haggenmacher, P. (1983), *Grotius et la doctrine de la guerre juste*, Paris.

Hamilton, Bernice (1963), *Political Thought in Sixteenth-Century Spain: a Study of the Political Ideas of Vitoria, De Soto, Suárez, and Molina*, Oxford.

Hart, H.L.A. (1961), *The Concept of Law*, Clarendon Law Series, Oxford, 1984.

Hartung, G. (1996), 'Von Grotius zu Pufendorf: Die Herkunft des säkularisierten Strafrechts aus dem Kriegsrecht der Früheren Neuzeit', in: Palladini, 1996, pp. 123-36.

Hauerwas, Stanley (1981), *The Peaceable Kingdom*, Notre Dame, Indiana.

Hervada, J. (1983), 'The Old and New in the Hypothesis "etiamsi daremus" of Grotius', *Grotiana*, 4, pp. 3-20.

Hittinger, Russel (1987), *A Critique of the New Natural Law Theory*, Notre Dame, Indiana.

— (1992), 'Natural Law and Virtue', in: George, 1992, pp. 42-70.

Hobbes, Thomas (1651), *Leviathan: on the Matter, Forme and Power of a Commonwealth Ecclesiasticall and Civil*, ed. M. Oakeshott, Oxford, 1960. (abbrev. *Lev.*)

Hollis, M., and Lukes, S. (eds.) (1982), *Rationality and Relativism*, Oxford.

Holmes, Oliver Wendell (1920), 'The Path of the Law', in: *Collected Legal Papers*, New York, pp. 167-84.

Honderich, Ted (1980), Review of Finnis's NLNR, *Times Literary Supplement*, Sept. 12.

Hont, Istvan (1987), 'The language of sociability and commerce: Samuel Pufendorf and the theoretical foundations of the Four-Stages Theory', in: Pagden, 1987, pp. 253-76.

Hume, David (1739-40), *A Treatise of Human Nature*, ed. L.A. Selby-Bigge, 2nd ed. rev. by P.H. Nidditch, Oxford, 1978.

James, William (1906), 'The One and the Many', in: William James, *Pragmatism in Focus*, ed. Doris Olin, London, 1992, pp. 71-85.

Jonsen, Albert R., and Toulmin, Stephen (1988), *The Abuse of Casuistry: A History of Moral Reasoning*, pbk. ed., Berkeley and Los Angeles, 1989.

Kant, Immanuel (1785), *Grundlegung zur Metaphysik der Sitten*, ed. Karl Vorländer, Hamburg, 1965.

Kelsen, Hans (1934), *Reine Rechtslehre*, Vienna, 1960.

— (1963), 'Foundation of the Natural Law Doctrine', in: Finnis, 1991, I, pp. 125-53.

Kline, Morris (1980), *Mathematics: The Loss of Certainty*, Oxford.

Kobusch, Theo (1996), 'Pufendorfs Lehre vom moralischen Sein', in: Palladini, 1996, pp. 63-73.

Koeck, Heribert Franz (1987), *Der Beitrag der Schule von Salamanca zur Entwicklung der Lehre von den Grundrechten*, Schriften zur Rechtsgeschichte, Heft 39, Berlin.

Kossmann, E.H. (1960), *Politieke theorie in het zeventiende-eeuwse Nederland*, Amsterdam.

— (1987), *Politieke Theorie en Geschiedenis: Verspreide Opstellen en Voordrachten*, Amsterdam.

— (1987a), 'Verlicht conservatisme: over Elie Luzac', in: Kossmann, 1987, pp. 234-48.

— (1987b), 'Bodin, Althusius en Parker, of: over de moderniteit van de Nederlandse opstand', in: Kossmann, 1987, pp. 93-110.

Kosters, J. (1924), 'Het jus gentium van Hugo de Groot en diens voorgangers', in: *Mededelingen der Koninklijke Akademie der Wetenschappen*, 58 (serie B), Amsterdam, pp. 71-87.

Krieger, L. (1965), *The Politics of Discretion: Pufendorf and the Acceptance of Natural Law*, Chicago & London.

Kühn, Wilfried (1982), *Das Prinzipienproblem in der Philosophie des Thomas von Aquin*, Amsterdam.

Kuhn, Thomas (1962), *The Structure of Scientific Revolutions*, Oxford, 1970.

Lakoff, George, and Johnson, Mark (1980), *Metaphors We Live By*, Chicago.

Laurent, Pierre (1982), *Pufendorf et la loi naturelle*, Paris.

Leibniz, Gottfried Wilhelm (1706), 'Opinion on the Principles of Pufendorf', in: *Political Writings*, ed. Patrick Riley, 2nd ed., Cambridge, 1988, pp. 64-75.

Leites, E. (ed.) (1988), *Conscience and Casuistry in Early Modern Europe*, Cambridge.

Locke, John (1661), *Essays on the Law of Nature*, ed. W. von Leyden, Oxford, 1954.

Lottin, Odon (1931), *Le Droit Natural chez Saint Thomas d'Aquin et ses prédécesseurs*, 2nd ed., Bruges.

— (1942-9), *Psychologie et morale aux XIIe et XIIIe siècles*, 2nd ed., 6 vols., Gembloux.

Luig, Klaus (1996), 'Von Samuel Pufendorf zu Christian Thomasius', in: Palladini, 1996, pp. 137-46.

MacCormick, Neil (1992), 'The Separation of Law and Morals', in: George, 1992, pp. 105-33.

McInerny, Ralph (1982), *Etica Thomistica: The Moral Philosophy of Thomas Aquinas*, Washington, D.C.

MacIntyre, Alasdair (1981), *After Virtue: a study in moral theory*, London, 1985.

Marsiglio of Padua (1324), *Defensor Pacis*, ed. and trans. Alan Gewirth, New York, 1956.

Martin, Christopher (1988), *The Philosophy of Thomas Aquinas: Introductory Readings*, London.

Mautner, Thomas (1991), 'Pufendorf's Place in the History of Rights-Concepts', in: Timothy O'Hagan (ed.), *Revolution and Enlightenment in Europe*, Aberdeen, pp. 13-22.

Mill, John Stuart (1863), *Utilitarianism,* introd. A.D. Lindsay, London, 1960.

— (1874), 'Nature', in: *Three Essays on Religion: Nature, the Utility of Religion, and Atheism*, 2nd ed., London, 1874, pp. 3-65.

Montaigne, Michel de (1577-80), *Oeuvres Complètes*, ed. A. Maurois, Paris, 1967.

Mullaney, Thomas O.P. (1950), *Suárez on Human Freedom*, Westminster, Maryland.

Nowak, Leszek (1980), *The Structure of Idealization: Towards a Systematic Interpretation of the Marxian Idea of Science*, Dordrecht.

O'Connor, D.J. (1967), *Aquinas and Natural Law*, London.

Pagden, Anthony (1986), *The Fall of Natural Man: The American Indian and the Origins of Comparative Ethnology*, 2nd ed., Cambridge.

— (ed.) (1987), *The Languages of Political Theory in Early-Modern Europe*, Cambridge.

— (1990), *Spanish Imperialism and the Political Imagination: Studies in European and Spanish-American Social and Political Theory 1513-1830*, New Haven and London.

— and Lawrance, Jeremy (eds.) (1991), *Francisco de Vitoria: Political Writings*, Cambridge.

Palladini, Fiammetta (1989), 'Is the *socialitas* of Pufendorf really anti-Hobbesian?', paper presented to the conference on 'Unsocial Sociability', Max Planck-Institut, Göttingen.

— (1990), *Samuel Pufendorf discepolo di Hobbes: per una reinterpretazione del giusnaturalismo moderno*, Bologna.

— and Hartung, G. (eds.) (1996), *Samuel Pufendorf und die europäische Frühaufklärung: Werk und Einfluss eines deutschen Bürgers der Gelehrtenrepublik nach 300 Jahren (1694-1994)*, Berlin.

Parry, J.J. (1940), *The Spanish Theory of Empire in the Sixteenth Century*, Cambridge.

Perry, Michael J. (1988), *Morality, Politics, and Law: A Bicentennial Essay*, Oxford.

— (1991), 'Some Notes on Absolutism, Consequentialism and Incommensurability', in: Finnis, 1991, II, pp. 55-70.

Pieper, Joseph (1964), *Das Viergespann*, München.

Pocock, J.G.A. (1985), *Virtue, Commerce, and History*, Cambridge.

Potts, Timothy C. (1980), *Conscience in Medieval Philosophy*, London.

Pufendorf, Samuel (1673), *De Officio Hominis et Civis Juxta Legem Naturalem Libri Duo*, trans. *On the Duty of Man and Citizen According to Natural Law*, ed. J. Tully, trans. M. Silverthorne, Cambridge, 1991. (abbrev. DOH)

— (1678), *De Statu Hominum Naturali*, trans. *On the Natural State of Men*, ed. and trans. Michael Seidler, Lewiston, N.Y., 1990. (abbrev. SHN)

— (1688), *De Jure Naturae et Gentium Libri Octo*, trans. C.H. and W.A. Oldfather, in: The Classics of International Law, Oxford, 1934. (abbrev. JNG)

Raphael, D.D. (1988), 'Hobbes on Justice', in: Rogers, 1988, pp. 153-70.

Raz, Joseph (1975), *Practical Reason and Norms*, London.

— (1978), 'Reasons for Action, Decisions, and Norms', in: J. Raz (ed.), *Practical Reasoning*, Oxford, pp. 128-43.

— (1994), 'The Obligation to Obey: Revision and Tradition', in: J. Raz, *Ethics in The Public Domain: Essays in the Morality of Law and Politics*, pbk. ed., Oxford, 1995, pp. 341-54.

Röd, Wolfgang (1970), *Geometrischer Geist und Naturrecht: Methodengeschichtliche Untersuchungen zur Staatsphilosophie im 17. und 18. Jahrhundert*, München.

Rogers, G.A.J., and Ryan, Alan (eds.) (1988), *Perspectives on Thomas Hobbes*, Oxford.

Rorty, R., Schneewind, J.B., and Skinner, Quentin (eds.) (1984), *Philosophy in History*, Cambridge.

Scheltens, D.F. (1983), 'Grotius' doctrine of the Social Contract', *Netherlands International Law Review*, XXX, 1, pp. 43-60.

Schneewind, J.B. (1996), 'Barbeyrac and Leibniz on Pufendorf', in: Palladini, 1996, pp. 181-9.

Scorraille, Raoul de (1913), *Francois Suárez de la Compagnie de Jésus d'après ses lettres, ses autres écrits inédits et un grand nombre de documents nouveaux*, Paris.

Scott, James Brown (1934), *The Spanish Origins of International Law: Francisco the Vitoria and his Law of Nations*, Oxford.

Seidler, Michael J. (1996), '"Turkish Judgment" and the English Revolution: Pufendorf on the Right of Resistance', in: Palladini, 1996, pp. 83-104.

Skinner, Quentin (1969), 'Meaning and Understanding in the History of Ideas', *History and Theory*, 8, pp. 3-53.

— (1978), *The Foundations of Modern Political Thought*, Cambridge, 1992.

Soder, Josef (1973), *Francisco Suárez und das Völkerrecht: Grundgedanken zu Staat, Recht und internationale Beziehungen*, Frankfurt a.M.

Suárez, Francisco (1612), 'Tractatus de Legibus ac Deo Legislatore', in: *Selections from three works of Francisco Suárez S.J.*, ed. James Brown Scott, trans. G.L. Williams et al., II, in: The Classics of International Law, Oxford, 1944. (abbrev. DL)

Truyol Serra, A., et al. (eds.) (1988), *Actualité de la pensée juridique de Francisco de Vitoria*, Bruxelles.

Tuck, Richard (1979), *Natural Rights Theories: Their Origin and Development*, Cambridge.

— (1983), 'Grotius, Carneades, and Hobbes', *Grotiana*, IV, pp. 43-62.

— (1987), 'The "Modern" Theory of Natural Law', in: Pagden, 1987, pp. 99-119.

— (1989), *Hobbes*, Oxford.

— (1993), *Philosophy and Government 1572-1651*, Cambridge.

Tully, James (1988a), 'Governing Conduct', in: Leites, 1988, pp. 12-71.

— (ed.) (1988b), *Meaning and Context: Quentin Skinner and His Critics*, Princeton.

Van Eikema Hommes, H. (1972), *Hoofdlijnen van de geschiedenis der rechtsfilosofie*, Deventer.

— (1983), 'Grotius on natural and international law', *Netherlands International Law Review*, XXX, 1, pp. 61-71.

Veatch, Henri (1981a), Review of Finnis's NLNR, *American Journal of Jurisprudence*, 26, pp. 247-59.

— (1981b), 'Natural Law and the "Is"-"Ought" Question: Queries to Finnis and Grisez', in: Finnis, 1991, I, pp. 293-311.

Vermeulen, B.P. (1983), 'Grotius' methodology and system of international law', *Netherlands International Law Review*, XXX, 3, pp. 374-82.

Villey, Michel (1968), *La formation de la pensée juridique moderne: cours d'histoire de la philosophie du droit 1961-1966*, Paris.

Virt, Günther (1983), *Epikie-verantwortlicher Umgang mit Normen: eine historisch-systematische Untersuchung zu Aristoteles, Thomas von Aquin und Franz Suárez*, Mainz.

Vitoria, Francisco (ca. 1532), 'De Jure Gentium et Naturale', in: Scott, 1934, appendix E.

Weber, Max (1904), 'Die "Objektivität" sozialwissenschaftlicher und sozialpolitischer Erkenntnis', in: *Gesammelte Aufsätze zur Wissenschaftslehre*, ed. Johannes Winckelmann, 5. Auflage, Tübingen, 1982, pp. 146-214.

— (1922), 'Der Sinn der Wertfreiheit der soziologischen und ökonomischen Wissenschaften', in: *Gesammelte Aufsätze zur Wissenschaftslehre*, ed. Johannes Winckelmann, 5. Auflage, Tübingen, 1982, pp. 489-540.

Weinreb, Lloyd L. (1987), *Natural Law and Justice*, Cambridge, Mass.

— (1996), 'The Moral Point of View', in: George, 1996, pp. 195-212.

Weinrib, Ernest J. (1995), *The Idea of Private Law*, Cambridge, Mass.

Welzel, Hans (1951), *Naturrecht und materiale Gerechtigkeit*, Göttingen, 1980.

— (1958), *Die Naturrechtslehre Samuel Pufendorfs: Ein Beitrag zur Ideengeschichte des 17. und 18. Jahrhunderts*, Berlin.

Westerman, Pauline (1992), Review of Buckle, 1991, *Grotiana*, 11, pp. 43-50.

— (1994), 'Hume and the natural lawyers: a change of landscape', in: M.A. Stewart, and John P. Wright (eds.), *Hume and Hume's connexions*, Edinburgh, 1994, pp. 83-104.

Wilenius, Reijo (1963), *The Social and Political Theory of Francisco Suárez*, Helsinki.

Williams, Bernard (1985), *Ethics and the Limits of Philosophy*, Cambridge, Mass.

Wolf, Erik (1927), *Grotius, Pufendorf, Thomasius: Drei Kapitel der Gestaltgeschichte der Rechtswissenschaft*, Tübingen.

Wyduckel, Dieter (1996), 'Die Vertragslehre Pufendorfs', in: Palladini, 1996, pp. 147-65.

Zwiebach, B. (1975), *Civility and Disobedience*, Cambridge.

INDEX